The purchase of this book
was made possible
by a generous grant from
The Auen Foundation.

DODGE CITY

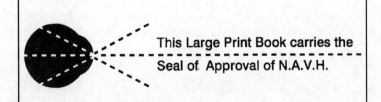

This Large Print Book carries the Seal of Approval of N.A.V.H.

DODGE CITY

WYATT EARP, BAT MASTERSON, AND THE WICKEDEST TOWN IN THE AMERICAN WEST

TOM CLAVIN

THORNDIKE PRESS
A part of Gale, Cengage Learning

GALE
CENGAGE Learning·

Farmington Hills, Mich • San Francisco • New York • Waterville, Maine
Meriden, Conn • Mason, Ohio • Chicago

GALE
CENGAGE Learning®

Copyright © 2017 by Tom Clavin.
Page 5: Left photo, Wyatt Earp, age 21. Right photo, Bat Masterson, age 24. (Kansas State Historical Society)
Map on pages 18–19 by Jeffery L. Ward.
Thorndike Press, a part of Gale, Cengage Learning.

ALL RIGHTS RESERVED
Thorndike Press® Large Print Bill's Bookshelf.
The text of this Large Print edition is unabridged.
Other aspects of the book may vary from the original edition.
Set in 16 pt. Plantin.

LIBRARY OF CONGRESS CATALOGING-IN-PUBLICATION DATA

Names: Clavin, Thomas, author.
Title: Dodge City : Wyatt Earp, Bat Masterson, and the wickedest town in the American West / by Tom Clavin.
Description: Large print edition. | Waterville, Maine : Thorndike Press, part of Gale, Cengage Learning, [2017] | Series: Thorndike Press large print Bill's bookshelf.
Identifiers: LCCN 2017012285| ISBN 9781432840358 (hardcover) | ISBN 1432840355 (hardcover)
Subjects: LCSH: Dodge City (Kan.)—History—19th century. | Earp, Wyatt, 1848–1929. | Masterson, Bat, 1853–1921. | Peace officers—Kansas—Dodge City—Biography. | Dodge City (Kan.)—Biography. | Outlaws—Kansas—Dodge City—History—19th century. | Frontier and pioneer life—Kansas—Dodge City. | Large type books.
Classification: LCC F689.D64 C55 2017 | DDC 978.1/76—dc23
LC record available at https://lccn.loc.gov/2017012285

Published in 2017 by arrangement with Macmillan Publishing Group, LLC/ST. Martin's Press

Printed in the United States of America
1 2 3 4 5 6 7 21 20 19 18 17

*To Kathryn Clavin and James Vunkannon
and their long life together*

AUTHOR'S NOTE

With Wyatt Earp, there is too much material, and with Bat Masterson, there is not nearly as much. To write about both, you hope to find a reliable middle ground you can hang your Stetson on.

There have been many books and films that feature Wyatt Earp and Bat Masterson. Almost all of the books are largely fiction, including the ones published as nonfiction. They contain exaggerations, embellishments, rumors, and outright falsehoods. The same goes for the onscreen efforts that began in 1932 with Walter Huston playing a character based on Wyatt Earp in *Law and Order.* The challenge for a writer today is to sift through all that has been done before to find the most reliable sources on both Wyatt and Bat and then tell how their stories intersected in Dodge City in the 1870s, where they became lifelong friends and met the one-of-a-kind characters who share many of those stories. Given what iconic figures these legendary lawmen are in American history and how over the years tall tales have stuck to them like barnacles on a boat, for me it was a challenge indeed.

As an individual subject, Wyatt Earp has been written about extensively. That would appear to be good news for an author taking a crack at a period in his life that has tended to be previously overlooked. Yes and no. While Wyatt had some notoriety during his lifetime, most of it was connected to the Gunfight at the O.K. Corral and the revenge ride that followed the shootings of his brothers Virgil and Morgan. Wyatt did not become a fully imagined legend of the Wild West until the publication of *Wyatt Earp: Frontier Marshal* in 1931, two years after his death. It sold briskly, even in the Depression, and Stuart Lake's biography would be the basis of movies and television episodes — and, alas, most "nonfiction" books and articles — for decades to come. Like *Frontier Marshal,* many such projects unashamedly played fast and loose with the facts. Even a classic motion picture like *My Darling Clementine* has Doc Holliday dying in the O.K. Corral gun battle, and Virgil Earp is not only portrayed as Wyatt's *younger* brother but is killed before the brothers even get to the corral.

Frontier Marshal is packed with stories and reads like a darn good yarn. The award-winning western and mystery writer Loren D. Estleman considers it "a pivotal work in the uniquely American process by which the common straw of history is spun into legendary gold." The problem is that some of the stories are inventions or at least embellishments. As Estleman immediately informs readers in his foreword to the 1994 edition of Lake's book, the book's contents are less fact than fable. Thankfully, with some Wyatt Earp stories, over the years diligent and dedicated researchers have found that there are sound, solid sources of information. A handful of those authors, particularly Casey Tefertiller and Sherry Monahan, have written accurately and wonderfully about Wyatt and the Earp family. Wyatt himself, though, and later his fourth wife, Josephine (also known as Sadie), had other priorities than being reliable raconteurs. At times his own recollections or those of his contemporaries were the only foundations for what may or may not be tall tales. From the time that Lake's book was published, the expanding and burnishing legend of Wyatt Earp became

11

more important than the real life of the man.

And there were those who wanted to do the opposite, to tear Wyatt down, to chip away at the statue of the most famous lawman of the American West while it was still being sculpted atop those faulty foundations. There were people who didn't like Wyatt or any of the other Earps or who simply were jealous enough of one western figure rising above the others that attacks were launched. As Estleman further explained, "If, for example, Lake's undisguised admiration for his subject compels him to paint an impossible picture of Wyatt Earp as saint, Frank Waters's personal grudge against Earp's widow moves him just as surely, in *The Earp Brothers of Tombstone,* to cast the lawman-entrepreneur in the equally untenable role of Antichrist."

As is usually the case in research, the truth lies somewhere in the middle. That is the course I have tried to steer when it comes to the lives and experiences of both Wyatt and Bat Masterson.

This writer's life would have been easier if more had been previously written about Bat. Aside from scholarly articles published from time to time, there are only three main sources of information. One is a series of

12

profiles of his contemporaries in the Old West, profiles that Bat himself wrote for a magazine and that were published as a collection in 1907 as *Famous Gunfighters of the Western Frontier.* They are colorful pieces indeed and should be, considering that Bat had led a colorful and adventurous life. But only some of what the profiles report is true. Bat relied primarily on his memory, and being in his fifties then, it was somewhat suspect, and to some extent he enjoyed the attention he received that was based more on legends than facts.

There are only two reputable, full-length biographies of Bat. The first, published in 1957, was written by Richard O'Connor. It is credited with being the basis of the *Bat Masterson* television series, and it reads more like popular screen fare than serious scholarship. But at least O'Connor tried to give Bat his due, and while the research is sketchy (beginning with Bat's place of birth), there are more accurate ingredients than knee-slappers. The second and, to date, last biography is by the eminent historian Robert K. DeArment and was published in 1979. It does a much better job of offering a full portrait of Bat. DeArment did his best to meet the challenge of Bat's life not being as well chronicled as

Wyatt's, and he regarded what had been written before — one example being Bat credited with killing twenty-two men in gunfights — as being more harmful than helpful.

Of course, there are other sources to draw from when writing about Wyatt Earp and Bat Masterson and all the truths, legends, and lies about Dodge City in the 1870s. Many writers have emphasized the "Wild West" reputation of the city, and correctly so, because for a time in the 1870s no other city west of the Mississippi was more of a free-for-all of cowboys, gunfighters, gamblers, prostitutes, entrepreneurs, prospectors, and others just passing through.

Even now, not just in the United States but around the world, to hear someone say "Dodge City" immediately conjures up images of lawlessness and violence, corruption and roughriding men in black hats. This overlooks that there were men and women in Dodge City working to establish a more civilized life, and they hired lawmen like Wyatt and Bat and Charlie Bassett and Bill Tilghman and Ed and Jim Masterson to forge a system of frontier justice that would eventually create the West we know today. If these men had failed, the history of America in the late nineteenth century would have been quite different.

The bibliography found at the back of this book offers a glimpse of the effort to cast a wide net to capture the facts and toss the falsehoods back into the sea of legend. But the more research I did, the more I realized that what is "known" was often contradictory or just plain hooey, perpetrated by public-relations men posing as writers, people with their own anti-Earp and/or anti-Masterson agendas, and Wyatt and Bat themselves. With this in mind, I did my own presorting before writing so that in this book there will be very little waffling. I would think that readers would find it frustrating to keep seeing "One version goes" and "Other accounts contend" repeatedly throughout the book. A few times this may be necessary, but for the most part, *Dodge City* is an attempt to spin a yarn as entertaining as tales that have been told before but one that is based on the most reliable research. I attempted to follow the example of the Western Writers of America, whose members over the years have found the unique formula of combining strong scholarship with entertaining writing.

However, despite how deeply devoted I was to using solid research and reasonable versions of events, there will be readers who disagree, often because they prize one source over another. So be it. And to those who disagree because I truly am in error, I apologize and take full responsibility. May Clay Allison or Dirty Dave Rudabaugh inhabit my guilt-ridden dreams.

The most famous line of dialogue in John Ford's late-career western *The Man Who Shot Liberty Valance* was, "This is the West, sir. When legend becomes fact, print the legend." For this book, most research sources revealed that legend and fact often overlapped and that the facts about the lives of Wyatt Earp and Bat Masterson before, during, and after Dodge City were usually at least as satisfying as the fictions. What mattered — in addition to being authoritative and to portraying a generation of lawmen and villains and everyone in between at a particular place and time — was sharing a lot of good stories.

So let's focus on that as you sort of sit around the campfire under a tall, dark sky. Once upon a time on the prairie . . .

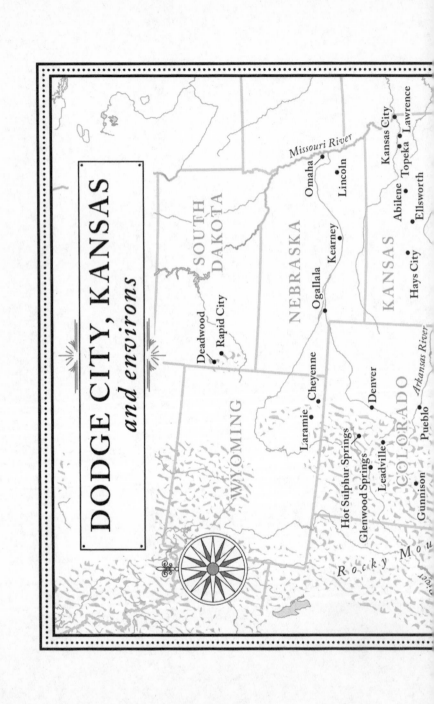

DODGE CITY, KANSAS
and environs

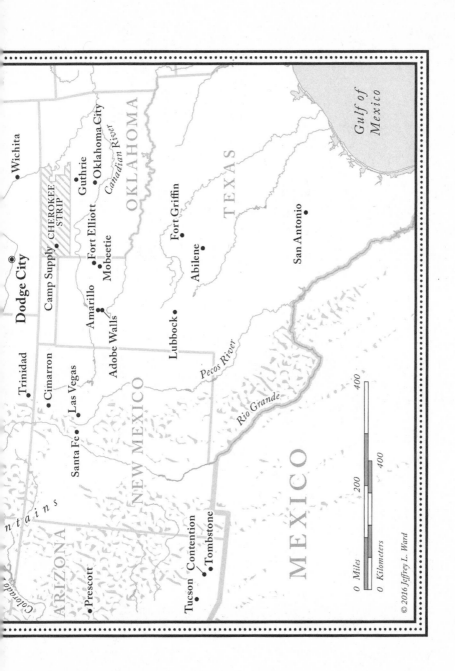
© 2016 Jeffrey L. Ward

PROLOGUE

It was decided that if a fight was all that would satisfy the mayor of Dodge — a fight he would have. — BAT MASTERSON

On a gleaming-bright morning in early June 1883, Bat Masterson was on a train bound for Dodge City. When he disembarked there, he expected to be greeted by Wyatt Earp. Neither man knew for sure, but they had a pretty good idea that whatever was to transpire that day — there were already national headlines about the "Dodge City War" — could mark the last time they would walk the streets side by side as men determined to do what was right. It was very likely that each would go his separate way, pursuing the myriad possibilities the American West offered . . . or on this day, their luck would finally run out.

The train, its plumes of puffing steam dissipating in the wide blue sky and dust-dry air above the prairie, traveled on the Atchison, Topeka & Santa Fe line. This was the railroad company that had done the most to connect the Kansas cow towns more than a decade ago and had made Dodge City, especially, the keystone not just of Kansas but of the entire frontier.

Bat had a fondness for trains. He had traveled on a lot of them since he and his brother Ed had first come to Dodge City and labored to lay tracks for them. They had been buffalo hunters and skinners then, and still teenagers. Both had become lawmen in Dodge, and his brother had died as one, gunned down by cowboys who then had to face Bat and his blazing six-shooters. Two years earlier, Bat had been on another train to Dodge City, arriving just in time to prevent a second lawman brother, Jim, from getting bushwhacked. Now, once again, Bat might have to step off with his pistols primed for sudden action.

None of his three remaining brothers were at risk, yet there was still a sense of urgency — and one of unfinished business. When he and Wyatt had gone their separate ways out of Dodge City several years earlier, the job of peacekeeping had been carried on by other men, capable ones like Charlie Bassett and Bill Tilghman. The town was tamed, so to speak, at least quite a bit compared to when "wicked" was the most common adjective for it and tales were told far and wide about dead men being hauled out to Boot Hill faster than graves could be dug. But now hell really had broken loose all over again. That was why Wyatt and Bat and their friends, most of them good with a gun, were back.

What had come to be called the Dodge City Peace Commission was Luke Short's doing, though he didn't intend it. He was a friend from back in their Dodge City days, and afterward he had landed in Tombstone. After first Bat then Wyatt had left that infamous Arizona town, Luke decided to go back to Dodge City and make a living gambling there. His stature fit his name. Maybe because some people looked at him as something of a runt, or because he did so himself, Luke Short could be a stubborn and hotheaded man. Bat described him as "a small package, but one of great dynamic force." He was a good and reasonably honest gambler and a hell of a dresser — the finest pants and shirt and vest, his head sporting a top hat, a diamond pin stuck in his tie — and he strode the streets of Dodge City with a gold-headed stick. More important, he had remained friends with Wyatt and Bat, and both men prized loyalty. That spring of 1883, their pal had been receiving the short end of the stick, and that had to stop.

However, Wyatt sure wasn't looking for a fight. The twenty months since the Gunfight at the O.K. Corral had not been easy ones. In December 1881, his older brother Virgil was ambushed on the street and hit with shotgun blasts. He survived, but his left arm was permanently crippled. The following March, as Wyatt shot pool with him in a saloon, his younger brother Morgan was killed.

The attacks on the Earps inspired what became known as the Earp Vendetta Ride. Wyatt recruited a posse of Doc Holliday, "Turkey Creek" Jack Johnson, Sherman McMaster, and younger brother Warren Earp and set off after the killers. For the most part, they were successful, but for a long time Wyatt was in legal hot water, charged with murder and other offenses. Another high-profile gunfight was not going to make life easier — assuming he survived it.

But Wyatt's code called for not letting a friend down. And he would be reunited with Bat. Already in the imagination of some of the American public back east they represented the toughest of the frontier lawmen, an undefeated duo who had been in any number of gun battles and had rescued the infamous Dodge City from being a modern-day Sodom and Gomorrah filled with desperadoes, drunks, and fallen women. (All three remained; they just were better at behaving themselves.) By doing so, Wyatt and Bat, their respective brothers, and the men they rode with had created the blueprint for law and order and justice throughout the frontier. The "Wild West" being no longer nearly as wild might make it less fun for some, but it was a lot more livable for families and others pursuing manifest destiny.

Wyatt and Bat had accomplished this without quite realizing it and while still very young men. Both had received little formal education, and they did not have enlightened or religious upbringings. Their fathers had to scrape out a living — in Wyatt's case, sometimes on the wrong side of the law — and their mothers bore and raised large broods of children, most of them boys. Somehow, Wyatt and Bat developed a rough sense of justice and how best to keep the peace. The Earp brothers and the Masterson brothers were, in a way, a gang who were tougher and more righteous than the other gangs in western Kansas and across the frontier. There were many setbacks, but as would later be portrayed in many Hollywood westerns, in the end the good guys won.

The ending in Dodge City had yet to be written. The six-shooters on the Peace Commission members' belts might be the pens that would do it. After all, giving fair notice, Wyatt had told Mayor Lawrence Deger and his followers just the day before, "Bat will arrive at noon tomorrow, and upon [his] arrival we expect to open up hostilities."

It had to be satisfying the way their faces had paled. Already, rumors had reached a fever pitch, that ruthless men including Dirty Sock Jack, Cold Chuck Johnny, Black Jack Bill, Dynamite Sam, Rowdy Joe, and Shotgun Collins had flocked to Dodge City when Bat and Wyatt had sent out a call to arms. The *Kansas City Daily Journal* had colorfully reported that Wyatt "is equally famous in the cheerful business of depopulating the country. He has killed within our personal knowledge six men, and he is popularly credited with relegating to the dust no less than ten of his fellow men."

Adding Masterson to the mix — who the *Journal* had declared was "one of the most dangerous men the West has ever produced" — meant that local lawyers may have been kept extra busy that night drawing up wills for the rattled "reformers." They had tossed Luke Short out so they could take away his gambling house, and increasingly that looked like a bad bet.

As Bat's train pulled into the station, he had to have mixed feelings about returning to Dodge City. He had told a newspaper reporter that Wyatt was "the best friend I have on earth," so he had to be looking forward to seeing him again. But he knew that corrupt tub of lard Larry Deger and his ilk were waiting for them. Gunplay was never Bat's first option, nor Wyatt's, but the scoundrels who had taken over the city might have different intentions.

When Bat stepped off the train, he had an ivory-handled six-gun on each hip and a double-barreled shotgun in his hands. Wyatt waited for him, along with Bassett, Frank McLain, Neil Brown, and several other men wearing pistols. Bat was curious as to the whereabouts of Doc Holliday, who he knew had joined Wyatt in Kansas City, but with the men already here — and this was just the reception committee; likely there were more in town — there was plenty of fire-power.

Wyatt and Bat greeted each other. Though different men physically — Wyatt tall and slender, Bat of average height and stocky — their grins were the same, indicating pleasure to see each other, even though the reunion was to settle a matter that might risk their lives. Then they set off, natural leaders, the rest of the men flanking them, starting down the dusty streets of Dodge City, ready for one last showdown to preserve the peace.

Act I

Dodge City in the 1870s, as viewed from Boot Hill.
Courtesy of Kansas State Historical Society

ONE

Little wonder that many early immigrants to the region thought of the vicinity of Dodge [City] as comparable to the Garden of Eden. There was a saying among the pioneers that God, after he created the heavens and the earth, chose to make a garden for Himself and thus He designed Kansas. — ODIE B. FAULK, *Dodge City: The Most Western Town of All*

That Dodge City was the gateway to the Great American Desert probably does not seem to be much of a recommendation for it. And not by a long shot was it the most populated, prosperous, or progressive city in middle America. Why, then, did it matter to anyone? Why did major daily newspapers to the east and ones in Denver and as far west as San Francisco and San Diego carry stories about the goings-on there in the 1870s? And why well over a century after

31

its "golden decade" is there still immediate name recognition when one hears "Dodge City"?

The small city in southwest Kansas came to symbolize both the American West and a nation seeking to fulfill its manifest destiny. Pioneer wagon after wagon deepened established trails and created fresh ones as a young generation of Americans sought new homes and opportunities. The search did not go smoothly. What happened in Dodge City was happening all across the western frontier, only more so.

On the first page of his memoir about Dodge City, Robert Wright, one of its earliest and most successful businessmen, writes that his image of the city then was "a picture ever changing, ever restless, with no two days alike in experience. In those days, one lived ten years of life in one calendar year. Indians, drought, buffaloes, bad men, the long horn, and, in fact, so many characteristic features of that time present themselves that I am at a loss where to begin."

What makes the Dodge City story such an enjoyable one is that it was a reservoir of tall tales, yet many of the facts are equally if not more fascinating. Most of the stories involve the explorers, cowboys, businessmen, gamblers, women from both sides of the tracks, lawmen, and others who came to call it home or who were simply stopping on their way to somewhere else.

By the mid-1870s, Dodge City had become the major "cow town" on the frontier — with all the good and bad that entailed — and was a doorway to the Great American Desert, the huge chunk of the country that was still largely unknown territory to many Americans. This was the plateau that rolled westward from the Missouri River to the Rocky Mountains. To strike west of Kansas City onto this plateau was to enter the vast unknown, where marauding Indians, wild animals, and all kinds of deprivations waited. Tales about such well-known trails as the Oregon, Santa Fe, and Chisholm followed by explorers, settlers, Mormons, prospectors, entrepreneurs, and some simply seeking adventure on the other side of the next hill were both captivating and frightening.

The exploits of Jim Bridger, John C. Frémont, Buffalo Bill, and Kit Carson captured the imaginations of young men who dreamed of joining their ranks. For many of them, the end of the Civil War in 1865 was a catalyst to begin their own adventures. Some found what they were looking for, some were disappointed, and some did not survive the occasionally harsh surroundings and even harsher people.

On the way west was a site known as Cimarron Crossing. This was where many early westbound explorers and settlers forded the Arkansas River and could then head into Colorado or go to Texas or on to New Mexico. It was near here that Dodge City was founded and took root.

Well before the Civil War, what had initially inspired the early explorations of an emerging America was the Louisiana Purchase. The transaction took place in 1803, and there was an immediate desire to explore the 828,000 square miles that President Thomas Jefferson and his administration had just spent fifteen million dollars on. That same year, Captain Meriwether Lewis and Second Lieutenant William Clark began their expedition, and many Americans would be enthralled by their reports about a strange and wonderful and intimidating land.

A territory called Kansas was right in the middle of the vast Louisiana Purchase property that stretched from Louisiana itself to portions of Montana and Idaho. There would be other explorers on the heels of Lewis and Clark, including the well-traveled Lieutenant Zebulon Montgomery Pike, who in 1806 crossed the region that would contain Dodge City. He observed "wind [that] had thrown up the sand in all the fanciful forms of the ocean's rolling waves" and cautioned that people on the eastern sides of the Missouri and Mississippi Rivers would be smart to "leave the prairies incapable of cultivation to the wandering and uncivilized aborigines of the country."

Pike was certainly not the first explorer of European descent. In 1542, the noted Spanish conquistador Francisco Vazquez de Coronado led a party of approximately fifty men, thirty of them on horses, east and then north into southwest Kansas. Coronado's men had taken an Indian captive who claimed that the Spaniards would discover a river as wide as five miles across and from which they could take fish as large as horses. The expedition had come up from the Rio Grande valley of New Mexico via the Texas Panhandle and a strip of Oklahoma to this flat country that they referred to as "plains." On their way to the valley of the Arkansas River they had encountered a black-brown sea of buffalo, a jaw-dropping sight. To add fish the size of horses to their discoveries was too tempting to resist.

The captive's claims turned out to be exaggerations, but Coronado and his fol-

35

lowers were still impressed by the vast plains east of the Rocky Mountains. They were filled with lush green shortgrass that rarely grew taller than sixteen inches. They also found twisted mesquite trees, shrubs with prickly thorns, sharp-needled cacti, and cottonwood trees along streams and creeks. They soon learned that in the summer hot air followed them up from the south, parching almost everything in its path. The shortgrass turned gold and brown and delectable for the literally millions of buffalo that roamed the plains. Other animals found in abundance were prairie dogs, skunks, badgers, ground squirrels, jackrabbits, coyotes, pronghorn antelopes, and dark-gray wolves, who thrived on all the available prey.

But most of all there were American bison, most often called buffalo. It is estimated that when European explorers like Coronado and those who came after arrived in future Kansas, there were at least five million and perhaps as many as eight million buffalo there. Big and shaggy, they didn't fear the wolves or other animal predators. They were safe in numbers as long as they remained on the plains and away from the Rocky Mountain foothills, where they would risk encounters with grizzly bears.

A bull buffalo could weigh a ton and be a ferocious fighter, but much of the herd's protection was thanks to the older cows with a highly developed sense of smell. The biggest danger buffalo posed to Coronado's contingent was their hooves. The explorer wrote to the king of Spain, Charles V, about the plentiful supply of buffalo meat for his hunters but that their trial-and-error efforts set off stampedes that ran down horses as well as men.

There were as many buffalo in the area that would later host Dodge City as anywhere else in Kansas. Explorers bearing "modern" rifles in the ensuing centuries had a lot more luck killing the lumbering beasts for their meat and hides. In the unlikely event that there wasn't a herd handy, other game would supply early settlers and others passing through, including ones with feathers: wild turkeys, prairie chickens, grouse, ducks, and geese. There was plenty of water and fertile farming soil. The weather could be a challenge, though, beginning with those hot winds up from Mexico. *Kansa* was an Indian word meaning "people of the south wind."

A sign that summer was giving way to autumn was when the leaves on trees along rivers and streams changed from green to gold, orange, and red. While the breezes no longer blew exclusively up from the south, the air and the ground remained dry. In winter, however, there was snow. Sometimes lots of it. It piled up in the mountains to the west and blanketed the plains. A blizzard could last several days, and just like in the 1800s, such storms today can claim the lives of people exposed to them. Finally, spring crept in when moderating winds from the south — ones that can be harsh and unforgiving in July and August — gradually melted the snow, water rushed down from the mountains, and the earth was ready to be tilled.

The original inhabitants, however, were not very interested in farming. Bands of Apache, Kiowa, and other tribes roamed the prairie, feasting on the wild game and buffalo, the latter supplying most of the Indians' food, clothing, and utensils. (A brutal but efficient harvesting method was practiced when the hunters stampeded a herd toward a cliff and the panicked buffalo plunged to their deaths.) When horses from the Great American Horse Dispersal that had begun in the Southwest in the late 1600s arrived in the plains and multiplied there, the domineering Apache could roam even farther and faster and send successful raiding parties against such enemy tribes as the Wichita, Kansa, Missouri, Oto, and Osage.

But in the first half of the 1700s it was the Apache's turn to be pushed around. Descending from the central Rocky Mountains, the Comanche proved to be the better horsemen. That and an especially fierce fighting ethos combined to spell doom for the earlier inhabitants when the interlopers reached the Arkansas River. The Apache were swept aside, forced to find less-dangerous surroundings, while the Comanche expanded into Texas and as far southeast as the Gulf of Mexico. Eventually, the remaining Apache and the Kiowa found ways to coexist with the Comanche. They might still steal each other's horses, both out of necessity and to earn status within their tribes, but the land offered enough food and resources for everyone.

Then white men began to show up. Most of them traveled east to west, finding a region of swaying green and brown grass and choking dust that gradually inclined toward the mountains, at its center twenty-five hundred feet above sea level. Zebulon Pike would be followed by another army officer, Major Stephen Long, who echoed his predecessor's opinion that this eastern portion of the Great American Desert was "uninhabitable by a people depending on agriculture for their subsistence."

Such sentiments certainly didn't persuade people back east to fill wagons with plows and seed and head to the Arkansas River area to begin farming. But a few entrepreneurs saw the explorations of Pike, Long, and others as opening the territory to traders. One of the very first was William Becknell. He loaded up mules in Missouri and took them to Colorado to trade with Indians for furs. Not finding any willing customers there, he accompanied a group of scouts to New Mexico, specifically to the settlement of Santa Fe. Trading there was brisk, and when he returned to Missouri, Becknell had blazed what would become the Santa Fe Trail.

In 1822, the year after his first sojourn, Becknell was back again, with a group of wagons and workers and more goods to trade. He was soon followed by others. In April 1824, the largest group yet, consisting of eighty-three men in twenty-four wagons, set off from Franklin, Missouri, and three months later reached Santa Fe. Coming and going, they passed near the site of the future Dodge City.

Still, the city could have become nothing

more than one of dozens of settlements that found ways to survive near the Santa Fe and other trails. What contributed greatly to this particular settlement's earning a prominent place on the map of Kansas was the founding of a fort, and there would be not one but two officers named Dodge associated with it.

The Comanche, Apache, and other Indian tribes did not have an inherent hatred of white people. At least, not initially. Encountering them here and there had the benefit for the Indians of trading furs and other animal products with them for trinkets and some clothing and, unfortunately, whiskey, for which the Indians had no immunity. Even just occasional exposure could lead to alcoholism and early death. This was also true of diseases like smallpox and cholera. During the decades of white migration west before the Civil War, the Santa Fe Trail was basically a commercial route for traders, though beginning in 1849, it also served as a stagecoach route. All this exposure to white travelers resulted in thousands of Indians dying from diseases, much more so than in armed conflict.

Many Hollywood movies would have viewers believe that the sight of any white people out on the prairie would whip Indians into a fury. For the most part, however, white people and their equipment were a curiosity to them. One example of the latter was the Conestoga wagon. It was constructed to resemble a longboat and was watertight so that it could "sail" across the vast ocean that was the Great American Desert. These wagons became known as "prairie schooners." Indians could not imagine riding in such contraptions, but rather than attack them, they watched as they moved on to westward destinations. The friction would increase years later when there were many more white people and more of them were stopping to settle or were killing the buffalo.

When Indians did attack with more frequency and savagery, migrants and miners petitioned the U.S. government for protection. The government did attempt to work out treaties with tribes and compensate them for allowing safe passage. Such treaties rarely lasted long, because they were broken by avaricious white traders and eager settlers, or because the Indians really hadn't understood what they were giving away and thus continued with their traditional practices of hunting and camping wherever they pleased. When white people got in the way or trespassed (according to the Indians) on sacred ground, or when an exchange of goods went wrong, arrows flew, guns that had often been gotten from traders blazed, and the white intruders had to fight to survive.

As the historian Samuel Carter III described it, "To the marauding Comanches and Cheyennes, still lords of the Plains whatever others thought of them, the wagon trains were like the Spanish galleons to the pirates of the Caribbean. Time and again they raided the caravans, killing and scalping the drivers for good measure. A favorite point of ambush was Cimarron Crossing, twenty miles west of the site of Dodge, where the Conestoga wagons trying to ford the shallow Arkansas made an easy target for the raiders."

The army sent units west to build forts in the Dakotas, Wyoming, Colorado, Nebraska, and Kansas. The southern ones became important when the ending of the war with Mexico resulted in a leap of trading along the Santa Fe Trail and the increase in conflicts with Indians due to more whites passing through the territory. A fort, or post, no matter how crudely constructed, offered some shelter from bad weather as well as from Indians in addition to being a place to resupply and rest.

One such post was built in April 1847. Captain Daniel Mann with forty men arrived at the Arkansas River eight miles west of the future Dodge City. There they fashioned logs into four structures within walls that were twenty feet high and sixty feet long. The geographical significance of the outpost was that it was roughly halfway between Leavenworth, the biggest city in Kansas then, and Santa Fe itself.

Mann's little fort on the prairie lasted only three years. In August 1850, Fort Atkinson was established one mile to the west and also close to the river. In its early days the fort went through a head-spinning series of names — first Fort Sodom, because the buildings were made of sod; then Camp Mackay, after an officer who had died the previous April; then Fort Sumner, because Lieutenant Colonel Edwin Sumner had led the contingent that had constructed it; and finally Fort Atkinson, after another officer who had died. This post also did not last long, sort of a victim of its own success.

In July 1853, the former mountain man and now Indian agent Thomas "Broken Hand" Fitzpatrick arrived with wagons filled with gifts and a mandate to hammer out a treaty with the Comanche, Apache, and Kiowa to allow safe passage on the

Santa Fe Trail in that region. He never needed to reach for the hammer. The Indians were agreeable to not attacking travelers in exchange for the gifts. Unlike many other treaties, the Treaty of Fort Atkinson stuck. The tribes stayed south of the Arkansas River, travelers on the trail went unmolested, and the government could not justify the expense of maintaining Fort Atkinson. By 1854, it was an empty shell.

Kansas was about to undergo a political upheaval that resulted in more fighting among whites than with Indians. The same year that Fort Atkinson was abandoned, the Kansas-Nebraska Act established the region as a territory. Slavery was coming west with a greater influx of settlers and hopeful businessmen; it was the same issue that had resulted in the Compromise of 1850. There was no compromise in Kansas.

Some migrants from southern states brought their slaves along. Those from the Midwest and some eastern states brought along their abolitionist views. Before there was a Civil War there was a civil war in the territory that became known as Bleeding Kansas, as pro- and antislavery settlers (and mercenaries) fought each other. This continued when the real Civil War began in 1861, and some Indians, taking advantage of the army having abandoned their western posts, attacked settlements along the frontier. For much of the war, Kansas was in chaos: the Garden of Eden had turned into hell.

By the end of the war, with the South clearly on its last legs, the U.S. government could once more pay attention to the West. Created was the Department of the Missouri, which stretched from Nebraska to Kansas (it had been admitted to the Union in 1861), Colorado, Utah, Wyoming, and Montana, and command of it was given to Major General Grenville Dodge.

In his later years, Dodge would view himself as a benevolent friend of the Indians he encountered in Kansas and elsewhere. This ran counter to the prevailing view, one attributed to General Philip Sheridan's sentiment: "The only good Indians I ever saw were dead." By the time he reportedly uttered this, most of the Indians in what had once been the Great American Desert were confined to reservations, and of their prominent figures, Red Cloud was long retired as a military leader, Crazy Horse and Spotted Tail had been assassinated, and Sitting Bull had recently been released from imprisonment at Fort Randall in South Dakota and was preparing to go on a stage tour that would include sharpshooter Annie Oakley.

General Dodge was not as benign and paternalistic in the 1860s as he later claimed. He saw safety of travelers as his top priority and he moved quickly to insure it. There were more frequent and larger wagon trains on the trails. Dodge did not want the prairie schooners shot full of burning arrows, so he sent a force under the command of Colonel James Hobart Ford to conduct a winter campaign against the Comanche. It was successful, pushing the tribe and some of its allies into Oklahoma Territory, also referred to as "Indian Territory."

But in March 1865, the "hostiles" were back, with an estimated two thousand Comanche, Kiowa, and Apache camped south of the Arkansas River. To tackle such a big task, Ford told his commander that he would need a fort as a base of operations. This resulted the following month in construction beginning on a new post on the north bank of the Arkansas River, twenty-two miles east of Cimarron Crossing. It was named Fort Dodge. General Grenville Dodge believed it was named after him, and it may have been, but there was also a Colonel Richard Irving Dodge who would be stationed there and eventually become the fort's commanding officer.

In 1883, after spending two years as aide-de-camp to General William Tecumseh Sherman, Colonel Dodge published a book titled *Our Wild Indians: Thirty-Three Years' Personal Experience Among the Red Men of the Great West.* Unlike the lurid tales about bloodthirsty Indians, which were quick to find audiences in the eastern United States and in Europe, Dodge's writings were mostly favorable, and he wrote about his experience: "For many years past I have been the most fortunately situated for such study, having been stationed directly among the wild tribes, whose characteristics have always been of most interest to me."

By the way, Colonel Ford would not be overlooked. Two years later, in 1867, when a new county was created, it was named Ford County.

Plans for a postwar campaign against the Indians — *they* were now the intruders — were dashed when the Andrew Johnson administration insisted on negotiating a new treaty, and emissaries were sent west to do so. The Treaty of Little Arkansas River was drawn up and "signed" by the tribes' leaders. Because the native residents could not read or write English and certainly did not have signatures to affix to these mysterious papers, when an Indian leader or "chief" (a title invented by the white man) agreed to whatever had been read to him, he touched the pen held by an army scribe, who then wrote the Indian's name on the document. The Little Arkansas treaty gave the Comanche, Kiowa, and Apache the right to hunt seasonally but otherwise be confined to reservations. With no fighting to do, in between forays to patrol along the Santa Fe Trail the army soldiers were put to work improving and expanding the fort.

These efforts didn't do much good. The compound and most everyone living in it were flooded during spring rains. The prairie heat of the summer was unbearable, and the troopers were riddled by a variety of diseases, exacerbated by the poor diet and poorer sanitary conditions. The autumn offered some respite, but the harsh winter with its seemingly incessant blizzards bottled the men up within the wooden walls. No doubt by the spring of 1866, the officers and troopers had to wonder why anyone would want to live in the area — and in any part of Kansas for that matter. They couldn't wait to be relieved and sent . . . anywhere.

Still, Fort Dodge endured, providing supplies, horses, livestock, shelter, and some support for campaigns to round up Indians who had left reservations to roam north from Oklahoma to hunt. The campaign in 1867 was led by two Civil War heroes, General Winfield Hancock and Lieutenant Colonel George Armstrong Custer and his 7th Cavalry. Battles were few and far between because as the army forces grew more daunting with their numbers and more advanced in their weapons, the Indians, with the dwindling populations of the tribes, could not put up much of a fight.

Again, what would become Dodge City might well have been nothing more than a frontier settlement supporting the inhabitants of a fort but for three uncontainable forces that intersected there: buffalo, railroads, and longhorn cattle from Texas.

The number of American bison on the Great Plains, including Kansas, indeed was an uncontainable and seemingly inexhaustible force. There were estimates contending that as many as seventy million buffalo blanketed the Plains by the mid-1800s, a substantial leap from Coronado's day. Men reported riding through a herd for more than one hundred miles. Others claimed that when they arrived at the top of a promontory and looked down, there were grazing buffalo as far as they could see.

Hundreds of men came west and south to kill the buffalo and sell their hides. An excellent place to hunt was in the vicinity of Fort Dodge. Hopefuls opened up simple stores housing supplies for the hunters, joining the crude saloons that were supplying the soldiers with whiskey. Henry Stitler, a teamster, constructed a sod house, and a hunter, Charlie Myers, built a trading post right next door to the fort.

As more buffalo hides were harvested, many lawmakers, government agencies, and private businessmen were in a hurry to lay track. The direction of most of the construction was east to west. The railroad companies would help bring civilization to the Great American Desert a lot faster than horses and wagons would. The creation of a transcontinental railroad would enable America to fulfill its "manifest destiny," a phrase first used in 1845 in a magazine article by John L. O'Sullivan, who was describing the desire to unite the two halves of the country into one great nation. At least just as strong a motivation was that a railroad line that could take livestock and what farmers were harvesting as well as passengers from one part of the country to another in days instead of weeks could make its backers literally carloads of money.

Because of its central location, Kansas was especially attractive to railroad entrepreneurs. But in the rush to get out in front of the transcontinental effort, some initiatives went . . . off the rails. One prominent example was the Kansas Pacific Railroad, first known as the Leavenworth, Pawnee and Western when the proslavery Kansas legislature created it in August 1855. Tracks were to be laid from Leavenworth west, following the Kansas River to Fort Riley and then following the Smoky Hill River to the 100th meridian.

Nothing happened for two years; then brothers Hugh and Thomas Ewing joined the LP and W. Their father was an Ohio senator. They were cousins of James G. Blaine, who would become a leading figure in the Republican Party, and brothers-in-law of an obscure army officer at the time, William Tecumseh Sherman. Thomas Ewing would later become chief justice of the Kansas Supreme Court.

Such a pedigree appeared promising. The brothers set about acquiring land grants from the U.S. government so track could be laid. When Indian tribes were found to be in the way, the Ewings worked out more treaties with them. But the process remained agonizingly slow. In 1863, a frustrated Thomas Ewing actually found enlisting in the Union Army to be more appealing. Two new players, Samuel Hallett and John C. Frémont, took over the company.

Frémont had achieved national fame in the 1840s as an explorer and for the best-selling books (actually written by his wife) about his adventures. He had lost to the Democrat James Buchanan in the 1856 presidential election. However, his star had lost its luster after he was fired early in the Civil War by President Abraham Lincoln for losses as a Union general and harsh treatment of Missouri slave owners. Frémont was looking for a soft landing spot. Hallett, the younger man, actually knew something about building railroads. Thanks to his efforts, ground was finally broken for the renamed Union Pacific Eastern Division in December 1863.

Sadly for Hallett, this success led to his demise. The ineffective Frémont was pushed out in April 1864, and supporters of his in the company followed him out the door. One of them was Orlando Talcott, who wrote a report critical of Hallett to Washington. Learning of its contents, one of Hallett's brothers looked Talcott up and slapped him in the face. That July, as Hallett walked to his office in Wyandotte, Kansas, Talcott approached him from behind and shot him in the back, killing him. Talcott offered his gun and to surrender to several people, including a police officer, but when no one took him up on it, he got on a horse and rode away. Hallett was about to preside over a ceremony for the opening of the first forty miles of track.

This was not the end of the UPED in Kansas. That December, the tracks reached Lawrence, then Topeka in 1865, Junction City the following year, and by September 1868 they were forty miles from the Colorado border. But without effective leadership the company lost its way. It would be up to the Atchison, Topeka & Santa Fe to connect the rest of the state to the profitable markets elsewhere in America, and to be responsible for the growth of Dodge City into a significant town and a legend.

This railroad had gotten a later start than the ill-fated Kansas Pacific, but it made up for lost time. In 1859, a founder of Topeka, Cyrus Holliday, and several partners obtained a charter to build a railroad. It would begin at the Missouri River, specifically Atchison, and go to Topeka. Four years later, after this had been accomplished, the Lincoln administration gave Holliday a land grant to continue the railroad to the border of Kansas and Colorado, with the eventual destination to be Santa Fe. It apparently bothered no one that much of the land being granted belonged to Indian tribes. To keep the grant, the railroad had to reach the border by March 1873.

This it did. Along the way, settlements to house workers and those who catered to them sprang up. Colonel Dodge was the commander by the time the tracks reached the Fort Dodge area, in 1872, and they went straight past a small collection of wooden buildings that was known as Buffalo City.

Appropriately enough, the settlement had been founded so that men could drink whiskey. The colonel had assumed command of the post that spring. Echoing what a fictional captain would say in the film *Casablanca* seventy years later, Dodge was shocked that his soldiers were drinking within the fort's walls and that some were even reporting for duty drunk. If any drinking were to be done, it had to be done elsewhere. The settlement near the new railroad tracks offered that opportunity.

That third uncontainable force came not from the east, like the railroad, or from the plains, like the buffalo, but from the south. After the surrender of Santa Anna to Sam

Houston and the end of the Texas Revolution in 1836, inhabitants of the new republic found themselves with land and cattle left behind by Mexicans who, fearing revenge for the slaughter at the Alamo, had fled. The most durable of the cattle was the longhorn, which meant that these bulls and cows were the best candidates to survive long drives to markets.

"Long" is an understatement. Before the Civil War there were cattle drives to California and New Orleans as well as Kansas City. The longhorn proliferated, which meant increasing supply for Texas ranchers, and the demand was high enough, but the ordeal and the length of the drives made for a barely profitable business. During the war there were even more longhorns but fewer ranchers and many fewer markets, with most of the closer Confederate markets closed by enemy forces or unable to afford to buy much of the meat available.

Thus, there was a lot of pent-up supply when the war ended. At that time, it was estimated that there were five million longhorns in Texas. Meanwhile, there was increasing demand for beef in the reunified country, especially in industrialized northern and eastern cities. The coming of the railroads was like pulling the cork out of a bottle. Cattle drives couldn't get going fast enough. It was a more tolerable trip to herd cattle from Texas to Kansas, the state right on the north side of the strip of land that was part of Indian Territory (later Oklahoma) and the Cimarron River. Less of an ordeal in transporting them meant more and fatter cattle surviving, and the soaring demand for meat plus the railroad providing faster travel to more major markets was a winning equation for the Texas ranchers, railroad operators, and ultimately the towns and cities along the way.

Dodge City was not the first to benefit by the intersection of a railroad and cattle drives. In 1861, a small settlement called Abilene, in Kansas a few miles north of the Smoky Hill River, consisted of a store, a blacksmith shop, a post office, and even a hotel. The town's handful of residents expected that once the Kansas Pacific Railroad came through, there would be an increase in population. That didn't happen, and there was very little business to be done. But when the Civil War ended and cattlemen from Texas resumed their drives north looking for railroad towns that would ship their cows to slaughterhouses to the north and east, Abilene was ready to make up for lost time.

However, for a year or so it was stymied by a quarantine on Texas longhorn cattle. They carried splenetic fever, which, inevitably, was called Spanish fever in Texas, and Texas fever by people outside of the state. Like Lyme disease today, this illness was transmitted by a tick. The Texas cattle were rarely sickened by the disease, but it was deadly to other cattle they encountered, such as those in Kansas. That state and Missouri enacted quarantine statutes. It was very frustrating to the would-be cattle barons that the railroad and shipping sites were enticingly right there but unavailable, as it also was to the would-be Kansas entrepreneurs, who saw their visions of riches and expanding towns turning into prairie dust.

Ultimately, the solution was to ignore the quarantine. In 1867 when thousands of head of cattle were driven north and sold, the proceeds far outweighed the fear of the fever. By the next year, Abilene was calling itself the "Queen of the Cowtowns." Similar claims were made by residents and officials in other towns touched by the railroad — Ellsworth, Hays, Newton, and Wichita chief among them. While all would be eclipsed by the expanding settlement at the 100th meridian, two-thirds of the way west across the state, they did offer a preview of Dodge City's near future. Abilene's busiest year for cattle was 1871, and there were eleven bars in town. (At least it had Wild Bill Hickok keeping the peace.) Two years later, Wichita could offer fifteen watering holes for prairie-parched cowboys.

Despite its very humble origins as a place to get drunk, Buffalo City was poised to prosper. Robert Wright, George Hoover, and John McDonald are credited with being its first businessmen, with the latter two having set up a saloon inside a tent. The original name had been a rather obvious one, given all the hunting being done around the settlement. After Albert Alonzo Robinson, chief engineer of the Atchison, Topeka & Santa Fe Railroad, laid out the blueprint for the town in 1872, the tracks and the trains that rumbled on them arrived early that September. The ranchers and their cattle appeared soon afterward. Three important trails found their way there — the Military Road, the Tascosa Trail, and the Jones and Plummer Trail.

Seemingly overnight, wooden buildings and sidewalks were erected just north of the Arkansas River. The tracks went through the middle of what became Front Street, consisting mostly of one-story buildings, some of them still simple shacks. "Meanwhile, what a tremendous business was done in Dodge City!" exclaimed Wright. "For months and months there was no time when one could not get through the place on account of the blocking of the streets by hundreds of wagons — freighters, hunters and government teams. Almost any time during the day, there were about a hundred wagons on the streets, and dozens and dozens of camps all around the town, in every direction." He added, "We were entirely without law and order."

With such an abrupt transition of the town from watering hole to a center of Kansas commerce, its administration, such as it was, was not ready for the overwhelming influx of buffalo hunters, who would be followed by cowboys who had just spent anywhere from thirty to one hundred days on sunburnt, fly-infested trails and had pay in their pockets.

There was no police force when things got out of hand. The nearest law enforcement was seventy-five miles to the north, in Hays City. And cowboys were not the only problem. Buffalo City was renamed Dodge City — it would not be a formally incorporated city for another three years — and was on the edge of the frontier, a place that for a variety of reasons drew thieves, drunks, deserters, guerrillas still trying to relive the looting and pillaging days of the Civil War, and others with a price on their heads.

All this combined to put Dodge City in the late summer of 1872 on the precipice of being a totally lawless young town. It was inevitable that murder was one of the crimes committed. The first recorded killing in the new Dodge City was that of a man known as Black Jack, because he was indeed a black man. That September, a gambler called Denver yanked out a gun and used it on Black Jack in front of a saloon. The man fell dead in the street, and Denver walked away. Soon after, another black man, Jack Reynolds, was shot six times by a railroad worker, and he too died. In November, J. M. Essington, owner of a hotel bearing his name, was killed by the establishment's cook.

Life in town quickly descended into chaos. Within a year fifteen men had been murdered, with the bodies being hauled up to the new cemetery, Boot Hill, for burial. It was into such lawless and dangerous surroundings that Bat Masterson, still a teenager, first arrived in Dodge City. Wyatt Earp would find his way there, too, and eventually both young men would be given badges

and a mandate to tame a town on the brink
of violent chaos.

Two

I had a six-shooter in my belt and could have stood the ten others off. There wasn't a one of them with any sand if you stood up to them, but they all had mean tempers and they were all thieves.

— WYATT EARP (age 16)

The man who came to be the most familiar image of the American West lawman did not even hail from anywhere west of the Mississippi River, but from Illinois. Born on March 19, 1848, Wyatt Earp was the sixth child of Nicholas Earp and the fourth with his second wife, Virginia Ann Cooksey. By the time Nicholas, who would not die until 1907 at age ninety-four and was one of nine children, was finished procreating, he had done his father one better, fathering ten children — six sons and four daughters.

The overall Earp story began even farther away, in Staffordshire, England, where John

Earpe was born around 1600. His son, Thomas, was born in Ireland in 1631. Thomas Jr., also born in Ireland, in 1665, was the first to spell his last name without the second "e" and the first to set foot on American soil, settling in Virginia. One of his sons was Joshua, born in 1700, and William Earp was born to him in 1729. One of his nine children, Philip, born in 1755, fought with fellow patriots in the American Revolution and was the first to leave Virginia, moving to Lincoln County in the western half of North Carolina. One of his sons, Walter, born in 1787, was a teacher, a preacher in the Methodist Episcopal Church, and later a justice of the peace. He and his wife, Martha Ann Early, added to the young country's population with their nine children. Their third child and second son, Nicholas Porter Earp, was born on September 6, 1813. The Earp family picked up stakes and moved to Tennessee, then to Kentucky. Only fifteen days after the birth of Nicholas, Abigail Storm was born, the woman who was to become Nicholas's first wife. They were married twenty-three years later, on December 22, 1836, in Kentucky.

The wanderlust that Wyatt and his brothers exhibited throughout their lives was clearly inherited from their father. Nicholas had the misfortune of becoming a young widower, and that contributed to his roaming farther and farther west. Newton was born to the Earps on October 7, 1837, and Mariah Ann on February 12, 1839. Then there were twin tragedies. Abigail, only twenty-six, died in October, and her daughter lived for only ten months, leaving Nicholas by himself with a two-year-old son.

Not for long, though. Virginia Ann Cooksey of Kentucky was nineteen when she married Nicholas Earp on July 30, 1840. They wasted little time, giving birth to a son, James, in June 1841 in Hartford, Kentucky. Virgil followed in July 1843, also in Hartford; Martha in September 1845; and Wyatt in 1848. Martha had been named for Nicholas's mother, and Wyatt, oddly, for an army officer.

When Wyatt came along, the family was living in a white two-story house in Monmouth, a town in western Illinois. They had moved there from Kentucky with Walter and at least two more of his sons. Nicholas was by 1848 a war veteran, though how much action he actually saw was debatable. Walter served as a justice of the peace in Monmouth — and was called Judge Earp by the citizens — and would eventually be buried there, in 1853. Nicholas did some farming, operated a saloon, and also was a justice of the peace. If Nicholas had not gotten restless, or patriotic, the growing family might have remained in Illinois indefinitely.

But then came the war with Mexico, in 1846, as a result of the United States having annexed Texas the year before. Though Nicholas was thirty-three and had a wife and children, he enlisted in the 2nd Company of the Illinois Mounted Volunteers. His commanding officer was a local merchant named Wyatt Berry Stapp. Nicholas admired his captain, and the company saw some fighting in Mexico, with a dozen men reported killed. Nicholas missed out on further action. As he explained in a statement included in his army pension file, "I received a specific disability occasioned by the kick of a mule in my groin . . . this disability being received at Magdalena, Mexico while in active service in the Mexican War for my country." By December 1847, Nicholas was back in Monmouth, and Wyatt Berry Stapp Earp was born four months later.

While he did not have a very distinguished military career, Nicholas's service did make him eligible for a land grant from the federal government. (His service also provided him, beginning in 1894, with a pension of twelve dollars a month.) He moved his family of four sons and a daughter west across the Mississippi to Pella, Iowa, where he farmed eighty acres and again served as a justice of the peace. There, he and Virginia Ann had two more sons, Morgan in 1851 and Warren in 1855.

In 1856, the family moved back to Monmouth, but this time the reason wasn't restlessness, it was grief. That May, Martha had died, four months shy of her eleventh birthday. No cause of death was recorded, but it was not uncommon for children to succumb to fevers or other ailments that today would be easily treated. It was in Monmouth, two years later, that Virginia was born. The presumably exhausted Mrs. Earp was to bear only one more child, who, fortunately and thanks to living into the middle of the next century, served as the Earp family historian for future generations.

It was a somewhat dizzying time for the family. Nicholas returned to farming and also became a constable . . . but not for long, and he and his brood were in Pella once again. All of this moving about up to the eve of the Civil War was not attributed completely to wanderlust. Nicholas had an uneasy relationship with the law, even though he himself had spent time administering it. While living in Kentucky, he had learned how to make moonshine whiskey. He supplemented his income by producing and selling it in Illinois, and whenever he was caught, he was fined. Nicholas was not particular about paying those fines. While Pella held the sad memory of a lost child, it was a familiar place in another state where he wasn't viewed as a criminal.

The Civil War caused disagreements within the family. Though a resident of Iowa as well as Abe Lincoln's Illinois, Nicholas considered himself a Southerner. He claimed that a reason he had signed up for the Mexican-American War was to defend Texas and make sure it became a Southern state. Nicholas was opposed to secession and slavery, however. His sons saw themselves as Northerners, so when Newton, James, and Virgil enlisted, they left home to do it and all entered the Union Army.

Newton was twenty-four when, on November 11, 1861, he signed up with Company F of the Fourth Cavalry, Iowa Volunteers. In September 1863, he was promoted to corporal, and three months later he apparently passed up the opportunity to go home by reenlisting. He was in the fourth year of service in the Union Army when he was discharged in Louisville, Kentucky, in

June 1865, having risen to the sergeant's rank.

Virgil's desire to join the Union Army may have been motivated by more than a call to arms. He was only seventeen when he fell in love with Ellen Rysdam, a daughter of the large Dutch community in Pella. In September 1861, the two teenagers eloped, getting married in the next county under the assumed names of Walter Earp and Ellen Donahoo. Just over nine months later Nellie Jane Earp was born and would be only a year younger than her aunt Adelia, born to Nicholas and Virginia in 1861. A couple of weeks later, on July 26, 1862, Virgil was back in Monmouth, exchanging the role of new father for the rank of private when, having just turned nineteen, he enlisted and went off to war.

Like Newton, Virgil was involved in some fighting and managed not to be severely wounded. He was a member of Company C of the 83rd Illinois Volunteer Regiment that was stationed in Tennessee and Kentucky. The muster roll of the company describes Virgil as five feet ten with "light hair, blue eyes, light complexion, single, farmer." Wyatt would become almost like a twin brother to Virgil, so close was their physical resemblance.

The regiment didn't fight in any major battles, but it did mix it up near Fort Donelson in 1863, against troops led by General Nathan Bedford Forrest. Most of the regiment's time was spent guarding roads and supply trains. Virgil spent almost three years in the army, and was discharged in Nashville in June 1865.

Yet in a way he was a casualty — he had been reported killed in action. Virgil didn't know this until he returned to Illinois. Don Chaput, in his biography *Virgil Earp: Western Peace Officer,* speculates that Virgil's doom was authored by Ellen's father with Nicholas Earp's approval because the two men had not wanted the marriage and the war offered a way out. Ellen was told that Virgil was badly wounded in a battle and a short time later he reportedly succumbed to those wounds. The Rysdams, with Ellen taking the "fatherless" Nellie Jane with them, emigrated west and south, settling in Kansas.

When Virgil came home, all he was told was that his wife and son were gone. Maybe he was relieved, because he did not set out in search of them. Ellen unknowingly committed bigamy when she married in 1867. Virgil would be reunited with his daughter, his only child, and his "widow," but that would not be until decades later.

James Earp would be the only one of the three brothers to sustain a serious injury in the war. During an early battle, in Fredericktown, Missouri, he was struck in the left shoulder by a musket ball. It went through the shoulder, shattered the joint, and flew out of his chest. In an age of routine amputation, James was fortunate to keep the arm, but enough agonizing damage had been done that he spent the next seventeen months in military hospitals. He could never get back to fit-for-duty status, because he would not recover full use of the arm. When he was discharged from the army in 1863, he returned to the Earp homestead.

While his brothers were off saving the Union, Wyatt had remained at home, and he wasn't happy about it. He was thirteen when the Civil War began and had no chance of following his brothers into the army. Worse, as the oldest of the Earp sons remaining on the eighty-acre farm — Morgan and Warren were only ten and six — many of the responsibilities fell to him. Wyatt did not like farming and he spent the rest of his life avoiding it. When the day came that he couldn't stand the plowing and milking and other onerous chores anymore, he ran away.

There are several versions to this story, but the gist of it is that Wyatt, thinking that his father had business to attend to in the western part of the county, took off in another direction, to Ottumwa, Iowa, intending to join the Union Army. Most likely, because he was still underage, he must have hoped to find a disinterested recruiter and one not familiar with the Earp family. What he found there instead was his father, who had either been tipped off or knew his restless son well enough. Wyatt was hauled home and ordered back into the cornfields.

According to a story he told in later years — which, like many of his stories, may or may not have been embellished by a biographer — Wyatt was about to be punished by a switch. As Nicholas moved in, Virginia Ann got between him and her son. Nicholas moved her aside. Wyatt viewed this as manhandling his mother and rushed his father. Nicholas was impressed by this bold action and canceled the punishment.

Despite his Southern sympathies, Nicholas was active during the war as a deputy U.S. provost marshal in charge of recruiting in his congressional district. This role was apparently not enough to satisfy him, because in the spring of 1864 he couldn't resist the temptation to take to the road again. But this time, the trek wouldn't be across the border to the adjacent state. The new destination was California.

Because of his Mexican War experience and a tall tale he told in which he had prospected for gold in that state in 1850, Nicholas was selected as the leader of a wagon train of 150 Pella residents ready to do their part in the manifest-destiny scenario. Sharing Nicholas's wagon would be his wife, Wyatt, Morgan, Warren, the still-recovering James, and Adelia. Specifically, the migrants aimed to wind up in San Bernardino and begin farming there.

Along the way, though, there was some friction between Nicholas and his fellow travelers. As leader, he was gruff, short-tempered, and a stickler for the rules he had laid down. One of the group was Dr. J. A. Rousseau, whose wife kept a diary during the trek. In one of her entries she notes that "Mr. Earp had another rippet" because Warren had gotten into a fight with another boy, and "then he commenced about all the children. Used very profane language and swore if the children's parents did not whip or correct their children he would whip every last one of them."

Nicholas was not necessarily being arrogant, though there was some of that in his personality. The fact was he was leading farmers and their families on a long and rugged journey across the Great American Desert and up and down mountains, and there would be all kinds of weather and other risks to face. In a letter written to a friend in Pella in 1865, Nicholas described one of them, a day when his troop of amateurs fought off an Indian attack.

In old age, Wyatt told a biographer that he had participated in the defense of the wagon train several times, and during one attack his quick thinking in provoking horses and oxen to stampede succeeded in turning back a force of onrushing Indians. This may have been an invented incident but it was Wyatt's story and he stuck to it. He told a nephew a story about his father tossing a Paiute Indian out of the wagon train's camp because he had the annoying habit of never leaving and possibly stealing from the travelers' wagons. When the Paiute returned, he had a group of braves with him. He pulled a knife and his comrades appeared menacing, but they backed down when Nicholas and his son drew pistols. "If he'd have got Pa, I aimed to cut him down," Wyatt told his nephew.

Wyatt also claimed to have met Jim Bridger in Utah. This is possible, as the legendary mountain man, though in his advanced years and arthritic by 1864, was still active as a scout for the army and private hunting parties throughout the Great Plains. Supposedly, Bridger taught the sixteen-year-old about hunting and fishing in the mountains.

Despite all the hardships, the wagon train did make it to San Bernardino that December, completing a two-thousand-mile trip with no loss of life.

The only "loss" was James. No, the wounds did not get to him; the lure of gambling and other entertainment did. As the wagon train neared Austin, Nevada, James veered off to it. He found a mining camp enjoying some prosperity. A man who could deal cards and pour drinks and tell war stories could find a decent job there. For James, this was the beginning of a lifelong career.

After Virgil found out that he was as single as he had put on his enlistment papers and there was nothing for him to do in Illinois or Iowa, he made his way west, too, joining the other Earps in San Bernardino. No chance he was going to be a farmer, though. With his physical strength and way with horses, driving a stagecoach was more to his liking. Virgil was hired to drive coaches in the triangle that was San Bernardino and Los Angeles and Prescott, Arizona. At times the triangle expanded to a rectangle when runs to Salt Lake City were included. Prescott was where shipments went to the goldfields and mining camps in the territory. His coaches always got through because Virgil had great stamina and he carried with him from the war a reputation as a tough man.

He couldn't do the entire job by himself, and by the late summer of 1865 he needed a sidekick. Who better than his brother Wyatt? Though Wyatt was still in his teens, there was no way that Nicholas could keep him on the farm, and maybe he didn't want to, because the routine chores of farming kept the seventeen-year-old in a chronic bad humor. From that point on, when Virgil climbed on a stagecoach, Wyatt was up top with him. His role was "swamper," which involved helping to load and unload the coaches and spell Virgil as driver, gaining valuable experience.

Then one time the two brothers went out from San Bernardino and didn't come back. According to their youngest sister, Adelia, interviewed many years later by a California newspaper, "When Virgil finished stage driving he and Wyatt went to Prescott, working for a big San Bernardino freight company with great wagons and long teams of mules and oxen."

This might not sound like very romantic work, but for young Wyatt Earp it was a big step toward a more adventurous life. Part of that life was getting schooled by Virgil and other freight-company workers on the joys of alcohol. For Wyatt, though, there was not much joy.

As Adelia wrote in her memoir, "When they arrived in Prescott, all the men went to a saloon in town to celebrate a mite. Wyatt had hardly taken a drink before and the whiskey soon had him reeling. Real drunk. He just passed out and Virgil and another friend took him off to his bed. When he woke up, he was in a terrible state all right, sick, headache, perspiring and trembling all over. Virge told him the only cure was to take a few more drinks. He did just that, and got as bad as before."

For the rest of his life, Wyatt's preferred drink was coffee, with the occasional exception of a small glass of beer. And there were times when being sober at a crucial moment probably saved his life.

THREE

"We're going to do well here, Caroline,"
Pa said. "This is a great country. This is a
country I'll be contented to stay in the rest
of my life."

Laura knew what he meant. She liked
this place, too. She liked the enormous
sky and the winds, and the land that you
couldn't see to the end of. Everything was
so free and big and splendid.

— LAURA INGALLS WILDER,
Little House on the Prairie

Portrayals of the Gunfight at the O.K. Corral do not include Bat Masterson. That is as
it should be because although he was in
Tombstone in 1881, Bat went off to a different adventure before the iconic fight took
place that October. But many portrayals in
books and movies and television episodes of
Wyatt Earp's adventures and activities
previous to Tombstone also don't include

Bat, even if he was present. When he is there, he's usually portrayed as being little more than a comic foil or coat holder to Wyatt in favor of giving Wyatt himself or even Doc Holliday more attention. Doc and Bat were not fond of each other, and if the latter could see into the future of American culture, this subservient role would only have given him even more reason to dislike the dissolute dentist.

The fact is, Bat Masterson was no one's Walter Brennan, Andy Devine, or Slim Pickens. Nor was he a retiring personality who let others do the talking, with their mouths or their six-shooters. His life was as adventurous as Wyatt's, probably even more so when one includes his cosmopolitan days in New York City, but Bat did not have a gunfight in Tombstone to burnish his legend to an iconic glow.

Most accounts of his life have had him born, like Wyatt and Wild Bill Hickok, in Illinois. He was not. Bertholomiew Masterson was born in Quebec, Canada, on November 26, 1853. When his supposed Illinois birth was reported during his lifetime, Bat did not try to correct it. Perhaps he didn't think it was important enough to make the effort, or as with the twenty or more men he was alleged to have killed in gunfights, the fallacy was more interesting and he simply went along with it. But here is an instance when the truth would have been at least as intriguing as the legend: if Bat never formally became a U.S. citizen, as a Canadian he never should have voted or held a federal office. William Barclay Masterson, the name he later claimed as his, did both.

On the other hand, the fact of how he acquired his nickname "Bat" is not as intriguing as the various published explanations. One was that as a child he was an especially talented baseball player and swung a good bat, as unlikely as this explanation was for a youngster in the 1850s. Another reason came about years later, when he was wounded in a gunfight, and thereafter walked with the aid of a gold-topped cane that he wielded as a weapon. But what is believed the most accurate explanation was that as a youngster his parents and siblings shortened the Anglicized "Bartholomew" to "Bat."

Thomas Masterson would live a life even longer than Nicholas Earp did, dying on his farm in 1921 at ninety-six. Also like Nicholas, there was some wanderlust, but only up to a point. Once he and his wife, Catherine, settled on a farm fourteen miles northeast of Wichita in the 1860s, they stayed put. After leaving Canada, the Mastersons had farmed in Upstate New York, in Illinois, then in Missouri after the Civil War ended, and then moved on to Kansas.

Bat was the second child, with Edward having been born in 1852. Bat would be closest to him and, though younger, was protective of him. Ed's gentle and unassuming nature may have made him the family favorite, and possibly by default it was Bat who grew up more eager and able to handle the rough-and-tumble life on the frontier. Ed was not a leader but a follower.

There were seven Masterson children in total, five boys and two girls. After Bat came James, then Nellie, Thomas Jr., George, and Minnie. From early on, Bat stood out from the bunch. According to the younger Thomas's recollections (interviewed late in life, in 1931) as well as his brother's own, Bat had a boisterous sense of humor, enjoyed practical jokes and teasing, was quick-witted and decisive, and had a strong constitution. In his 1957 biography, which was the basis for the *Bat Masterson* television series starring Gene Barry and which repeated some of the untrue stories about him, Richard O'Connor wrote, "He was the eternal Huck Finn, and the scant provision for education among the sod huts of the Kansas homesteaders did not dismay him in the least. Self-education and a resourceful mind later supplied much that should have been instilled by a prairie schoolmarm."

The youngster enjoyed the trips he took with his father by wagon from the farm in Sedgwick County to Wichita. It provided Bat with his first exposure to an emerging frontier town. There he observed the saloons, gambling houses, dance halls, theaters, more saloons, a variety of one-story wooden shops, and the people who frequented all of them — cowboys, girls who were dancers or singers or prostitutes or all three, gamblers on hot streaks in their new fine clothes, bloodstained buffalo hunters, travelers shaking the prairie dust out of their clothes, store owners and clerks, tough men and those trying to look that way wearing gun belts and pistols, and farm boys like himself spending a few precious hours away from the hoe and the plow. As would soon be proven, Bat much preferred town life.

In 1871, after another summer of working the farm with his father and before he turned eighteen, Bat determined to strike out on his own, or almost on his own. Ed was not so inclined, but the affable older brother pretty much did what Bat wanted him to do. Together, the teenagers headed south to a small settlement where buffalo hunters bought supplies, a town that would soon become Caldwell. Here, the brothers signed on with a hunting party. Roaming in search of large animals to kill must have seemed to them more adventurous than farming.

Much of the story of the American West and the long chapter of the decline of Indians is the story of buffalo — first their abundance, then the destruction of their population. The 1840 U.S. Census clearly underreported that there were seventeen million American bison on the prairies and plains west of the Missouri River, but as mentioned earlier, as the years went on, estimates expanded. Explorers returned east or sent back stories of buffalo covering the land the way we might see ants covering an anthill. One frontiersman came upon a herd that he insisted he had measured as seventy by thirty miles.

In 1846, Francis Parkman, the young explorer from Boston who was living with the Oglala Sioux, recorded an encounter with "one vast host of buffalo. In many parts they were crowded so densely together that in the distance their rounded backs presented a surface of uniform blackness."

While some tales were most likely exaggerated, there was every expectation that buffalo would be an almost overwhelming presence in the West for decades. And then they weren't.

Buffalo were a necessary source of food and clothing for dozens of Indian tribes. They ate the organs, stomach, tongue, intestines, and bone marrow in addition to the meat; the hides were used for tepees, robes, and shields; and other body parts became bowstrings, eating utensils, and glue. Even with this consumption, however, over the decades the hunting by the tribes had had no impact on the animals' population. They took as much as they had to and left the rest, and thus the harvest did not outpace the breeding of more animals. Each buffalo was fully exploited, and the meat could feed the tribe year-round, especially when thin strips of it were dried and pounded with berries or other ingredients to create pemmican, or *pimihka•n,* a Cree word for a high-protein food that could be stored for the winter and that would sustain Indians while traveling to and from hunting grounds.

Early white explorers pretty much did the same, perhaps not so thoroughly, as a way to survive while traveling far from settlements and other food sources. But stories that drifted eastward about the strange, hulking bison caused a new market to spring up: buffalo tongues. They were viewed as something of a delicacy by diners in St. Louis, Philadelphia, New York, and Boston. Suddenly, as early as the 1830s, there was a demand for tongues, and after they were cut out the rest of the beast was left to rot. The frontier artist George Catlin was at Fort Pierre on the Upper Missouri and observed a keelboat off-load barrels of whiskey and the captain announce that he would trade them for buffalo tongues. (Actually, he would trade only the whiskey, as the tongues would be soaked in brine and loaded into the emptied barrels.) A large Sioux hunting party went out, found a herd of buffalo, killed hundreds of them, and severed their tongues. Such incidents not only changed the Indians' relationship with the buffalo but began a pattern of repeated slaughter on a grand scale.

That relationship, for most Indians, was a source of increasing conflict between them and white hunters. "The Indians claimed they only killed for meat or robes, and, as soon as they had sufficient, they stopped and went home," Robert Wright explained. "Whereas, the [white] hunter never knew when to quit or when he had enough, and was continually harassing the buffaloes from every side, never giving them a chance to recover, but keeping up a continual pop-pop from their big guns."

The near eradication of buffalo did not happen overnight in the 1860s and early 1870s. For example, in the mid- to late 1820s, hundreds of thousands of robes made from buffalo hides the Indians themselves had tanned were shipped to New Orleans and its eager white consumers and manufacturers. But it was a sensational decline, considering that in only a few decades a population in the tens of millions was reduced to thousands. Still, as late as 1870, the army estimated that as many as fifty million buffalo remained on the prairie and plains west of Fort Dodge. That same year, though, the introduction of a new technology spelled doom for the beasts: their hides could be tanned more efficiently and turned into high-grade leather products. More than ever before there was a rush of killing buffalo.

Buffalo Bill Cody, of course, became the popular image of the great white hunter perusing the prairie and plains for herds to harvest. His boast that he had once killed over four thousand buffalo in eighteen months was astounding to the people back east, some of whom wanted to believe that they were wearing an item that originated from an animal that Bill himself had shot. But Cody was easily surpassed by a new breed of buffalo hunter bearing a Sharps rifle and the knowledge that just one hide would earn him $3.50. Even the least educated frontiersman could calculate that felling ten buffalo a day would equal $35, an amount many men west of the Missouri River could not make in a month.

For some hunters, $35 was the floor, not the ceiling. One of the more well known and obviously ruthless hunters was Tom Nixon. During a thirty-five-day hunt in 1873, his rifle sent 3,200 buffalo to their deaths, and this included a banner day of shooting 120 of the overmatched animals in forty minutes. Demonstrating a preindustrial flair for mass production, Brick Bond had fifteen skinners in his employ and he kept them busy by killing 250 buffalo a day. With the prizes being the hides and the tongues, most of the meat was left on the ground, providing belly-bursting feasts for wolves and coyotes at night and putrefying during the hot summer afternoons.

Slaughtering buffalo became easier thanks to the .50-caliber Sharps rifle. It was a hefty weapon, weighing nine and a half pounds unloaded, and a bit heavier when containing a three-inch-long cartridge, 120 grains of black powder, and a bullet that was a tenth of a pound. The rifle made a loud bang when fired, and the bullet could travel with accuracy — especially when the rifle was perched on a couple of rest sticks — over a thousand yards.

By the time that Bat and Ed Masterson decided to take up buffalo hunting, the population was in severe decline, but little thought was given to conservation of what remained. In the winter of 1873–1874 alone, more than 1.5 million buffalo hides were carried by train from the western hunting grounds to eastern buyers. The first winter that Dodge City was being served by the Atchison, Topeka & Santa Fe line, Wright and fellow businessman Charles Rath had shipped over 200,000 buffalo hides "besides two hundred cars of hind quarters and two cars of buffalo tongues." Sights like hundreds if not thousands of buffalo skulls piled high and bleaching in the sun near railroad stations did not deter the hunters from killing the beasts nor such getting-rich-quick entrepreneurs from buying the hides and body parts.

The obvious reason for such deliberate

slaughter was greed: kill and harvest as much as you can as rapidly as you can or earn less than the next guy. Another reason was a mixture of fascination and disrespect: the animals were just so damn stupid and appeared to be begging to be killed. With most animals on the prairie and plains, getting shot at, and especially having one of your own killed, resulted in flight as fast as their paws or hooves could carry them. Not so the buffalo. A hunter could walk to within a hundred yards of a feeding herd, stretch out on the ground, aim, and fire. A good kill shot was through the lungs. After the animal collapsed and died, the others kept eating as though nothing had happened. If the herd began to move — and at full tilt, buffalo can run more than thirty miles an hour — the hunter killed the lead buffalo, which stopped the followers in their tracks.

On the farm where the Mastersons lived, though Ed was the oldest, Bat had been the one in charge of herding the children to and from the nearest one-room schoolhouse, which was several miles away. From time to time there were reports of Indians nearby, and every frontier town had stories (some of them accurate) of white children being kidnapped. One afternoon, leading his siblings, Bat spied an Indian who appeared to be hiding in the tall grass, studying them. It was for this reason that Thomas Masterson had gone along with his son's request for a rifle, trading for an old musket. The local blacksmith straightened out the barrel, and after hours of practice in the fields, the boy was able to hit just about anything he aimed at.

So with some buffalo still blanketing the prairie — though in smaller and fewer herds — especially during the late-spring northern migration, and with prices high and Bat by his late teens being a crack shot, it made sense to go hunting as the Masterson boys' first attempt to earn real money. Though a hardy and confident young man, Bat may not have been prepared for how grim a job this was. One had to stomach the constant carnage along the Arkansas River, particularly what happened after an animal was killed. Despite his prowess with a rifle, Bat did not begin his hunting career as an actual hunter but as a skinner. His and Ed's job was to slice the hides off, stretch them out using stakes on the ground so the sun would dry them, cut the tongues out, and in the process dismember some of the carcasses, which resulted in wallowing all day in blood and other noxious fluids.

There was the danger of Indian attacks, more so than before. The tribes had woken up to the fact that by allowing and even participating in the mass murder of buffalo, they had robbed themselves of their basic source of survival. White hunting parties faced an increasing risk of being pounced upon by angry Indians. That anger was stoked by the waste. The stripped carcasses left to rot in the harsh sun were a form of disrespect beyond that shown just to the buffalo. They fouled the landscape that had more meaning as a homeland to the native peoples than it did to the white interlopers.

Bat was not concerned with the larger issues; he simply wanted to earn a living and keep his scalp while at it. He and Ed joined a hunting outfit typical on the prairie in 1871. It consisted of several wagons and their drivers, a cook and his wagon, hunters, and skinners. Not all hunters carried Sharps rifles; some had Hawken, Henry, or Springfield rifles and whatever other rifles had been lugged home from the Civil War, but the one that became the bane of the buffalo was the Sharps rifle because of its unique combination of power and accuracy.

The hunting party that Bat and Ed belonged to worked an area of Kansas called the South Fork that fall of 1871 and again the following year. There were other hunting parties in camps on the prairie, and around them buffalo carcasses piled up by the hundreds, then thousands. The hides were hauled to the nearest train station, where they were lifted into railroad cars and shipped north and east. The hunting parties were not necessarily rivals, because there were still plenty of buffalo to go around. It was more like each encampment was its own little squadron, led by a top man who sold the buffalo hides and tongues and paid out the wages. Bat and Ed probably took a few breaks to visit their family in Sedgwick County, and it's likely that Bat was the one who was less hesitant about returning to the bloody, nasty work, especially when his shooting abilities earned him a promotion to hunter, at higher wages.

According to some accounts, it was during one of these buffalo-hunting trips that Bat Masterson and Wyatt Earp first met. In an essay written in the early 1900s, Bat wrote, "I have known Wyatt Earp since early in the seventies, and have seen him tried out under circumstances which made the test of manhood supreme." He describes Wyatt as "weighing in the neighborhood of one hundred and sixty pounds, all of it muscle. He stood six feet in height, with light blue eyes, and a complexion bordering on the blonde." In contrast, Bat was five feet nine with a slightly stocky but muscular body, broad shoulders, dark eyebrows and hair, and his mouth was quick to turn up into a grin, unlike the taciturn Wyatt.

Wyatt was to tell the biographer Stuart Lake that he first met Bat when both were working for buffalo-hunting outfits. And in his 1957 biography of Bat, O'Connor takes both Bat and Wyatt at face value and goes on to write that Bat was so impressed by "the tall, blue-eyed, and steadfast man six years his senior" that "Masterson made a conscious effort to pattern himself after Earp, cultivating a quietly confident manner and learning to hold his tongue."

Bat may indeed have acquired these traits at that time, but not from associating with Wyatt, who was actually five years older, was still having trouble being steadfast, and other, more-recent accounts claim that in 1871–1872 he was not off buffalo hunting. Here is a case of choosing to believe the recollections of the two men who contend their fast friendship began on the blood-soaked prairie or the speculation of others reading the tea leaves of conflicting documents.

Bat was no stranger to Buffalo City and

then Dodge City during this time. It was there, along with many other hunters and trail-riding cowpunchers, that he acquired a lifelong taste for gambling and alcohol. Suppliers of whiskey could readily be found at the camps themselves, and Bat probably took advantage of this "room service," but more enjoyable was to drink while socializing in a saloon. And he could play cards. There is no indication that Bat ever became addicted to alcohol or gambling, but both activities would be a big part of his life, and he had a high tolerance for and took much pleasure in both.

It was during one trip to Buffalo City that Bat and Ed decided to give up buffalo hunting, at least for a while. The prospect of another summer roasting under the prairie sun and surrounded by gore may have been too dismal. In 1872, the Atchison, Topeka & Santa Fe was getting closer to Buffalo City, close enough that the railroad and its subcontractors always needed workers. Bat and Ed were hired to grade land near Fort Dodge where tracks would eventually be laid. They were joined by Theodore Raymond, a friend from Sedgwick County who brought with him a wagon and a team of horses. The three young men went to work.

It was hard-enough work that maybe Ed,

at least, thought fondly of being back at the farm, where Jim, George, and Tom Masterson had taken over their routine chores alongside their father. On the blistering hot prairie the three new railroad workers choked on dust all day, the air shimmering around them as though about to reveal a mirage. A milestone was achieved when they worked their way to Buffalo City, and Bat, Ed, and Raymond were able to witness the streets being laid out by the engineer Robinson. Then it was back to work.

As it turned out, the pay promised them was the mirage. A fellow named Raymond Ritter had hired them, then left, claiming he had to get the money owed them from the company to the east that had hired him. It was only then that the exhausted trio learned from people in town that this particular subcontractor was known to take a trip when a job was done. Ed and Raymond, despondent, returned to Sedgwick County and home-cooked meals and beds under roofs that offered protection from the sun and rain. Maybe farm life wasn't so bad after all. Bat was furious. The young men were owed three hundred dollars, and he decided he'd stay put and find a way to collect it.

He found enough work as a teamster to

eat and sleep out of the autumn rains as the railroad extended beyond the new Dodge City to the west, toward Colorado. But as much as Bat enjoyed the drinking and gambling pleasures of Dodge City, the real money was still in hunting buffalo, especially with railroad-related work moving on. That fall, when he was offered a job as a hunter with an outfit camped on Kiowa Creek, led by Tom Nixon and Jim White, Bat took it.

Nixon was already a legendary hunter. White had had a more exciting and less one-sided experience than hunting a few years back, during what had become known as Red Cloud's War. In 1866, over two thousand warriors from several tribes, led by the Lakota Sioux warriors Red Cloud and Crazy Horse, had vowed to stop any incursion into Pahá Sápa, the "Black Hills," which straddled the border between South Dakota and Wyoming and was considered sacred territory by the Sioux. The construction of Fort Phil Kearny by a U.S. Army force led by Colonel Henry Carrington was indeed an incursion.

On December 21, 1866, one of Carrington's officers, Captain William Fetterman, led eighty men in an attack on what he thought was a small group of Indians riding with Crazy Horse. He fell into the trap planned by Red Cloud, and the army contingent was wiped out. The following year there was another battle, this one called the Wagon Box Fight, in northeast Wyoming. It wasn't as fierce or as deadly as what had become known as the Fetterman Massacre (to the Sioux, it was the Battle of the Hundred Hands), but it was a close call for Jim Wilson and the others pinned down by attacking Indians for much of a hot August day. The next year, Wilson and another man got into trouble in Las Vegas, New Mexico, and the incident included killing four men. To try to hide his violent past, when Wilson showed up in Kansas to hunt buffalo, he was "Jim White." (Mayhem would always follow White, who was killed in 1880 at his hunting camp in Wyoming.)

From Dodge City west into Colorado there were dozens of hunting camps operating at a brisk and bloody pace into 1873. Tens of thousands of buffalo were felled and skinned. Though some buffalo meat was sold to the railroad to feed its construction crews, the harsh, hot breezes scouring the frontier carried the smell of rotting carcasses. Hunters were looked at with some disgust when they came to town because of the gagging scents they carried and their unkempt, gore-stained appearance. But everyone was making money and would continue to as long as the population of the animals held out.

Before 1872 ended and around the time of Bat's nineteenth birthday, Jim Masterson arrived in Dodge City. At seventeen, he too had had enough of farming and he wanted to experience the adventures his brothers Bat and Ed — who had returned to hunting with Bat — were having. Skinning the hides off animals his brothers shot might not have been Jim's idea of adventure, but he made more money than on the farm because the hunting was good right up until Christmas, when the last of the buffalo that had remained that far north with winter coming on were killed. The first week of January 1873 saw the brothers break up, with Ed and Jim heading to Sedgwick County and Bat staying in Dodge City.

Ed returned the following month. The brothers signed up again with the Nixon-and-White outfit even though there was little hunting to be done between snowstorms. Ed spent more time in town, working at a saloon, and probably served his brother drinks, when Bat rumbled in with a wagon full of hides. It was around this time that the patient and persevering Bat exacted his revenge on Raymond Ritter.

A friend who had been laying tracks in Colorado arrived in Dodge City and informed Bat that Ritter was on his way east, possibly on the very next train. Grabbing his six-shooter, Bat headed to the Dodge City station.

When the train pulled in, Bat got on board. He went from car to car until, sure enough, there was Ritter, who had to be shocked to see the young man who had become hardened by hunting since the last time Ritter had seen him. Bat hadn't been pointing a pistol at him last time, either. Bat hauled the scoundrel out onto the platform. Word of the confrontation spread quickly, and a crowd gathered.

When Bat demanded the three hundred dollars, Ritter called for help, claiming he was being robbed. But he hadn't left a good reputation behind, and in the time that Bat had lived in Dodge City, people had come to know a hardworking, reliable, and personable young man. No one came to Ritter's aid. Instead, Bat was encouraged to pull the trigger, but he'd seen enough blood every day on the prairie and he just wanted the money he and his two companions had earned. Bat pressed the gun into Ritter's ribs and tried to appear as menacing as his nineteen-year-old face would allow.

"I'm only collecting what you owe me, and everybody here knows that," Bat said. "You ran out on me and Ed, but now you're going to pay up."

This explanation coupled with the pistol was persuasive enough for Ritter. He produced a round roll of bills, peeled off three hundred dollars, handed those bills to Bat, and boarded the train, which to his mind couldn't depart fast enough.

Another thing the people of Dodge City had discovered about the young Masterson man was that he could hold his liquor and could be friendly and outgoing. He proved this all over again when he led the crowd to the Front Street saloon where Ed tended bar and dipped into the three hundred dollars to buy everyone a round of drinks.

FOUR

While a northern attorney was visiting in Wichita he dropped into the court room to see how the law was administered in that locality. A placard above the judge's seat read: "No smoking allowed," but the judge, nine of the jurymen, and half of the attorneys were smoking pipes or cigars. —
The Girard Press

Wyatt took to being a teamster right away. The work wasn't any easier than plowing and harvesting and other responsibilities on the farm, but at least he wasn't looking at the same fields every day. By the spring of 1866, Wyatt and Virgil Earp were very busy transporting cargo to and from towns and cities that included San Bernardino, Salt Lake City, and Las Vegas in New Mexico.

After two years of that, Wyatt changed jobs, being hired to haul supplies to construction sites of the Union Pacific Railroad.

If one of his goals was to see more of the American West, he certainly succeeded, because his routes allowed him to cover hundreds of miles between destinations. The hard work and being exposed to all kinds of weather and long stretches when he was driving alone and isolated in a vast, changing landscape hardened Wyatt in several ways. By the time he was twenty in 1868, he was a tall, strong, handsome man with piercing, cold blue eyes who had to depend on his strength and wits and patience to deal with a variety of places and people.

He and the protective Virgil relaxed together when not working together. While Wyatt never quite got the handle of hard liquor, he learned how to gamble and do it well at saloons and mining camps. He also took a shine to boxing. He was quick and packed a powerful punch. This came in handy when disputes, especially if the other person was drunk, could have led to shooting. Wyatt learned that a fast and well-placed fist or butt of a pistol could end a fight before it escalated.

But boxing became more than just recreation for him; it was a lifelong interest. Wyatt did not become a prizefighter himself; he instead learned how to referee boxing matches — and, of course, to bet on them.

He would do one or both with boxing matches for most of his life, including high-profile championship bouts.

If he and Virgil weren't already as close as two brothers can be, it was during this time that they became the best friend each other could have. In his biography of Virgil, Don Chaput has him as "an experienced farm hand and well-traveled stage driver [who] would be described in the coming years as a smiling, pleasant, rough frontiersman, with a keen sense of humor, afraid of nothing, eager to help, and all-around good company, for campfire, gambling hall, fence mending, and chewing the fat with friends, neighbors, and relatives." Wyatt was not nearly as outgoing, but he and his brother had each other's back.

Wyatt's career as a peace officer might never have happened if he had remained traveling to and from California and the towns and camps in between. There was no indication that anything to do with being a lawman interested him at all. Probably, men like him worked and played with as little contact with the law as possible. And the restlessness in Wyatt had to be satisfied by hauling freight over hundreds of miles, not patrolling a city street.

Life changed thanks to the unabated

restlessness of his father. Nicholas, even at fifty-five, was not content to stay put, and in 1868, only four years after making the perilous trip west, he was on the road again. After a short stay in Wyoming, the family arrived in southwestern Missouri. Nicholas and Virginia Ann and their youngest sons and daughter found a place to live in Lamar, and somehow he wangled a job as constable. Also living in Lamar was one of Nicholas's brothers, Jonathan, who was a minister, like their father, Walter, had been.

Nicholas may have felt more comfortable being back in the South. Lamar, founded as recently as 1852, still showed signs of having been in the thick of the fighting. Only seven of the town's buildings were still standing when the Civil War ended. When the Earps arrived, Lamar was recovering, as evidenced by the construction of a courthouse and a bank. Soon, Wyatt showed up in the town. Perhaps he'd had enough of the dust of the Great American Desert in his nostrils and clothes, or even as a full-grown man he didn't want to be too far away from family. Wyatt's reason for giving up an itinerant life to try to settle down in Missouri can only be conjectured, because until the end of his days he refused to talk about Lamar.

It was there that Wyatt received his first taste of being a lawman. When a justice-of-the-peace position opened up, Nicholas took it, and his son was appointed to take his place as constable. Around the same time, in late autumn 1869, Wyatt experienced another life-changing event: he fell in love. In his travels as a teamster, Wyatt may have been smitten more than once with an appealing young woman, but it didn't take long for him to conclude that his feeling for Aurilla Sutherland was the real thing.

William and Permelia Sutherland were real city folk, originally from New York. Aurilla was the sixth child and second daughter born to the couple, on January 10, 1850. Like Wyatt, she had been born in Illinois. When she was ten years old the Sutherlands moved south, to Missouri, to own and operate William's Exchange Hotel right in the Lamar town square.

The twenty-one-year-old Wyatt and Aurilla could have met each other simply when Constable Earp stopped into the hotel. Or it may have been at a social event in Lamar, a town that had only sixteen hundred residents. Sherry Monahan, in her book *Mrs. Earp,* about all the women who were or fancied themselves wives of the Earp brothers, points out that the peripatetic and enterprising Nicholas Earp sold baked goods and oysters from a shop three doors down from William's Exchange Hotel. It is even possible that they met at church, with members of both families attending Methodist services on Sundays.

In any case, Wyatt did not waste any time courting his new love in the fall of 1869 and through the holidays. With Nicholas officiating, Wyatt and Aurilla were married six days after her twentieth birthday, on January 16, 1870. Perhaps Wyatt had sown enough wild oats as a teamster and freight hauler out west that he would be content for many years with a wife and family and a steady job in Lamar.

Wyatt did not waste any time, either, starting that family. Aurilla became pregnant soon after the wedding. In August, to provide a home for his wife and expected child, Wyatt paid seventy-five dollars for a small house next to ones where Nicholas and Virginia Ann and their youngest children lived and where Newton resided. Also living in Lamar by then was Virgil. He too may not have wanted so much distance between himself and family. On May 30, also with Nicholas doing the honors, Virgil married Rozilla Draggoo. She was just seventeen.

The 1870 U.S. Census, conducted in Lamar on September 3, listed Nicholas and Virgil as grocers, Virginia Ann as keeping house for her husband, the children Warren and Adelia as members of the household, and Newton Earp as a farmer. Wyatt and Aurilla were listed as constable and homemaker. Life, it would seem, was good.

It got better when Wyatt won the election (receiving 137 votes) that month to remain as constable. He did it by defeating his own brother. Newton had not run against him out of any sibling rivalry but more likely to ensure the office stayed in the family. With Nicholas still justice of the peace, the Earps had the local legal system sewn up. They could look forward to the holidays with some financial security and an expanding family.

And then Aurilla died. The baby did not survive.

There is no record of a cause of death, though typhus or childbirth has been speculated. Wyatt's never talking about Lamar certainly meant not mentioning anything about his first wife. Even in his later years, the memory must have been too painful, in addition to risking the jealousy of his fourth wife.

In November, the dreams of a home for

his family dashed, Wyatt sold the lot, making a twenty-five-dollar profit on the transaction. It probably would have been best if he'd left Lamar and its painful memories. He didn't, and he would soon live to regret it. He would go lower than the loss of his wife.

The first sign of Wyatt heading for trouble was when there was a brawl between Virgil and Wyatt (Newton or James may have been involved, too) and two of Aurilla's brothers and three of their friends. There may have been some bitterness over her marriage and subsequent death, or it was a financial dispute. It is even possible that Wyatt was in a reckless mood — and Virgil, too, after Rozilla apparently left him — and went looking for mischief. In any event, the boxing Earp brothers took on five men, and no one was badly hurt.

Then early in 1871, Wyatt was hauled into court, accused of stealing or not repaying a loan of twenty dollars. The charge was dismissed, but clearly Wyatt was in a downward spiral, driven almost mad with grief. He resigned as constable, and his next step after that — decidedly a step down — was to become a horse thief.

The two horses stolen belonged to a man named William Keys, who lived in Indian

Territory. Wyatt must have made his way to what is now eastern Oklahoma, because in the company of two men, John Shown and Edward Kennedy, he showed up at the home of Keys in Fort Gibson. A strange statement later given to the court by Shown's wife alleges that Wyatt and Kennedy got Shown drunk and they rode for three nights into Kansas with two horses stolen from Keys. They were arrested and arraigned on April 14, and Anna Shown claimed that Wyatt and Kennedy threatened to kill her husband if he testified against them.

Wyatt somehow came up with five hundred dollars to make bail. He was never convicted; it is believed that after Kennedy's trial resulted in his acquittal, Wyatt was let loose. There is a story that Kennedy and Wyatt were kept in a jail in Van Buren, Arkansas, from which they and five other prisoners escaped on May 8. In any event, if he had been tried and convicted of what was a very serious crime, there may not have been lawman Wyatt Earp.

It would have been that autumn, perhaps trying to stay as far away from peace officers as possible, that Wyatt joined up with a buffalo-hunting outfit and crossed trails with Bat Masterson. Corroboration comes from two other sources. Bat's good friend Billy Dixon, in a book written many years later, recalled meeting Wyatt in the hunting camps and that he "was a shy young man with few intimates. With casual acquaintances he seldom spoke unless spoken to. When he did say anything, it was to the point, without fear or favor, which wasn't relished by some; but that never bothered Wyatt."

Another source is Bill Tilghman, who would become one of the more famous frontier lawmen. He recalled meeting Wyatt while buffalo hunting, and noted that what separated him from the other men was that Wyatt never drank alcohol.

And many years later in her family memoir, Adelia Earp Edwards recalled an incident: "Morgan was in a fight with a buffalo hunter one day and it would have come to shooting if Newton had not gotten between them and talked them into shaking hands. Morgan had a terrible temper while Newton was always very even in his ways. I recall he used to say, 'Morg and Warren will be the death of me.' " Hundreds of young men had turned to buffalo hunting to make good money, and with no other prospects, it makes sense that Wyatt was one of them.

In March 1872, he turned twenty-four.

He was already a widower and a fellow who had had repeated brushes with the law. He had no home and no real prospects and, writes Sherry Monahan, he "apparently continued his downward spiral into the depths of depravity." Wyatt was a lonely man touched by tragedy, who was reluctant or unable to make friends and to let anyone get close to him. It would have been very easy for him to fall in with the wrong crowd and repeat the ill-advised horse-stealing escapade, or worse.

Instead, Wyatt went to Wichita and found redemption.

FIVE

Bat was a handsome young fellow with a reckless devil-may-care look. He was already an experienced plainsman and a noted shot. — BILL TILGHMAN

Jim Masterson mostly stayed in Dodge City while his brothers Bat and Ed continued hunting. But the harvest in the summer and fall of 1873 was down significantly — a combination of incessant hunting having thinned the herds and a smaller migration than usual of buffalo coming north to the Arkansas River. And there was a national economic downturn that year. What was being called back east the Panic of 1873 reduced consumer demand across the board. Some men gave up hunting. The ones who remained found that they had to go farther afield to find the herds. This carried risks, chiefly being confronted by Indians also seeking a share of the dwindling resource.

One of those hunters was Bat, and after his confrontation with Indians, he almost went the way of the buffalo. But the result of his stomach-knotting experience was another bump up in his emerging reputation.

It was not smart for a hunter to set out alone, but that is what Bat did one day in the third week of December. He was unaware that his search for buffalo brought him near the camp of a Cheyenne band led by Bear Shield. Bat was happy to have found a stray buffalo, and he killed it. But as he was skinning the animal he was surrounded by five warriors. Before Bat could move, one Cheyenne lifted his Sharps rifle up off the ground, another yanked his pistol out of the holster, and when Bat turned to try to grab it back, the first Indian bashed him with the rifle barrel.

Blood flowed from a gash in his head. Bat fought to remain conscious, afraid that if he collapsed the Indians might choose to do to him what he'd been doing to the buffalo. He concluded from their gestures that the Cheyenne wanted him to leave the dead buffalo to them and go away . . . on foot, because they were keeping his horse, too. Bat had no choice but to make tracks.

Somehow, he managed to find his camp, where other hunters stitched up his wound.

He was glad to be alive but furious at being robbed of everything except the clothes on his back. Putting him in an even worse mood was the decision by the hunters to set out for Dodge City rather than face any of Bear Shield's warriors, whether there be five or fifty. Bat borrowed a couple of guns. He wasn't going anywhere. As with that railroad crook Raymond Ritter, he would be patient and exact his revenge. This time, he didn't have to wait nearly as long.

Accompanied by fellow hunter and friend Jim Harvey, Bat went in search of Bear Shield's camp. They found it Christmas night, and apparently it was not guarded well, because as the Cheyenne warriors slept, Bat and Harvey made off with a few dozen of the band's horses. They must have pushed them hard because the men made it to Dodge City before Bear Shield's irate (and embarrassed) warriors could chase them down. They did try: Bat was later told by a hunter that he had seen forty Cheyenne hurrying in the same direction he and Harvey had just traveled. A providential snow squall slowed them down, and as they drew closer to Dodge City without spotting their prey, the warriors accepted that they were out a herd of horses.

Bat and Harvey sold the horses for twelve hundred dollars. Once again at the Front Street saloon, drinks were on the man who was obviously not to be trifled with.

Though still only twenty years old in March 1874, Bat had acquired some notoriety in the Dodge City area for his dash, perseverance, and pluck. An event that cemented his reputation for courage under fire that year was the Battle of Adobe Walls.

There had already been one Battle of Adobe Walls. It had occurred ten years earlier, during the Civil War. Adobe Walls, north of present-day Amarillo, Texas, had been a trading post then, and rumors reached Kit Carson, the former mountain man and scout who was then a colonel in the Union Army, that Comanche had overtaken it. With few Confederates around to occupy his troops, Carson believed that his mission was to find and kill whatever hostiles were available.

He led three companies of army cavalry and infantry east — 335 soldiers and 72 Ute and Apache scouts — along the Canadian River into the Texas Panhandle. There were indeed Comanche at Adobe Walls, and Carson attacked them. Though an experienced frontiersman, he had underestimated the number of Indians — as many as a thousand, and they were angry as hornets — and he was surprised by their ferocity and tenacity. Carson and his troops barely escaped disaster, and they declared victory as they rode back to Santa Fe. He was actually credited as a hero for not having his force annihilated.

In March 1874, an expedition was formed that would go well south of the Arkansas River, across the western strip of Oklahoma, and into the Texas Panhandle, and thus severely trespass on Indian hunting grounds. There was no way around it; this was an incursion, a clear violation of the Medicine Lodge Treaty. But with buffalo becoming more scarce, it was every white and red man for himself. There was a sense of urgency, too, because if the scarcity of buffalo meant their products fell out of favor back east, prices could plunge further than they had during the previous year's depression. It wouldn't pay to wait around. This could be the last big buffalo expedition on the frontier.

The endeavor was organized by several Dodge City merchants who wanted to establish a new outpost on the Panhandle. They included James Hanrahan, a saloon owner; Tom O'Keefe, a blacksmith; the already successful duo of Charles Rath and Robert Wright, who needed to keep up a steady stream of hides being shipped from Dodge City; and several storekeepers, including Charlie Myers and Fred Leonard. A trading post had been established in 1845, and an adobe fort had been erected to house it — thus the name Adobe Walls. The small settlement lasted only three years because the Indians kept attacking it. Perhaps, in 1874, they would no longer be as aggressive.

The original handful of merchants and twenty-eight buffalo hunters were supplemented by whiskey haulers and even William Olds and his wife, Sybil (the only woman on the journey), who would seek to open a restaurant at the new trading post. Bat was the youngest participant. Sharing this adventure was twenty-four-year-old Billy Dixon, still a staunch friend. Bat wrote about him in a preface to the *Life of "Billy" Dixon,* a memoir by Olive Dixon published in 1914: "Billy Dixon was a typical frontiersman of the highest order. The perils and hardships of border life were exactly suited to his stoical and imperturbable nature. This does not mean that Billy was not a kindhearted, generous and hospitable man, for he possessed all these admirable qualities to a high degree, but he was cool, calculating and uncommunicative at all times."

Bat and Billy would have the least-interesting names of this wild bunch and the frontiersmen they expected to encounter in the Panhandle. These colorful characters included the Hoodoo Kid, Shoot 'Em Up Mike, Prairie Dog Dave (who, like his namesake, will pop up in this narrative from time to time), Dirty-Face Charlie, Bull Whack Joe, Hurricane Bill, Light-Fingered Jack, the Stuttering Kid, and Dutch Henry Born, who was soon to become a legendary frontier horse thief. While some of these names are probably true, we can also assume that storytellers over the years added and embellished others. The plain-named Dixon would go on to be possibly the only buffalo hunter to win the Medal of Honor, which was authorized for his valor during battles with Indians later that year. No matter what they were called, many of the men soon to set off south were tough and experienced travelers who wouldn't back away from trouble.

Demonstrating the disrespect for Indians or possibly the foolhardiness of the time, members of the hunting party did not heed the warning of Amos Chapman. As a grizzled veteran of the frontier, he'd had plenty of experience with Indians, and his credibility was even stronger for having a Cheyenne wife who had kept close ties with the tribe. When Chapman heard of the expedition being formed, he took it upon himself to inform the organizers that the Comanche and Kiowa down there were likely to come after the trespassers. The injury was killing their sustenance, the buffalo that remained on the Panhandle, and the insult was the blatant intrusion to do it.

With more bravado than brains, the merchants and the others ignored Chapman. The thinking was that with all these men and guns and ammunition, the Indians were the ones who had to be careful. An attack by hostiles, Dixon later recalled, "meant fighting to the last ditch, and victory to the strong."

The expedition left Dodge City, cheered on by a crowd that had gathered to bid them farewell. It was smooth going at first, with the clear air mild during the day and chilly at night, with a wide, dark, star-filled sky. The first challenge was to get the wagons across the Cimarron River, which in the spring was a swollen three-hundred-plus yards wide with pockets of quicksand along the shore. The calm and experienced teamsters managed to get the wagons across the churning, ice-cold water, and it was on to the Canadian River country.

The hunting party arrived in Texas without incident. Chapman had either been wrong about the bruised feelings of the Comanche and Kiowa, or their leaders had observed a force too big and with too much firepower to attack. When Bat and the others rolled up to East Adobe Walls Creek, they set up camp there. A few may have been well aware of Kit Carson's near debacle of a decade earlier. The famous frontiersman, mountain man, and scout had died in 1868, at fifty-eight, at Fort Lyons in Colorado, apparently from grief a month after his wife had died giving birth to their eighth child. (Helping to perpetuate the Carson truths and myths of a trailblazing career well into the twentieth century was a nephew born as William Carson, who took on the Kit Carson name, playing his uncle in circuses and other popular shows. This second Kit Carson died in 1957, at age ninety-nine.)

Not by a long shot were Bat and his companions the first ones to visit the Adobe Walls area since the Civil War. It was a remote area, and at that time of year it was a beautiful one, thanks to the blooming chinaberries, willows, and cottonwoods along the Canadian River and the sand hills to the east. Despite its distance from white civilization (it was 150 miles from Dodge City) and being in Indian country, men had journeyed there seeking treasure. Stories had persisted for many years that centuries earlier Adobe Walls had been a Spanish settlement. Expecting an Indian attack, the residents had buried chests crammed with gold and silver. The settlement was wiped out, and supposedly the treasure was still there, waiting to be uncovered. So far, it had not been found.

The group from Dodge City didn't believe or care about the rumors of buried treasure; they had more practical work to do. Using wood and especially sod, new buildings were constructed about a mile from Carson's battleground, for living in, for storing material, and for a saloon, a blacksmith shop, a restaurant, and a corral. This kept them busy into the end of May, when it was expected the northward-migrating buffalo would appear. Brave or desperate hunters who had gone farther south were already showing up at Adobe Walls with buffalo hides, and they bought ammunition and supplies at the trading post before leaving to go south again. A few, though, having had their fill of killing and with full pockets (and still full heads of hair), went north out of the settlement. Their earnings would further boost the business of the bars, saloons, and brothels in Dodge City.

For Bat, this may have been an idyllic time. He was exploring new, picturesque territory in the company of older, experienced men, there was plenty of whiskey and food, the days were growing long and warm, the fragrant nights offered a view of seemingly every star in the universe, and the arrival and killing of buffalo would be a bounty for all. A bonus was a sense that the Indians either didn't know or didn't care about the trespassers from Dodge City.

About that last part, they were very wrong. The Comanche and Kiowa and even Southern Cheyenne and Arapaho had taken notice and were not inclined to be gracious hosts. Worse for the white intruders, the tribes determined that this deliberate violation of their land would make the perfect example of justified Indian retaliation. It was as if a line in the sand as well as the Arkansas River had been crossed. To keep their sovereign land and remaining hunting grounds, it wasn't enough to chase the white invaders back to where they came from. They had to be exterminated.

To that end, the tribes did something

unusual — they banded together to fight a common foe, and under one leader: Quanah Parker. He would be assisted by a medicine man who some Comanche believed was also a magician. He sent out a call for warriors to converge for a Sun Dance, a ceremony that includes singing and drumming as well as dancing. Many answered the call, congregating on the Red River. The "star," though, the one who would lead them into battle, was the half-breed warrior Parker.

Chances were the Dodge City party did not know who he was, though they probably knew the widely circulated story of his mother, Cynthia Ann Parker. At the age of nine in 1836, she had been captured by Comanche warriors raiding a fort in East Texas. She grew up living with the tribe and married one of its leaders, Peta Nocona. The couple had three children, with Quanah being the oldest. In December 1860, during the Battle of Pease River, U.S. Army soldiers captured Cynthia Ann and her daughter, Topsana, and they were sent east to live with white family members. Both were dead within a decade, Topsana in 1863 and Cynthia Ann in 1870. Peta Nocona was killed in a battle in 1864. While still a young man, Quanah formed the Quahada band of the

Comanche, known for their cunning and ferocity.

In 1867, at age twenty-two, Quanah had attended the final negotiations for the Medicine Lodge Treaty but refused to abide by it. Though still not yet thirty in June 1874, he was already a respected and dramatic leader, a warrior who inspired other Comanche, and members of his band were veterans of skirmishes and battles with white migrants and army soldiers. As the recognized leader of the Comanche, he was naturally the one to lead the coalition as well because they deferred to the especially aggressive and powerful tribe who claimed, with some justification, to be the finest horsemen west of the Missouri River.

By 1874, the most visible enemy of the Comanche and their allies was Colonel Ranald Mackenzie, and his presence ratcheted up the tension between Indians and whites. He had been sent by the Ulysses Grant administration as head of an army force to kill or capture Indians who had refused to live on reservations. He knew who Quanah Parker was, and he vowed to catch him. To that end, Comanche and members of other tribes who were found by Mackenzie's troops were being killed.

On top of the injury and insult, the inhabitants of the new Adobe Walls settlement were targeted as revenge for Mackenzie's raids. The Dodge City party had put themselves in the wrong place at a very wrong time, and prospects for a long life were dimming.

At the end of May, as several hundred members of the tribes rallied to Quanah Parker and he prepared to lead their attack — which included teaching warriors assault tactics he'd witnessed used by the U.S. Cavalry — Bat and the other hunters were busy killing and skinning the buffalo who had traveled in the forefront of the northern migration. Early wagering suggested that this could turn out to be one of the most successful hunting expeditions ever.

But then in June there were rumors of Indians attacking settlements and other hunting camps in the Panhandle. A man named Joe Plummer arrived to tell those at the new Adobe Walls settlement that his two hunting partners at a nearby camp had just been killed and scalped and their bodies mutilated beyond recognition. Another man told a similar story a few days later. More hunters arrived, having left their camps, favoring their lives over future profits.

Several of the hunters wanted to take what had been harvested so far and head back to

Dodge City. The merchants talked them out of abandoning Adobe Walls. They pointed to how good the hunting was, which would result in fuller pockets when they did return home later in the summer. Of equal or more concern was not wanting to have to clear out and leave behind merchandise not yet sold or traded. The twenty-eight hunters, several of the merchants, and Bill Olds and his wife agreed to stay. Everyone else packed up their wagons and pointed them toward the Arkansas River.

It was not a good sign when that prophet of doom Amos Chapman showed up at Adobe Walls. He was acting as a scout for an army sergeant and four troopers who were tracking horse thieves. Chapman met privately with the remaining merchants to inform them that according to the post trader at Camp Supply in the Cherokee Strip — the horizontal sliver of Oklahoma just south of Kansas — the word was that the Comanche and their allies were to attack at the next full moon, which was a few days away. Using the excuse that more supplies were needed from Dodge City, the merchants hastily began the trip north toward the safety of Kansas. Either the nervous merchants drew straws or he couldn't bear to abandon his wares, but

James Hanrahan stayed behind as the caretaker.

The hunters were not stupid men — well, some of them weren't — and they recognized people high-tailing it when they saw it. Bat and the rest didn't follow, but they were extra vigilant.

It was on the night of June 26 that the gleaming white full moon hung in the seemingly endless North Texas sky. Fortuitously for the small army led by Quanah Parker, the night was hot with just the barest breeze. It was expected that the doors and windows of the handful of buildings would be open. If they were quiet, as soon as there was enough light the raiders could ride down from a bluff above the Canadian River and be upon the sleeping white men before they became aware of an attack. The men and one woman, it would seem, had only minutes until suffering a violent death. The lucky ones would be those who died the quickest.

That this did not happen is either because of a faulty ridgepole or the remaining merchant who almost got himself and the others killed by being too clever. At about two in the morning, a sharp crack echoed loudly in the saloon. Hanrahan shouted, "It's going to collapse!"

The men jumped up and set right to work shoveling dirt off the roof to lighten the load and cutting poles to support the supposedly failing ridgepole, the saloon's main support beam. Why "supposedly"? Some accounts suggest that Hanrahan couldn't bear to abandon his saloon and its contents by informing the hunters of Chapman's warning, yet he couldn't risk them being slaughtered in their sleep, either. The ridgepole may have been perfectly fine — Billy Dixon, for example, reports in his memoir that when he examined it, the pole was intact — but Hanrahan's shouting and what may have been a rifle shot simulating the sound of a cracking wooden pole and the resulting rescue of the saloon had everyone wide awake. Thus, when the first light of dawn licked the eastern horizon, the inhabitants of Adobe Walls could see that coming down at them, offering a Technicolor display of war paints and armed with rifles, lances, knives, and shields of thick buffalo hides, were hundreds of warriors led by Quanah Parker.

According to Dixon's memoir, the Indians "were coming like the wind. Over all was splashed the rich colors of red, vermillion and ochre, on the bodies of the men, on the bodies of the running horses. Scalps dangled from bridles, gorgeous war-bonnets fluttered their plumes, bright feathers dangled from the tails and manes of the horses, and the bronzed, half-naked bodies of the riders glittered with ornaments of silver and brass. Behind this headlong charging host stretched the Plains, on whose horizon the rising sun was lifting its morning fires."

It was easier for Dixon writing decades later to appreciate all that dangling and the scenery surrounding the attackers. At the moment, however, the urgent task for Bat and his hunting brethren was to not get killed.

Most of the men acted quickly by slamming doors and barricading the other openings in the buildings with grain and flour sacks, leaving just enough space to poke the barrels of their Sharps and other rifles through. Knowing they had an abundance of ammunition, they began blazing away from all three main buildings. Bat, one of the nine hunters in Hanrahan's saloon (the others were divided up between the two stores), was especially effective because he had excellent eyesight and he had learned to shoot by firing at moving animals, not ignorant, nearly motionless buffalo. The tables had been turned: now it was the Indians startled by the ferocity of the Adobe

Walls defenders.

There were immediate casualties, however. Two brothers named Shadler had been caught in a freight wagon and were killed. Trapped in the buildings, the hunters watched them die. The warriors were all over the structures now, looking for any openings to ride or jump through. Flaming arrows landed on the roofs.

The defenders were helped greatly because the buildings were mostly made of sod, and thus, despite the Indians' relentless efforts, they would not catch fire. Also, the way the structures were positioned allowed those in the saloon to provide flanking fire to relieve some of the pressure on the men in the other two buildings. Still, sheer numbers might be the deciding factor, with Indian forces outnumbering the whites by at least ten to one. With the Indians right outside the doors and windows and on the roofs, the Sharps rifles were not of much use. Bat and the others relied on their pistols and even knives and bare hands when warriors managed to work their way inside.

Their leader, Quanah Parker, was relentless, too, backing his horse into doors to try to break them down and leaping onto rooftops to fire his rifle down into the buildings. The men inside piled boxes and tables against the doors to make them harder to force open, and prayed they weren't standing in the wrong spot when a bullet came from above.

"So close would they come that we planted our guns in their faces and against their bodies through the portholes, while they were raining their arrows and bullets at us," Bat later recounted. "At times the bullets poured in like hail," Billy Dixon later reported, "and made us hug the sod walls like gophers when an owl is swooping past."

No owl would be as dangerous as Quanah Parker. But he and his warriors began to be withered by the firepower of the Sharps rifles and pistols before many could get close enough to the buildings, and the defenders had a virtually inexhaustible supply of bullets, especially the .50-caliber kind. The same bullets that could kill a buffalo weighing a ton could do incredible damage to a man, and it had to be disheartening for the Indians to see their fellow warriors — and their horses — shredded as well as killed.

One of the hunters in the Myers and Leonard store, Billy Tyler, was shot in the chest. During brief lulls in the shooting, the men in the saloon could hear him pleading for water. Bat grabbed a pail. To get to the well, he would have to expose himself to the attacking Indians. Just as Bat was about to throw open a door, an older man, Bill Keeler, persuaded Bat that he should go because he was well known among several tribes and might not be killed. Accompanied by his dog, Keeler ran to the well. He was wrong about not being shot at, but he returned unwounded with the water. Not as lucky was the dog, who died.

Bat focused on firing as fast and as accurately as he could. Dixon would later write, "Bat Masterson should be remembered for the valor that marked his conduct. He was a good shot, and not afraid."

He and the other good shots combined to turn the tide of the battle. When Quanah Parker's horse was shot out from under him, at around 10 A.M., the attackers withdrew.

The raid had not produced the expected result. The medicine man had convinced the Comanche and their allies that they were invincible against the white man's bullets, and the damage of the Sharps rifles had proved him dreadfully daft. To make matters worse, after the Indians had retreated to what they thought was a safe distance, a bullet found Quanah Parker, hitting him in the shoulder, and another bullet killed the medicine man's horse. They kept retreating farther, and the white men's sharpshooting still found them. Several hunters later corroborated Billy Dixon's claim that he shot an Indian off his horse at fifteen hundred yards, meaning the victim was too far away to even hear the shot and literally didn't know what hit him.

Among the many casualties the attackers suffered were fifteen dead, or this was the number of bodies the Indians had failed to carry off with them. With Parker wounded and the Indians not wanting to come within range of the powerful rifles, the battle was over. Bat and the others could now tend to their own wounded, repair damage to the buildings, and bury their own dead. There would be a fourth fatality, when a few days after the attack, with Indians still surrounding Adobe Walls, William Olds, while descending from the roof of Rath & Wright's, accidentally shot himself in the head. More hunters arrived to swell the population of the settlement, and finally the discouraged Indians and their wounded leader rode away.

The event had been a transforming experience for Bat, as the young man had faced death and displayed courage equal to or greater than that of the older, more experienced men. As Dixon wrote about his friend, "He was a chunk of steel and anything that struck him in those days always drew fire."

As a final note to the Second Battle of Adobe Walls story, it was the beginning of the end of Quanah Parker's position as leader and of the Comanche as a feared tribe. The battle was the opening salvo in the Red River War, with Colonel Mackenzie redoubling his efforts against the Comanche. He scored a victory against them that September in the Battle of Palo Duro Canyon, which included destroying the tribe's village there and killing fifteen hundred of their horses, the main source of the tribe's domination. The following year, with the remaining Comanche harassed and starving, Parker surrendered.

He spent the rest of his life on a reservation in Oklahoma. He lived in some prosperity there, fathering sixteen children, and died in 1911 at age sixty-six. Bat Masterson and Quanah Parker may have met up again seven years before that when Bat's friend Theodore Roosevelt was being inaugurated for the second time as president and Parker rode in the festive parade seated in the back of a car with the Lakota Sioux leader Spotted Tail and the legendary Apache warrior Geronimo.

Six

He had always kidded her, in the days when she was a sporting girl in Dodge, that she would end up respectable, though even he couldn't have guessed that she'd marry a sheriff.

— LARRY MCMURTRY, *Lonesome Dove*

Wyatt didn't go to Wichita directly. He still had some wandering and grieving and sorting out to do. In his book *Inventing Wyatt Earp,* Allen Barra notes, "For a couple of years after the death of his wife, Wyatt Earp was a loner; he would retain some of the qualities of a loner the rest of his life."

It is indeed likely that he tried his hand at buffalo hunting and met Bat Masterson, Billy Dixon, and some of their colorful colleagues along the way. It was still a way for a man with few skills to make pretty good money, and Wyatt was one who had skills with horses and, inevitably, guns from the years of hauling freight. It was also an occupation for someone who had no other pressing business to attend to.

"I'll admit that no other buffalo hunter of my acquaintance — myself, least of all — planned his work as a crusade for civilization," Wyatt told a biographer many years later. "I went into the business to make money while enjoying life that appealed to me."

It couldn't have appealed to him that much, because at some point in late 1871 or early 1872 he was back in Illinois, in Peoria, where he lived in a brothel operated by Jane Haspel. Reportedly, Virgil was also living in Peoria, and in February 1872 Wyatt and Morgan were arrested "on a charge of being found in a house of ill fame." Wyatt would be arrested twice more on the same charge but in different brothels. He may have been a steady customer at these houses of prostitution in Peoria, but it is more likely that he and probably Virgil and Morgan worked as bouncers at such places.

However, at some point in 1873, when he was twenty-five, Wyatt realized he had to quit Peoria and its court system for good. He could go back to buffalo hunting, but soon after he did, he put his nose to the Panhandle breeze and whiffed the scent of a dying industry. He may have also detected the pungent odor of a new one emerging, that of shipping cattle north and east. In their camps, hunters had to notice the trail drives coming up from the south and passing through Texas and Oklahoma to Kansas towns like Wichita and Abilene and others connected by railroad tracks. A young man with a talent for gambling and who could keep a cool head unfettered by whiskey could leave the bloody work behind and strive to make a good living in one of those towns.

The cow town that Wyatt went to first was Ellsworth. It was smack in the middle of Kansas, north and west of Wichita, connected by the railroad to Abilene. It lay on the treeless banks of the Smoky Hill River, surrounded by tall-grass prairie. In 1871, with the Kansas Pacific Railroad having come through on its gradual way west, Ellsworth had rivaled Abilene as a cattle-shipping town. The railroad had helped to fund the survey of a new cattle trail southeast to the Chisholm Trail, laying out a long welcome mat to Texas ranchers. They took full advantage of it, and in 1873 tens of thousands of cattle were filling the holding pens and railroad cars.

Why Wyatt would travel that far north

from the Panhandle is not known, other than that Ellsworth may have appeared a more promising town to try before Wichita and Dodge City became more active cow towns. Until the financial panic back east that year curbed its activities, Ellsworth was a gambler's paradise and an oasis for cowboys looking for other forms of recreation. The dance-hall girls were kept busy, and a few were pretty formidable gamblers, too. One, known as Prairie Rose, bet a cowboy fifty dollars that she would shed her clothes and stroll down the main street. Never figuring a woman would do that, the cowboy accepted the wager and reported it back to his comrades. At five the next morning a naked Prairie Rose did walk down the street, but she held two cocked six-shooters and shouted out that she would put a bullet in the first cowboy face that appeared in a window.

An incident that places Wyatt in Ellsworth in 1873 involved two of the frontier's more dramatic characters. In June, after a bunch of cowboys had shot up the town, the police department was expanded to five officers. These included the brothers Ben and Billy Thompson, gunmen and gamblers who believed that the police force, headed by Marshal Brocky Jack and his chief deputy,

Happy Jack Morco — who had wound up in Ellsworth after leaving behind in Oregon a wife and charges of killing four men — was corrupt and populated by men who were more degenerate than the men they tossed in jail. However, Chauncey Whitney, the sheriff of Ellsworth County, was a respected lawman and a Civil War veteran. The problem for citizens was that Whitney had only limited jurisdiction within Brocky Jack's territory.

Ben Thompson, in particular, was not a man to aggravate. He had been born in West Yorkshire, England, on November 2, 1843. While he was a child, the Thompson family emigrated to America, settling in Austin, Texas. As a teenager, Ben learned how to set type, and he was bent on becoming a printer. The Civil War changed those plans: two months after the attack on Fort Sumter, he enlisted in the 2nd Regiment, Texas Mounted Rifles, H Company, and somehow his brother, Billy, barely sixteen, managed to join the Confederate Army, too. Ben was wounded during the Battle of Galveston in 1863, but he returned to his regiment, and he and Billy saw further action.

When the war ended, Ben became a mercenary, finding work fighting for Emperor Maximilian in the Mexican Revolution.

Along the way Ben acquired a wife. When word reached him in Mexico that his wife had been attacked by her own brother, Ben returned to Texas and beat up the abuser so badly that Ben was tried and convicted of attempted murder and sent to Huntsville Prison. His stay was a short one, though, as he received a full pardon. Ben hit the road as a gambler, working his way up into Kansas, and could be recognized for his fine clothes, mustache, and top hat.

Thompson would soon play a crucial role in Bat Masterson's life. Years later, Bat reminisced that the debonair gunman "was a remarkable man in many ways and it is very doubtful if in his time there was another man living who equaled him with the pistol in a life and death struggle. The very name of Ben Thompson was enough to cause the general run of 'man killers,' even those who had never seen him, to seek safety in instant flight."

Ben had tussled with lawmen before, including the most feared one: James Butler Hickok. As with Wyatt Earp, Illinois could not contain a restless man, especially one who would earn the name Wild Bill. As a spy and scout in the Civil War, Hickok had fought against the Confederates in Arkansas and Missouri, with many of the rebs being from Texas. Having an understanding of such men was an advantage when he began wearing a badge in the Kansas cow towns and most of the cowboys were from Texas. What helped more, of course, was his tall, lean stature, long auburn locks and mustache, and that he could outdraw any man in a gunfight.

Hickok wore two Colt Model 1851s. Each was a .36-caliber percussion pistol weighing less than three pounds and which had been engraved at the Colt factory by the master engraver there, Gustav Young. The guns were nicknamed "Navy" across the West because of the naval warfare scene depicting a battle between Texas ships and the Mexican navy that was inscribed on the cylinders of the first run produced in 1850. General Robert E. Lee had carried an 1851 Colt pistol during the Civil War, and another owner was Richard Burton, the English explorer. It is not known for certain how Hickok acquired his guns in 1869. One story has them being a gift from Senator Henry Wilson of Massachusetts when Hickok guided him and friends through the Arkansas River territory. Another has them being presented to the quick-handed lawman by the Union Pacific Railroad as a reward for getting Hays, Kansas, under control. Wild Bill rarely used his left hand to shoot; the second gun was more of a backup in case the right-hand gun misfired or ran out of bullets. One photo shows him wearing the Navy Colts with the butts pointing forward, known as a "crossdraw" style.

The ivory-hilted and silver-mounted pistols impressed the men, and his looks as well as his shirts of the finest linen and boots of the thinnest kid leather impressed the ladies. But what impressed frontier people the most was his shooting. Tales of his legendary accuracy made the rounds, going back to July 21, 1865. On that day in Springfield, Missouri, Hickok was challenged to a duel by Davis Tutt. Standing sideways and seventy-five yards away, Tutt must have assumed he was safe from serious injury and that his honor would be restored. He died honorably, at least, when Hickok shot him through the heart.

Hickok became marshal of Abilene in 1871, just as all hell was beginning to bust loose there. He already had enough of a reputation as a gunslinger that he could allow the cowboys enjoying the saloons and prostitutes between trail drives to wear their guns and know that would not instigate trouble. Indeed, using a frontier form of reverse psychology, the intimidating marshal knew the cowboys would figure out that either they would never want to cause trouble while wearing a gun and have to go up against Wild Bill, or the smartest play was to leave their gun belts in their saddlebags.

That same year, Ben Thompson and a partner, Phil Coe, arrived in Abilene and established the Bull's Head Tavern & Gambling Saloon. Ben's first brush with the law there was when he painted a huge and lewd bull on the outside wall. Citizens complained, Hickok ordered it removed, and Thompson refused. Instead of going for his gun, Hickok went for a can of paint and a brush and covered the bull. As tough as Thompson was, he was not about to go up against the marshal himself.

A different strategy presented itself when John Wesley Hardin hit town. The precocious gunslinger, then eighteen years old, was on the run from an arrest warrant in Texas. After a few visits to the Bull's Head, Thompson pointed out to him that Hickok hated rebels and was a damn Yankee who needed killing. Hardin looked Hickok up. However, the young man immediately saw Wild Bill as an idol, and the marshal took a liking to the fugitive kid. He made Hardin a deal: he would pretend he had no knowledge of the Texas warrant if the teenager refrained from killing anyone while in Abilene.

The deal did not last long. One night while Hardin was asleep in the American Hotel, an intruder entered. Not waiting to learn of the man's intentions, Hardin grabbed his gun and fired, killing him. Also not waiting long enough to even pull on pants, Hardin jumped out a back window as Hickok hurried into the front lobby. Hardin landed in a small wagon, which he drove south, possibly preferring Texas to Wild Bill's six-shooters. Along the way, he found a cowboy and took his pants and horse. Hardin told the cowboy to return the wagon and "give Wild Bill my love." He never set foot in Abilene again.

Ben Thompson would soon have another reason to dislike Hickok. Phil Coe became infatuated by a saloon girl named Jessie Hazel. As it happened, Wild Bill was drawing her under his spell, embittering Ben's partner. One night during a card game that included Hickok and Coe, there was an accusation of cheating. Coe went for his gun, but his fate was sealed as soon as the marshal's cleared leather. Unfortunately, Hickok fired more than once, and a stray bullet killed one of his deputies. The marshal was furious. He kicked all the cowboys out of Abilene and patrolled the streets with a shotgun, daring anyone to show himself wearing a weapon.

With his partner in the ground, Thompson decided to relocate, and that is how, with his brother Billy, Ben wound up in Ellsworth. One day in August 1873, the brothers and Happy Jack and another policeman, John Sterling, were gambling in a saloon owned by a man named Brennan. The combination of alcohol and charges of cheating proved combustible. Arguing led to Sterling punching Ben Thompson in the face, which led to guns being drawn. The combatants spilled out into the street and shots were fired. What prevented bloodshed was the appearance of Sheriff Whitney, whom the Thompsons trusted. They agreed to join the sheriff for a drink back in the saloon.

Unfortunately, Billy still held a shotgun with the hammers up. When Happy Jack, unhappy with Whitney's interference in the dispute, confronted Ben with a brandished pistol, Billy's immediate (and drunken) reaction was to pull the triggers. He shot the sheriff. According to witnesses, Ben said, "My God, Billy, you have shot our best friend." Worse than that, the shot would prove to be a fatal one.

Ben told his brother to get on a horse and ride like hell out of town. Billy did just that. The mayor of Ellsworth, James Miller, appeared and told the remaining brother to give up his guns. Ben refused. Brocky Jack, Happy Jack, and another policeman stood with their hands on their guns. Flooding out of the nearby saloons were cowboys eager to fight alongside another Texan. When the standoff continued long enough, the frustrated mayor fired the entire police department. Now what?

Stuart Lake's biography claimed that Wyatt Earp arrived on the scene to see what all the commotion was about, and the mayor immediately made him the new marshal of Ellsworth. However unlikely this is, it does seem that Wyatt intervened to help defuse the situation. He may have encountered Thompson before, perhaps only just weeks earlier as fellow gamblers in the saloons, or maybe he simply didn't want to see his new hometown shot up. A mortally wounded sheriff may have tipped the scales. In any case, this was Wyatt's first confrontation that began to build his reputation as a lawman.

Wyatt told his third wife a few years later that he squared off against Ben Thompson:

"I thought he would shoot me. I really expected to be killed unless I could see his wrist move in time to draw and fire before he could pull the trigger. I just kept looking him in the eye as I walked toward him. And when he started talking to me I was pretty sure I had him. I tried to talk in as pleasant a voice as I could manage and I told him to throw his gun in the road. He did and that's all there was to it."

Thompson was arrested by a county deputy sheriff named Edward O. Hougue. As soon as Ben was securely behind bars, a posse was formed to go find Billy. They went on their way, and shortly afterward a gambler friend of Ben's, Cad Pierce, offered a thousand dollars for the formation of a new posse that would chase down and stop the first posse. There were no takers, but the first posse lost Billy's trail, anyway.

The next day, Ben Thompson was brought before a judge. He was fined twenty-five dollars, he paid it, and then he rode off to track down his brother. A new police force was installed in Ellsworth, and one of its members killed Cad Pierce in a gunfight. Billy eventually returned to Ellsworth and was acquitted of murder. Before Whitney died, the sheriff stated that his shooting had been an accident.

When Wyatt finally arrived in Wichita, in 1874, the town was at its peak in transporting cattle, with one reasonable estimate being eighty thousand of them packed into railroad cars and sent off to the slaughterhouses. Some years before, the site had been little more than tall, waving prairie grass on the bank of the Arkansas River, and now it was a bustling, noisy, dusty Eden for ranchers selling their animals. Wyatt's older brother James, now married to a woman named Bessie, had already settled in Wichita, working at a saloon. Bessie operated a brothel. (In a census taken the following year, Bessie's occupation was listed as "Sporting.")

With a steady flow of cowboys into town, saloons were springing up on every corner. Officials went so far as to post signs on the trails leading in that read EVERYTHING GOES IN WICHITA. At night, wafting through the dry air and vying with the stench of the penned-up cattle, were the scents of beer and whiskey, horses, cheap perfume, and men who had gone too long between baths.

The tinkling of pianos came from the saloons, background to the laughter and the occasional crashing sounds when a fight broke out. It took a lot of rambunctiousness to put a cowboy in jail, where he could not spend money. Besides going to alcohol, that money was taken readily enough by the card players who stayed glued to chairs at saloon gaming tables. Young women in fluffy dresses offered songs and other favors. In Wichita, prostitution was legal as long as the ladies were licensed.

The city was gaining the sort of reputation that would soon be replicated and exceeded by Dodge City's. "Wichita resembles a brevet hell after sundown," intoned *The St. Louis Republican.* "Brass bands whooping it up; harlots and hack drivers yelling and cursing; dogs yelping, pistols going off; bullwhackers cracking their whips; saloons open wide their doors, and gayly attired females thump and drum up pianos, and in dulcet tones and mocking smiles invite the boys in and night is commenced in earnest."

One of those fights led to Wyatt becoming a Wichita lawman. In May 1874, a brawl broke out in one of the saloons that spilled out into the streets, inviting more participants to join in. Somehow, Wyatt got mixed up in it and was arrested. He was being escorted to the jail by the deputy marshal when a new group of rowdy cowboys entered town. With the deputy marshal looking for a way out, Wyatt talked the newcomers out of causing further damage. When Marshal Bill Smith heard about this, he offered Wyatt the deputy marshal's job. Wyatt took it, though it was not a full-time position, more of an as-needed job.

Wyatt joined not a moment too soon. That same month, Charley Sanders returned home to find two Texas cowboys attempting to have their way with his wife. He was a strapping, black hod carrier, and the cowboys were no match for him. Sanders beat them both badly and tossed them out in the street. This humiliation had to be avenged. The next day the two bruised men and several other cowboys rode into town, found Sanders working at the construction of a building, and shot him twice. Rather than wait for the marshal, the men went and found Smith, who wouldn't dare challenge so many guns. He stepped aside and the cowboys sauntered off. Clearly, a more aggressive form of policing was needed in Wichita.

The town got it, Wyatt's way. Ida May was the owner of a brothel who provided a piano from Kansas City purchased for $1000 as additional entertainment. Actually, she had paid a quarter of that price and didn't bother forking over the remaining $750. The piano store owner wired the marshal's office in Wichita, requesting that the piano be repossessed and held until he could come get it. Wyatt showed up at the brothel with several men to do just that. When he found the parlor filled with drunken cowboys, he shamed them into passing the hat for money to make a payment on the piano. It stayed in the parlor, but the Texans were angry with Wyatt's manner.

The next day, about fifty of them banded together on the southwest side of the Arkansas River, led by a man named Mannen "Gip" Clements, who was a cousin of John Wesley Hardin. It was time to remind the law who really ruled Wichita. Expecting trouble, Wyatt had recruited a force of gun-toting citizens to support the police force, and they waited on the Wichita side of the river. When the cowboys rode across the bridge, they were surprised to be confronted. Wyatt, with a shotgun crooked in his arm, ordered Clements and his men to holster their pistols. There was a tense standoff for a few moments; then the cowboys returned to their camp.

By now, a host of Hollywood screenwriters would have concocted plots based on a chance meeting in Wichita between the man who would become the most famous lawman of the West and a thirteen-year-old who would become one of its most notorious outlaws. There are accounts of Henry Antrim and his mother living in an apartment near the courthouse where Wyatt worked. He had been born William Henry McCarty Jr. in New York City, and after his mother married William Antrim, the boy was called by his middle name. He and his mother were stopping for a while in the bustling Wichita on their way to New Mexico, where he would achieve infamy as Billy the Kid. Alas, here is a case of the legend being more enticing than the fact: his mother had married Antrim and they had settled in New Mexico the year before, and in 1874 she died of tuberculosis.

In late October, Wyatt was called upon to chase down a group of men identified in the local press as the "Higgenbotham outfit." These "scalawags," as *The Wichita City Eagle* called them, had toted up over twenty thousand dollars in debts and run out on them by stealing a man's new wagon. The theft victim filed a complaint, and officers John Behrens and Wyatt set off. They tracked the wagon for seventy-five miles. One has to think there was a more effective way for the fugitives to make good their escape, or they never expected the lawmen to be so persistent. In any case, Behrens and Wyatt confronted the Higgenbotham outfit with shotguns and six-shooters, and restitution was arranged.

In Wichita, Wyatt was putting his life back together, but he was no choirboy. In between his deputy responsibilities he was a gambler and, evidence indicates, working again as a bordello bouncer or manager. This would not necessarily be redemption in the modern sense, but in Wichita at that time that was a legitimate occupation. Someone had to protect the "soiled doves," as prostitutes were often condescendingly called, from the cowboys, miners, mule skinners, and other ruffians who could be violent. Moonlighting lawmen often made for good guardians, much the same as policemen today moonlight as security guards — though not, presumably, where prostitution is being practiced.

That Wyatt was wearing a badge regularly and was gaining the trust of the citizenry in Wichita was a form of redemption. And it would seem his grieving over Aurilla had faded, because there was a new woman in his life, one who would be considered his second wife, even if they never wound up standing in front of a preacher.

Sarah Haspel was sixteen at the time that Wyatt worked for her mother at the brothel in Peoria. Their "wedding," such as it was, had occurred in September 1872, when Sarah and Wyatt were arrested and a Peoria newspaper identified her as Sarah Earp. (Wyatt was identified as "the Peoria bummer.") Sarah's father, Frederick Haspel, a German immigrant, had lost a leg while fighting in the Union Army and did not return to Illinois afterward. By then, Jane Haspel had three youngsters to feed and house, and she did so by opening a brothel. During Sarah's teenage years, she became one of her mother's employees.

Whatever detours Wyatt took in 1872–1873, when he arrived in Wichita he had Sarah with him. Carrying on the family tradition — both families, it seems — she joined forces with Bessie Earp in operating a brothel. This was not anything like the domestic life that Wyatt had envisioned and had begun to live in Lamar, but now he was older and wiser about life and how much to expect from it. Wichita was home now, he had a "wife," at least one of his brothers was a neighbor, and once again — at least, most of the time — Wyatt was working on the right side of the law. For now — maybe for good — this was enough.

Seven

You who live your lives in cities or among peaceful ways cannot always tell whether your friends are the kind who would go through fire for you. But on the Plains one's friends have an opportunity to prove their mettle. — WILLIAM F. "BUFFALO BILL" CODY

Bat was glad to be back in Dodge City. Unlike some of the others from Adobe Walls who wanted to return there while it was still hunting season and the army had Quanah Parker and the Comanche occupied, Bat intended to stay put.

Not that Dodge City was an oasis of calm in the summer of 1874. Many people were frightened by the outbreak of violence and the threat of marauding Indian bands. It was said that over a hundred white people had been killed between the Arkansas River and the Rio Grande, a high enough total

156

that some homesteaders and hunters sought the shelter of Fort Dodge. Bat wasn't about to do that, either. The Adobe Walls adventure had left him without nearly as much money as he had anticipated, and he had to do something about that. For a time, that something was gambling.

But Bat's luck must have been all used up by surviving the Battle of Adobe Walls and the subsequent trip back from the Panhandle to Dodge City with his scalp still attached to his skull. Though short of his twenty-first birthday, Bat was mature and experienced enough to know that a man down on his luck could get into a lot of trouble in Dodge City. Thus, in August, when his friend Billy Dixon signed on as an army scout, Bat decided to do the same.

The campaigns being waged by Colonel Mackenzie and affiliated commands meant such scouts were in high demand. Nelson Miles was in charge of eight cavalry companies and four companies of infantry being organized at Fort Dodge. Miles had risen to the rank of general during the Civil War and had been wounded in battle four times, his actions during the Battle of Chancellorsville had earned him the Medal of Honor, and when Lee surrendered to Grant in April 1865 he was, at just twenty-six, an infantry corps commander. Now a colonel — after the war, many officers were reduced in rank or lopped off the active list altogether — Miles was about to lead a force from Fort Dodge south and he needed scouts who knew Indian Territory. Bat and Billy did, and they were welcomed. In turn, the young men welcomed the pay of seventy-five dollars a month plus the possibility of bonuses if the campaign was successful.

There would be thirty-seven scouts working for Miles, twenty of them Delaware Indians. Most of the seventeen white men were former buffalo hunters. They joined the Bluebellies on the banks of the Arkansas River, and on August 11, 1874, they crossed over and began the journey across the Cherokee Strip and into Texas. It was a hot, dry summer, especially for men whose horses kicked up choking dust from sunup to sundown. Still, it didn't seem very long before Bat and Billy were in familiar surroundings.

While hunting Comanche and Apache war parties, Miles and his force paid a visit to the Adobe Walls settlement. At least a dozen hunters were still there. Not much hunting was being done, because a war party could appear at any moment, but the hunters, with plenty of supplies and whiskey, figured they were better off inside the walls than making a run for it across the Panhandle. Bat agreed with the wisdom of this when he observed two hunters who had gone out to pick wild plums only to be attacked, with the Indians managing to kill one of them.

With the inhabitants in relatively good shape, the army soldiers moved out, heading west and south, away from Adobe Walls. The battle there in June had earned Bat the admiration of his fellow hunters. The adventure he was about to undertake would earn him his first taste of true frontier fame.

Near the Canadian River the soldiers and scouts fought their first engagement. It was a minor one against a small group of Indians, with one being killed and another wounded. Believing that more hostiles must be close by, Miles's command picked up the pace the last week of August. This made for tough going for men and horses, as the territory being covered was even hotter and drier than in Kansas, with temperatures sometimes topping 110 degrees. Saloon ceiling fans and ready access to water and whiskey back in Dodge City must have seemed very appealing to Bat and Billy.

Finally, soon after sunup on August 30, the hard-riding scouts found a large force of Indians. More accurately, the Indians found them. As Bat and the others were riding on a trail between two lines of bluffs, at least two hundred warriors appeared above them and opened fire. The scouts jerked their carbines out of their saddle holsters and jumped off their horses. From the ground and behind rocks and withered brown bushes they returned fire. It was touch and go until the cavalry arrived and routed the Indians.

Helping them do that was a recent addition to the firearms of the West, a Gatling gun. The Indians were astonished as the ancestor of the twentieth-century machine gun, bolted onto a baggage wagon, spewed bullets faster than a dozen men could shoot. Once again, the technological advances of the white man forecast the ultimate defeat of the Southwest and Plains tribes.

The scouts got back on their horses and the chase was on. For twenty miles they and the army were in hot pursuit — too hot, as men suffering from incredible thirst and heat exhaustion fell by the wayside. Still, Bat and those with stronger stamina persisted, day after day, with the army soldiers and their exhausted horses trailing behind them.

Finally, the chase ended. The whites were in an area known as the Staked Plains, so named because of a series of poles or stakes that had been driven into the ground to mark a route for cowboys to direct their herds to sources of water. Miles ordered that camp be made there. He hadn't scored the decisive victory he sought, but he wasn't going to retreat, either.

A few days turned into a few weeks. Miles sent scouts to Camp Supply inside the Cherokee Strip with dispatches on his lack of progress, and they returned with supplies. One of these trips was taken by four troopers guided by Dixon and the grizzled Amos Chapman, who had warned the merchants at Adobe Walls back in June that Quanah Parker was organizing an attack. At a site called Buffalo Wallow the six men were ambushed by over a hundred Comanche and Kiowa. This time there was no cavalry on the way, so the scouts and soldiers kept firing as fast as they could, keeping the Indians at bay until nightfall, when they retreated. One soldier was killed and the others were wounded, including Chapman, who lost a leg. It was for his bravery and deadly accuracy with his rifle during this engagement that Billy Dixon would receive the Medal of Honor.

Essentially, Miles had pinned his own command down, neither advancing to find

161

and engage the Comanche bands nor moving back toward Fort Dodge and offering the Indians an opportunity to raid prairie settlements. Meanwhile, an event back in Kansas would have a powerful effect on Bat Masterson.

Over four years earlier, a man named German and his wife left Georgia bound for Colorado. Accompanying the couple were their seven children, six of them girls. They stopped several times as they made their way west, earning enough money each time to resupply and move on. For the Germans, Colorado was viewed as a dream to be realized.

Their migration turned into a nightmare. The family's last stop before expecting to reach the Colorado border was in Ellis, Kansas. On the morning of September 11, 1874, their wagon and a few head of cattle left Ellis, expecting an easy trip to Fort Wallace. It wasn't. The family was ambushed by seventeen Cheyenne Dog Soldiers led by Kicking Horse. As the four youngest daughters watched in horror, their parents, brother, and two older sisters were killed and scalped. Katherine, Julia, Adelaide, and Sophia German, ranging in age from nine to fifteen, were dragged off as captives of the Cheyenne.

When word of this reached Miles and his men, finding the four kidnapped girls became their new mission. The scouts learned that the Dog Soldiers had entered the Panhandle. They also heard that the German sisters had been separated, with two girls going with a band headed by Gray Beard and the other two with Stone Calf. Bat and a few of the other scouts had crossed trails with Stone Calf before, at Adobe Walls, when his son was one of those killed during that June attack.

The Cheyenne bands and the white girls with them proved very elusive as the weeks passed. Especially frustrating was the thought that two or all four of the German sisters had been brought hundreds of miles to Mexico and traded away there. If so, they would never be recovered. The scouts consoled themselves that Cheyenne were not known to go that far south, away from their hunting grounds and familiar surroundings. They kept searching and hoping.

The scouts found Gray Beard's camp on November 8. A few days earlier, the more experienced ones had speculated that the Cheyenne would follow their routine and begin to set up a winter camp near McClellan Creek. Miles dispatched a contingent of soldiers and scouts to find out. On the morning of the eighth they arrived atop a slope near the creek, and looking down, they spotted dozens of tepees there. When the army soldiers arrived, led by the chief of scouts, Lieutenant Frank Baldwin, another Civil War recipient of the Medal of Honor, an attack was launched. As Baldwin would later write in his report, they rushed down the hills and charged the Cheyenne village "yelling like demons."

During the brief battle, most of the inhabitants of the village fled. Those left behind were either too petrified to fight or dead. Also left behind, discovered trembling under a buffalo robe, were Julia and Adelaide German. The girls had not been harmed but were as malnourished as many of the Cheyenne children. Bat later recalled that "their little hands looked like bird's claws."

For the rest of the fall of 1874 and into the winter, Bat continued to do some scouting for the army as well as working as a teamster hauling supplies to and from the ongoing Miles expedition. The search continued, this time focused on finding the two sisters who were supposedly still with Stone Calf's band.

That search was derailed by the early and unusually harsh onslaught of winter. Bat's stamina and luck were put to the test on December 16. The War Department had decided to establish a new outpost not far from Adobe Walls, on Sweetwater Creek. A large train consisting of over a hundred wagons carrying a million pounds of grain and over half a million pounds of other goods was to set out from Camp Supply to travel south of the Canadian River to help establish the new outpost.

It set out well enough, but after only forty miles the men, Bat among them, and their teams of oxen and horses were battered by a sudden blizzard. Some drivers, blinded, veered off and disappeared into the storm, never to be seen again. Disoriented animals froze in their tracks. After the blizzard barreled on, what was left of the wagon train continued, with only a couple of dozen drivers and their supplies reaching their destination. It would be another six weeks before a new supply train tried another trip.

The severity of the winter produced Colonel Miles's desired result for him. What had become an annual agony for tribes was that many of them were unable to find enough food on the frozen plains, with the women and children suffering the most. As Miles's troops neared the border with New Mexico, an emissary from Stone Calf appeared, informing the colonel that the Cheyenne band was nearby. Their leader wanted to discuss laying down their arms in exchange for food.

Bat was one of the men who, understanding the risk that it could be a trap, volunteered to talk to Stone Calf. On March 1, 1875, without weapons, they rode into the Indian camp. The scouts could see immediately that Stone Calf must be serious because his people were clearly starving. It was explained to the Cheyenne leader that the German girls must be returned before an ounce of food was provided . . . if they were still alive. Bat and his companions were brought to a tepee and ushered in. There they found Katherine and Sophia lying on animal skins, as close to starvation as the others in the camp. It had taken almost six months, but all four German sisters were found alive.

Five days later, Stone Calf led eight hundred men, women, and children to the Cheyenne and Arapaho Reservation, where they hoped to be fed. A hero of the Civil War, General Philip Sheridan, who commanded the Missouri District, declared that the Miles campaign "was not only very comprehensive, but was the most successful of any campaign in the country since its settlement by the whites."

Bat Masterson's role in it elevated him to hero status. But he had turned twenty-one while living out on the plains, and he had grown weary of that rough and dangerous lifestyle. It was time to ride back to Dodge City.

EIGHT

The integrity of our police force has never been seriously questioned. — *The Wichita Beacon*

Wyatt Earp would lose another wife in Wichita. And just like he had done in Lamar, he would get into a peck of trouble and hit the trail. This time, his next stop would be Dodge City . . . with a third wife in tow.

Sarah Haspel had the unhappy habit of being arrested for being an operator — sometimes with James Earp's wife, Bessie — of a brothel. This was bothersome to Wyatt, not for moral reasons but because it cost money to keep bailing her out and hiring lawyers. It also drew unwanted attention to him and his contradictory position of being a police officer. Chances were that Wyatt saw being a lawman in Wichita as a more promising pursuit than making a living gambling or being a brothel bouncer, but an added incentive was keeping his wife out of trouble.

In April 1875, he was appointed a regular member of the police department, making his somewhat ambiguous status official. During the 1870s, Bill Smith and Mike Meagher would trade the position of marshal in Wichita as the whims of the voters dictated. It was Meagher who would help Wyatt's lawman career along.

Mike and his twin brother, John, had been born in Ireland in 1843. The Meagher family emigrated to Illinois, and when the Civil War began the brothers joined the Union Army. Both survived the war, and they made their way to Kansas as stagecoach drivers. Whatever skills Mike Meagher had, they were enough to become the city marshal of Wichita in 1871. He appointed his brother and Bill Smith to the police force. The latter became marshal in 1874, when Mike became a deputy U.S. marshal.

Mike was back the following year, and in the election he beat out Smith and once more led the police department. In addition to hiring Wyatt on full-time, he appointed John Behrens and James Cairns (who would later be brother-in-law to Bat Masterson) as assistants. Wyatt earned sixty dollars a month, so he continued to moonlight as a gambler. His specialty was a game popular at the time called faro.

Mike Meagher did Wyatt another favor, in addition to giving him his first position as a full-time lawman. He taught the young policeman a tactic known as "buffaloing," one that would be a big help to Wyatt in the coming years of confronting desperadoes and other rough characters. In buffaloing, when it looked like a confrontation could get violent, the lawman would strike first by hitting the dumbfounded drover over the top of the head with the barrel of a gun. The unconscious cowboy would recover, either in jail or in a saloon, where he could resume being free with his money. Not having to resort to gunplay probably kept the mortality rate in the police department down and certainly allowed for more repeat customers in the saloons. Wyatt was especially suited for buffaloing because he was taller than most men of that time.

Meagher proved to be an especially effective marshal, managing to juggle the interests of saloon owners, shopkeepers, cowboys, bordello operators, and the citizens who wanted to feel safe on the streets. He did so while rarely firing a shot. He would not kill a man until 1877, when the only one he dispatched was Sylvester Powell. At some point in the past Marshal Meagher had arrested Powell, maybe buffaloed him, too, and the man harbored a grudge. On New Year's Day, he saw an opportunity for revenge. Meagher went out the back door of a saloon and stepped into an outhouse. Powell moved in close and began shooting. Though wounded, Meagher was angry as a yellow jacket when he busted out of the outhouse with his gun blazing. One of the bullets took care of Powell and his grudge.

It was no coincidence that Sarah was not arrested after Wyatt became one of Meagher's policemen. Or there may be another reason: Sarah left Wichita, and her "marriage."

In the 1875 census conducted by the state of Kansas, the names of Wyatt Earp and his brother and sister-in-law are listed, but not Sarah's. There is no mention of her again in Wichita. According to the sleuthing done by Sherry Monahan, Sarah can next be found in 1883, living under the name Sadie Haspel in Kansas City. For a time during that decade she lived with a prizefighter named Murphy, then married a man named Bollman. She died as Sadie Bollman on July 29, 1919, at the age of sixty-six, in Oak Forest, a suburb of Chicago.

Wyatt did not suffer anything like the grief when Sarah left as he had when Aurilla died. He already had her replacement picked out. In fact, he may have met her before Sarah.

More so than any of the Earp brothers, Wyatt had complicated relationships with women. The others would find steady relationships, even James, whose wife was involved in prostitution. After he had branched off from the California-bound wagon train led by his father to give Nevada a try, James lived in Idaho, Washington, Wyoming, and Montana, which proved to be his favorite. But he didn't stay there, either; he looked up his parents in Missouri, then tried Kansas City, then returned to Missouri, where as a wounded Union veteran he received a land grant of 145 acres in Boonville.

Somewhere along the way James met Bessie Nellie Catchim, a divorcée from New York City with a son named Frank and a daughter named Hattie. James and Bessie were married in Illinois in April 1873. Apparently, farming was not for them, because James wound up re-uniting with Wyatt in Wichita the following year, now with a family to support. Either James could not support them well enough or Bessie wanted to continue making use of business skills she had developed, because she became a brothel operator.

Virgil was not long out of his twenties when he married for the third time. His marriage to Rozilla Draggoo may have ended with her death because there is no further record of her, and apparently Virgil was free to marry again. He did, probably in 1873, to Alvira Packingham Sullivan, a girl of Irish descent known as Allie.

She was born in Florence, Nebraska, in January 1851. The family moved to Omaha, and when the Civil War began, her father, John Sullivan, enlisted in the Union Army despite (or maybe because of) having a wife and eight children. Louisa, Allie's mother, died a year later. With John still away, the children were separated and taken into foster homes. Allie ended up in an abusive one and she ran away. She was taken in by other families, and then when she was sixteen she was back in Omaha, living with an older married sister. It was there she first encountered Virgil Earp, in late 1872.

Allie was working as a waitress, and when the tall, handsome stagecoach driver entered the restaurant, she was smitten. He noticed the attractive waitress and maybe sensed the same kind of wandering spirit the Earps had. "He always said I was just getting ready to take a bite out of a pickle when he first saw me," Allie wrote many years later. "When I was mean he used to say I was just as sour. But mostly he said I was no bigger than a pickle but a lot more sweet."

She and Virgil began to live and travel together in 1873. It is uncertain if they actually married, but their union would be a permanent one, lasting until Virgil's death.

Morgan had gone up to Montana to join James Earp. His older brothers had been a bit protective of their boyish brother because Morgan hadn't developed some of the rough edges they had. In Allie's reminiscences about the family, she recalled that Morgan was "the nicest to us of all the Earps, the most good-natured and handsomest. His face was lean like Jim's and Wyatt's but more sensitive. His thick straight hair never did stay combed and his moustache was always scraggly."

After Montana, Morgan returned to Missouri and became a bartender in St. Louis. In 1875, he was in Wichita, with James and Wyatt. Apparently, he was no stranger to their establishments, because Morgan was arrested during a raid on a brothel. He was fined three dollars, but when it was all sorted out that he was the brother of a city cop, it was rescinded. A woman named Nellie Spalding was Morgan's girlfriend at the time and may have been in the same business as Bessie and Sarah. Morgan would not be married until a few years later, and not to Nellie.

Warren Earp, almost fourteen years younger than James, was still living with Nicholas and Virginia Ann Earp and his youngest sister, Adelia, and marrying anyone was not much on his mind.

At that time, the Earp brother with the most stable marital situation was the half brother, Newton. After his return from the Civil War he married Nancy Jane Adam, known as Jennie, in Missouri. They accompanied Nicholas and Virginia Ann to California, where Newton became a saloon manager, and returned east with them. Newton, a farmer, and Jennie were the neighbors of Wyatt and Aurilla in Lamar. Their first child, a daughter, was born in Missouri, and their second, a son named Wyatt Clyde, was born after they had moved to Kansas. The couple would have two more daughters and a son, Virgil Edward.

Mattie Blaylock would become Wyatt's third "wife." A photograph of her was taken in Fort Scott, Kansas, in 1871, and Wyatt was believed to be in the vicinity at that time as part of his post-Lamar wanderings. It is possible that is where he first met Mattie. This would turn out to be the most turbulent relationship with a woman that Wyatt had in his life.

Celia Ann Blaylock was born in January 1850, the third of six children of Henry and Elizabeth Blaylock, in Monroe Township, Iowa. The family farmed land there. Celia Ann's parents were Lutherans and strict enough in their ways to be a burden to at least two of their rebellious children. As teenagers, Celia Ann and a younger sister, Sarah, ran away from the farm. Nothing is known about Celia Ann until, under the name Mattie Blaylock, she was living in Fort Scott. Sarah would return home and eventually marry, accepting the more conventional life.

Mattie, apparently, was not similarly inclined. According to E. C. Meyers in his biography of her, in the summer of 1871, Wyatt was living on Newton's farm outside Fort Scott. How they met was not necessarily unconventional at the time on the frontier, but their life together would be. "When Mattie Blaylock met Wyatt Earp she was a garden-variety prostitute quietly residing in a pleasure palace operating just off the main street," writes Meyers.

Initially, the attraction may have been one-sided. Mattie noted that Wyatt was "tall, slim, with blond hair and neatly trimmed mustache, he was very handsome. She could not have helped but to also notice his blue eyes and ice cold they were." She might have fared better, Meyers claims, "by walking away instead of tying her wagon to his erratic star. From that day and for the next eleven years, she went where he went, stayed where he stayed and did his bidding." Mattie began to call herself Mrs. Wyatt Earp "and to her final day identified herself as such."

In what could have become fodder for a French farce, Mattie went with Wyatt or at least joined him when he landed in Peoria, where he took up with Sarah Haspel. Mattie may even have been one of the women who worked at Jane Haspel's brothel, but at some point she went to work for another madam, Jennie Green. Much of the confusion about the time before Wyatt went to Wichita is that Meyers and others assert that Mattie and Sarah are the same person and the same "wife," because in front of a judge on September 10, 1872, Mattie reportedly said, "My name is Sarah Earp. I am Mrs. Wyatt Earp." There are also assertions that after fleeing the overzealous law enforcement of Peoria, Mattie accompanied Wyatt back to Newton's place, and he spent 1873 farming, not buffalo hunting and making an impression in Ellsworth. Given his lifelong antipathy to plowing, harvesting, and other farming chores, it isn't likely that this was what Wyatt was doing.

In any case, when Wyatt had arrived in Wichita, he had Sarah, the real Sarah Haspel, with him, not Mattie, who had been left behind with Newton and Jennie on the farm. Supposedly, the plan was that Wyatt would settle in with James and Bessie, establish himself as a gambler, and send for Mattie. By November 1873, she still hadn't heard from him. One can conjecture that Sarah's position was that Wichita wasn't big enough for her and Mattie at the same time. Wyatt had to choose who would be his wife.

Walking the streets to patrol Wichita at night — either boisterous or quiet ones, depending on whether a cattle drive had just concluded — probably offered relief to Wyatt. Whatever his women issues, they did not deter his law-enforcement efforts. An account in *The Wichita Beacon* of May 12, 1875, tells of Wyatt's no-nonsense practice of policing. It had been reported that a man named W. W. Compton had stolen two horses and a mule in nearby Coffey County, and the previous Tuesday evening the misspelled "Erp" spied a man matching the thief's description: "Erp took him in tow, and inquired his name. He gave it as 'Jones.' This didn't satisfy the officer, who took Mr. Jones into the Gold Room, on Douglass avenue, in order that he might full examine him by lamp light. Mr. Jones, not liking the look of things, lit out, running to the rear of Denison's stables. Erp fired one shot across his poop deck to bring him to, to use a naughty-cal phrase, and just as he did so, the man cast anchor near a clothes line, hauled down his colors and surrendered without firing a gun. The officer laid hold of him before he could recover his feet for another run, and taking him to jail placed him in the keeping of the sheriff."

Contradicting his previous restlessness, Wyatt did not seem of a mind to be on the move again. However, other Earps were. As usual, it began with Nicholas. Though over sixty, he again wanted to wander, thinking of giving California another try. Newton said he and his family would go along. Farming in Kansas had lost its allure in the summer of 1874, when a grasshopper plague of biblical proportions had wiped out the crops on many of the farms in and around Hutchinson. Virgil and Allie decided to go along, with the latter hankering to see what the West Coast was like. The Earps were part of an eleven-wagon train that rendezvoused at what was left of Newton's farm. (Also along was a man named Bill Edwards, who would later marry Adelia Earp.) Nicholas gave the order, and the wagon train headed west.

For a time, Wyatt had done pretty well for himself in Wichita, whatever his domestic situation actually was. Being a member of the police force, he no longer had to pay fines for the activities of his wife . . . or wives. As a lawman, he was an important part of Marshal Meagher's pretty successful effort to tame Wichita's tougher elements and help the business district to grow. In just a couple of years, the city became somewhat civilized.

There were still colorful characters who passed through, though. Abel Head "Shanghai" Pierce, for example, was one of the most successful cattlemen of the era. After a stint as a butcher in the Confederate Army, he wound up owning a ranch on Matagorda Bay in Texas (though he hailed from, of all places, Rhode Island). He and his nephew introduced the American Brahman breed of cattle, which were immune to tick fever. At six feet five, Pierce was especially tall for the time, and he carried 220 pounds. He sported a white beard and a voice that people claimed could be heard half a mile away. He called his cattle sea lions, contending they had been bred in the bay, and in the 1870s he sold tens of thousands of them in the Kansas cow towns. In 1875, Wichita was a favorite watering hole, and he enjoyed raising hell there.

One night in a saloon, Pierce was drunk and wearing a gun, an ominous combination. Wyatt walked in and ordered the cattleman to leave town and not return until he was sober. Pierce obeyed, but his unhappiness must have been more than evident back at camp, because soon after, twenty or so of his cowboys rode into Wichita demanding to see Wyatt. He presented himself, and a loaded shotgun, and Wyatt must have been accompanied by others, because the reported outcome was that all twenty were disarmed, escorted to jail, and fined. (This may have been the only time that James Earp stood shoulder-to-shoulder with his brother and holding a gun.) The next morning, a rueful Shanghai Pierce, twirling a walking cane, arrived at the jail and paid to bail his cowboys out to the tune of two thousand dollars.

Such extravagances were not unusual for

the charismatic cattleman. A few years later Pierce paid ten thousand dollars for a twenty-foot-tall bronze statue of himself. It now overlooks his grave in Blessing, Texas.

Wyatt must have kept his nose clean and done a good job, because there were several additional mentions of doing his duty and keeping the peace in the Wichita newspaper. The December 15, 1875, issue of *The Beacon* tells of Wyatt finding a man so drunk he was just lying in the street. "He took him to the 'cooler' and on searching him found in the neighborhood of $500 on his person." The drunk slept it off in the city jail, and, as the newspaper reported, when he faced a judge the next morning, he could pay his fine from the bankroll Wyatt had returned to him.

Sarah Earp may have questioned Wyatt's integrity and found it wanting, because she apparently left town. Perhaps Wyatt and Mattie, now the sole Mrs. Earp, would have remained where they were for years to come. But the end for Wyatt in Wichita was the 1876 election, in April. This time Bill Smith hoped to unseat Meagher. He watched the counting of votes on election day while nursing some bad bruises.

During the heated campaign, Smith had accused Meagher of having a plan to pack the police department with Earps, meaning Morgan and James or Virgil would be appointed to serve alongside Wyatt, and the citizens of the city would have to foot the bill for these extra and unnecessary officers. Wyatt was furious that his family was being used in this way. The next time he encountered Smith on the street, Wyatt gave him a good beating and was arrested for disturbing the peace. Reluctantly, Meagher had to follow the wishes of the city council and fire Wyatt for conduct unbecoming an officer.

Meagher prevailed in the election. He wanted to rehire Wyatt, but the city council vote on the matter was a tie. Feeling betrayed by them, Wyatt considered his options, and instead of requesting a new vote, he and Mattie began packing. James and Bessie had established a brothel elsewhere in Kansas. In May, Wyatt and his wife set out for Dodge City.

There, he would renew his friendship with Bat Masterson, and together they would clean up the "wickedest town in the West."

■ ■ ■ ■

ACT II

■ ■ ■ ■

Wyatt Earp as a young man.
Courtesy of Denver Public Library

NINE

Of course everyone has heard of wicked Dodge; but a great deal has been said and written about it that is not true. Its good side has never been told. Many reckless, bad men came to Dodge and many brave men. These had to be met by officers equally brave and reckless. As the old saying goes, "You must fight the devil with fire." — ROBERT WRIGHT

Many of the myths about the Wild West are connected in some way to Dodge City. During what some writers and public relations practitioners have labeled the "golden decade" of Dodge City, that being the years from 1872 to 1882, some of the frontier's most famous and infamous characters passed through. Quite a few of the stories about people and events evolved into myths or began their lives as tall tales. Thankfully, some of them are true or at least contain a solid kernel of truth.

Wyatt Earp and Bat Masterson, of course, were two of those famous characters, and shortly we'll pick up where we left off with them. Doc Holliday will be along soon enough. There was Wild Bill Hickok, until he was shot in the back in Deadwood, South Dakota. We'll visit again with Ben and Billy Thompson. The actions of that decade in the American West, related to Dodge City one way or another, made or enhanced the reputations of many a gunfighter, whether he be a law-man or an outlaw.

The word "gunfighter" in America can be traced back to 1874, but it wasn't until around 1900 that it was more commonly used. The term that most people used in the 1870s was "shootist," or the more specific "man killer." An example of one was John Wesley Hardin.

Hardin spent some time in Dodge City, but he was more associated with Texas and another Kansas city, Abilene, where he had been photographed before escaping the long gun of Wild Bill. By then, the son of a Methodist preacher was already a veteran man killer. In 1867, his precocious criminal career had begun at age fourteen, when he was expelled from school for knifing a classmate. The following year he gunned down a former slave on an uncle's plantation in Moscow, Texas. Three army soldiers were dispatched to arrest him. Hardin ambushed and, depending on the account, killed one or all of them.

The saying "I never killed a man who didn't need killing" has been attributed to Hardin, and he obviously lived in needy times because he is "credited" with sending as many as thirty men to the hereafter. A few were killed while he worked as a cowboy on the Chisholm Trail; there was that one man dispatched in the hotel in Abilene; and he had a run-in with some lawmen in Texas. But then he seemed to go straight, marrying a Texas girl in Gonzales County, and they had three children.

But for Hardin, domestic bliss didn't last. A killing spree ended the lives of four men, and he was arrested in Cherokee County by the sheriff. He escaped from jail, fled to Brown County, where he killed a deputy sheriff, and, after collecting his wife and kids, he went east, to Florida. It wasn't until 1877 that Hardin was located and arrested, in Pensacola by Texas Rangers. He was found on a train, and when he grabbed his pistol it got caught in his suspenders. His companion, nineteen-year-old James Mann, was less clumsy but also less of a marksman. His bullet went through the hat of Ranger John Armstrong, who shot Mann in the chest, killing him.

After being convicted it was hard time for Hardin, seventeen years of it in the state prison in Huntsville, where among other occupations he studied law and headed the Sunday school. When released, he was admitted to the Texas bar and opened a law practice. During his incarceration his wife had died, so he was free to marry, which he did to a fifteen-year-old, but the union was short-lived. So were the rest of his days.

In 1895, Hardin was in El Paso to testify in a murder trial. One day he was standing at the bar shooting dice with a local merchant. John Selman, a man with a grievance — and who the year before had killed the appropriately named Bass Outlaw — came up behind him. Right after Hardin said, "Four sixes to beat, Henry," Selman shot him in the head. While Hardin was on the floor, Selman shot him three more times in the chest, just to be sure. Enough hometown jurors believed Selman's ridiculous claim of self-defense in killing Hardin that he was released. He was slain the following year by lawman George Scarborough, who in turn was killed in 1900 while pursuing outlaws in Arizona.

Jesse James passed through Dodge City from time to time, and he certainly enhanced the reputation of the entire frontier as a place where legendary gunmen came to live and die. Born in Missouri, he was only seventeen when he joined Quantrill's Raiders in 1864, riding alongside the likes of Bloody Bill Anderson as they made Kansas bleed, following up on a massacre in Lawrence the previous year that killed 150 people. In the early 1870s, Jesse, too, was glad to see the railroads expanding westward because that meant more targets that he and his brother Frank and the Younger brothers could rob.

What can be gently labeled an "innovation" by Jesse was being an early prairie practitioner of public relations. He did this by creating a press release about himself and his gang in advance of robbing a train in 1874. The train was in Gads Hill, Missouri, and the robbery resulted in a good haul of cash and jewelry. Before leaving the train, Jesse handed the conductor a written message and told him to have it telegraphed to the *St. Louis Dispatch.* The "press release" was titled "The Most Daring Train Robbery on Record!" It described what had just taken place, and ended, "They were all mounted on handsome horses. There is a hell of an excitement in this part of the country."

A bank was the gang's downfall, the First National Bank in Northfield, Minnesota. The attempt to rob it in September 1876 was a disaster, with brothers Jesse and Frank James barely escaping and Cole, Bob, and Jim Younger captured. (When Cole was finally paroled twenty-five years later, he and Frank James entertained audiences with a Wild West show.) Jesse and Frank went on the run, with sightings reported all over the frontier.

What most of the men who came to Dodge City in the 1870s had in common were horses and guns. Few feared the former, but the latter could cause a lot of harm. Cowboys carried sidearms, as did the lawmen, who also often shouldered shotguns when making their rounds. The weapon found in many holsters was the Colt revolver.

Samuel Colt's fascination with guns began when he was a child in Hartford, Connecticut, and his maternal grandfather, a former officer in the Continental Army, bequeathed to him his flintlock pistol. In 1830, at the age of sixteen, Colt went to sea on a brig bound for Calcutta. It was on this voyage that he observed that the spokes in the ship's wheel, no matter the direction it was spun, always synchronized with a clutch to hold the wheel in place.

Colt was familiar with the multibarreled, if cumbersome, handgun called a "pepperbox revolver," which required the shooter to rotate the gun's cylinder, like a pepper grinder, after each discharge. He became transfixed with the idea of eliminating that time-wasting step. Using scraps from the ship's store, he built a wooden model of a five-shot revolver based on the movement of the brig's wheel, wherein the cocked hammer would rotate the cylinder, and a pawl would lock it in place on the tooth of a circular gear.

Back in the United States two years later, Colt secured American and European patents on his invention, founded the Patent Arms Manufacturing Company in Paterson, New Jersey, and set about raising funds. He was spectacularly inept. He toured the eastern United States and Canada with what can only be described as a carnival act that incorporated nitrous oxide, wax sculptures, and fireworks in his demonstrations. He gave theatrical speeches and threw elaborate dinner parties awash in alcohol, to which he invited wealthy businessmen and military officers in hopes of luring investors and securing army contracts. The problem was, Colt usually ended up outdrinking them all. His sales did spike briefly when the army ordered a consignment of five-shot Paterson Colts during the Second Seminole War. It was not enough. In 1842 the assets of the Patent Arms Manufacturing Company were sold at public auction in New York City.

Colt tried his hand at other inventions — underwater electrical detonators and, in partnership with Samuel Morse, inventor of the telegraph, a cable waterproofing company to run undersea communication lines. Then Colt returned to his revolver. At about the same time he was tinkering with its original design, and had even scraped together the money to hire a New York gunsmith to begin limited production, lightning struck when a veteran of the Seminole War knocked on his door with an order for one thousand guns. The man's name was Samuel Walker, and he had recently been promoted to captain in the Texas Rangers. Walker's Ranger company had used the five-shot Colt to great success against marauding Comanche Indians, and he proposed adding a sixth round to the cylinder. Their collaboration produced the Walker Colt, the template for a generation of western handguns.

President James Polk approved succeeding editions of Colt's handgun, most famously the Navy Revolver, as the official sidearm of the U.S. Army. It would be said after the Civil War that "Abe Lincoln may have freed all men, but Sam Colt made them equal." By then, however, Walker was long dead — killed in a skirmish during the Mexican War in 1847 — and the fifty-seven-year-old Colt, wealthy beyond description, had only five more years to live before he, too, died, of gout. But his gun lived as the six-shooter that participated in many a confrontation across the American West.

Especially in Dodge City. That fifteen men would be gunned down there in a year beginning in the summer of 1872 surely did not indicate that a golden decade had begun, unless it was for the undertaker. However, the outbreak of violence should have surprised no one. Business was booming in Dodge City. "And such a business!" exclaimed Robert Wright, reminiscing in an article written five years later. "Dozens of cars a day were loaded with hides and meat and getting supplies from early morning to late at night."

Being on the edge of the buffalo hunting grounds and connected to the big cities back east and to the north meant that hides were shipped as soon as they were hauled in. When the hunters, many of them retaining the foul odors and wretched stains of their gory work, were in town, they wanted whiskey and women. Good manners would only result in them having to wait longer for both.

The hunters' work remained hard and dangerous, and not just in the summer. The winter of 1872–1873 was an especially harsh one for those men camped or traveling out on the prairie. In December, as Wright and a group of teamsters he had hired were hauling twenty wagons loaded with corn to Fort Dodge, they were hit with a blizzard. After two days, it was still raging. To stay alive in their makeshift shelters, the men had begun to burn the wagons. Finally, two men set off on mules for the fort. Almost immediately they became lost in the blinding snow. However, the mules found their way to Fort Dodge. The two men arrived frozen in their saddles, but alive. They told about the stranded party, and Wright and the others were rescued. During the entire winter the surgeon at the fort amputated the frostbitten arms or legs of seventy hunters, and Colonel Richard Dodge estimated that as many as a hundred men froze to death.

Like the hunters, when the cowboys came to Dodge City, they wanted their entertainments, too. Filled with energy and pockets filled with their pay, they enjoyed riding down Front Street firing their pistols, sending citizens diving under their beds, and shopkeepers behind their wooden counters. It had been a long, dusty journey guiding thousands of cows to the cattle pens adjacent to the Dodge City railroad station, and the drovers' thirst and appetites had to be satisfied without delay. No one, not even a lawman, was to get in their way.

Prospectors, new settlers, would-be settlers heading farther west, men on the run from some trouble back east, and outlaws looking for more trouble were in Dodge City, too. Violent urges percolated in the kind of melting pot that the former Buffalo City had become. In his colorful memoir *Our Wild Indians,* Colonel Dodge considered such men "the most reckless of all the reckless desperadoes developed on the frontier" and "the terror of all who come near" them. Their arrival in town was "regarded as a calamity second only to a western tornado."

A few of these reckless desperadoes did not leave town alive. North of the city was a treeless bluff that became one of the most notorious sites in the West. One night, two cowboys were camping up on that bluff and a quarrel began. It escalated to the point that one of the cowboys drew his gun and shot the other one. The killer hurried down the slope to his horse and rode away. The body he left behind was discovered the next morning. No one knew what else to do with the anonymous cowboy, so a grave was dug there and he was dropped in it with his boots on. The grassy knoll became known as Boot Hill.

It became the final resting place of those who didn't pull the trigger fast enough. And occasionally, an odd place to find humor. On the marker of a man who had been shot dead had been carved, DIED OF LEAD POISONING.

In the face of all this rampant incivility, many of the citizens of Dodge City were trying to construct a civilization. The railroad had officially arrived that late summer of 1872, when a locomotive hauling banana-yellow cars chugged into town. The line carried in people looking for a fresh start and carried the buffalo hides and cattle out. The downtown area was growing. Tents had been replaced by wooden buildings that contained, in addition to the rapidly multiplying saloons, grocery stores, a barbershop, a gunsmith and a blacksmith, a drugstore, and dry-goods stores.

In November, a visiting reporter from a newspaper in Leavenworth counted between sixty and seventy buildings. Front Street and Bridge Street constituted the main intersection. The unpaved streets allowed for dust storms to kick up when the hot winds blew from the south, and during rainstorms horses, wagons, and pedestrians sank into the slick mud. Merchants banded together to construct wooden sidewalks on Front Street that were eight feet wide, and when there was enough mud, foot-wide planks were extended from one side of the street to the other.

Visitors to the city had two choices for accommodations. One was the Dodge House and its thirty-eight rooms. It had been the hotel J. M. Essington owned until his cook killed him. The other was the Great Western Hotel. One advantage was that the latter hotel had wild game on its menu, but a disadvantage for thirsty travelers was that no alcohol was allowed. There soon would be a building that served as a church for several denominations, a schoolhouse, a boot shop, a butcher shop, a courthouse, and restaurants such as Delmonico's; and two newspaper offices, one each for the

Dodge City Times and the *Ford County Globe,* would open within the next few years.

It was in 1872 that the first doctor set up shop. Thomas L. McCarty had studied medicine at Rush Medical College in Philadelphia, then at the tender age of twenty-two had traveled west to visit a relative in Indian country. The following year he was in Dodge City, opening up an office in Herman Fringer's pharmacy. The appearance of Dr. McCarty and his wife, Sally, was a benefit to the town in another way, too. The first baby born after Buffalo City became Dodge City represented the tenuous nature of the new community.

One morning a man who had been serving as a sawbones came into the drugstore and said, "I did something last night that I never thought is possible to fall to my lot and I am so ashamed. I delivered an illegitimate child from a notorious woman in a house of prostitution." Fortunately for local moralizers, not long after, Claude McCarty was born, and soon after came Jesse, the son of Charles Rath and his wife. Sadly, Jesse Rath died as an infant, but still, the number of "legitimate" babies was soon in the majority.

Robert Wright, Rath, A. J. Peacock, Frederick Zimmerman, Jim "Dog" Kelley, A. J. Anthony, Peter L. Beatty, and Henry Beverley were among those merchants who envisioned a future for Dodge City as a place to make a good living and raise a family. In this regard, it was representative of a frontier community, inhabited by people who shared that dream of a new American West. But this dream was endangered by the eruptions of lawlessness. In his memoir, Wright estimated there were two dozen unlucky occupants of Boot Hill.

Taming such lawlessness in Dodge City would create a blueprint for establishing a system of law and order everywhere in the West. Its reputation had sunk quite low. A story was told of a despondent man riding on the Atchison, Topeka & Santa Fe line; a curious conductor tapped his shoulder and asked where he was going. "To hell, most likely," the man muttered. The conductor responded, "That's two dollars, and get off at Dodge City."

Another tale was told of a wagon train that had come to a stop just east of Dodge City. The migrants were exhausted and a few were injured. The canvas atop the wagons had a porcupine appearance, with dozens of protruding arrow shafts, evidence of the Indian attack the travelers had just endured.

They climbed down out of the wagons and got on their knees, circling their minister, who pleaded, "Oh Lord, we pray thee, protect us with thy mighty hand. On our long journey thy divine providence has thus far kept us safe. We have survived cloudbursts, hailstorms, floods, thirst, and parching heat as well as horse thieves and raids by hostiles. But now, oh Lord, we face our gravest danger. Dodge City lies ahead and we must pass through. Help us, save us, we beseech thee."

There was an inauspicious beginning to law-and-order efforts. In 1873, a group of men banded together to form the Society of Vigilantes. They tried to keep their identities secret, but it was known the leader was the prolific buffalo hunter Tom Nixon. Never mind that a few of the members of the group were barely a cut above the ones who needed taming; it was time to try something. As it turned out, this was not it.

One day Colonel Dodge had his servant, William Taylor, travel into town to pick up some supplies. While he was in a dry-goods shop, two of the Society members tried to steal his wagon. He came running out hollering, and the two men opened up and shot him dead. The Fort Dodge commanding officer was furious. He received permission from the governor to ride into the city and arrest the murderers. Nixon declared that he and his men wouldn't allow that.

Undeterred, Colonel Dodge and his Bluebellies saddled up and thundered across the prairie. Waiting for them were fifty armed vigilantes. The colonel had faced armed men before and he didn't hesitate. With bugles blowing, the 4th Cavalry charged through the streets of the city named after his predecessor, rifles and six-guns blazing. The Society of Vigilantes had never counted on this, and its members ran in every direction, diving behind saloons and under haystacks. The killers were cornered, and Colonel Dodge dragged them back to the fort for trial.

A more promising approach was possible that same year when Ford County was incorporated. Dodge City was made the county seat, and when Charlie Bassett was selected to be the county sheriff, that meant for the first time Dodge City had a lawman closer than Hays City. Bassett had a reputation as a steady, levelheaded man, not dramatic at all — which is what the county needed, with plenty of others available to provide fireworks. He would become one of the more well respected lawmen of the frontier, come through several confrontations unharmed, and not turn in his badge and retire until the late 1890s.

But beginning that June 1873, when he was appointed (he would be elected to the office in November), Bassett had a whole county to cover and couldn't be expected to spend all his time and energy slowing down the Wild West chaos in Dodge City. But if he only had some help. . . . Merchants and other citizens passed the hat and collected enough money to pay a marshal's salary.

But this approach had its problems, too. One was that although Dodge City had been declared the official name in October 1872, it was not yet an incorporated city, so it could not have an appointed or elected peace officer. Another was that Bill "Bully" Brooks was the man hired as the first "marshal" of Dodge City. The qualification that he had played that role in Newton, Kansas, overrode the fact that Brooks was responsible for one of the graves on Boot Hill, after he had killed a railroad employee. This quickly was regarded as an ill-advised hire. Brooks's lawman strategy was to shoot them before they could shoot him, and during his first thirty days he killed or wounded at least a dozen men.

Violence begets violence. Tom Sherman operated a saloon, and he had a dispute with one of his customers, who ran out the door when Sherman pulled a gun. The proprietor chased him and shot him in the street. As the man writhed on the muddy ground, Sherman called out, "I'd better shoot him again, hadn't I, boys?" He did, putting a bullet in the man's brain. Brooks declined to arrest him.

Another disturbing incident occurred when one of the faux marshal's victims had four brothers, and they went gunning for Brooks. He learned of this and waited for them on Front Street, each hand gripping an unholstered six-shooter. As the brothers turned the corner onto the street, without warning Brooks opened up. By the next day, all five brothers resided at Boot Hill.

The citizens of Dodge City discovered that having a psychopath as a marshal would mean more and more killing, and that sure wasn't moving the dream of civilization any closer to reality. The final straw was when Brooks became smitten with Lizzie Palmer, who worked at one of the new dance halls. But she already had an admirer, Kirk Jordan, who was almost on the same level as Nixon as a buffalo slayer. Jordan did not believe in sharing, and one day he went looking for the marshal. When he found Brooks on Front Street, the startled lawman dove behind a water barrel. Jordan shot several holes in it, and thinking those holes were in the marshal as well, he left town. Brooks at first believed he was drenched in blood, but the wetness was water from the barrel.

The citizenry concluded quickly that it was worse to have a coward than a killer as marshal, and Brooks, too, left town. He would have a short, unhappy future. Bully returned to a previous occupation, as a driver for the Southwestern Stage Company. By June 1874, a rival company put it out of business and Brooks lost his job. Bitter about that, he and two confederates stole several mules and horses belonging to the rival company. All three were caught and thrown in jail. As an indication of how much Brooks had rubbed people the wrong way in Kansas, on July 29, while awaiting trial, a mob dragged him out of the jail and lynched him.

A man named Billy Rivers became marshal, but for unknown reasons he did not last long in Dodge City. It appeared that the violence would. Two factions formed in the town. One, which become known as the Dodge City Gang, included Wright, Rath, Beatty, and the others with interests in saloons, gambling, restaurants and music halls, and brothels (though never officially), as well as the cowboys, hunters, and other men whose wages supported their enterprises. They were not in favor of drastic change, because there was more money to be made that way. Their opponents were George Hoover, Ham Bell, Dan Frost, and others who saw the gang's view as short-sighted, believing Dodge City would wither and possibly die if it depended on quick profits from sordid ventures.

With Dodge City having become incorporated in November 1875, the following month a committee of business leaders set municipal elections for the next April. In the interim, Beatty would be the acting mayor. When the ballots were tallied in April, law-and-order champion George Hoover was the winner.

His mandate was to enact laws to reduce the violence — exactly what Beatty hadn't bothered doing during his four months in office. That was the easy part. The next goal was to enforce those laws. The man Hoover chose was Lawrence Deger. (Though of questionable character, he could be effective at tracking down outlaws, and decades later Deger was suggested as the model for Rooster Cogburn in Charles Portis's *True Grit.*) Though a big and physically imposing man, he was not a gunfighter. A man named Jack Allen was known as a fast draw, and Deger appointed him as his deputy.

This approach looked more promising, but still there was a problem. It is not known where Deger was at the time, but one day when a particularly rowdy gang of cowboys got to town, instead of confronting them, Allen hid out at the railroad station. He cowered there as the cowboys fired their pistols and roped dance-hall girls like cattle. The cowboys were still at it when the next train came through, and Allen jumped on it, probably not caring if it was heading east or west.

Deger already knew that taming Dodge City was not a one-man job, and it wasn't a two-man job, either, if he didn't have the right man. Finding him was now his and the new administration's top priority.

TEN

I don't like this quiet; it augurs ill. In 1875 I was in General Miles' cantonment in Texas. Along with the government employees and soldiers there were 400 buffalo hunters. Everything was quiet, like this camp, for two or three months and then things went lickety-bang. — BAT MASTERSON

On his way back to Dodge City in the spring of 1875, Bat Masterson made a detour that almost got him killed. Mobeetie was located in the northeast corner of the Texas Panhandle. The rancher and cattle baron Charles Goodnight, who traveled the prairie and plains extensively, once characterized it as "patronized by outlaws, thieves, cut-throats, and buffalo hunters, with a large per cent of prostitutes. Taking it all, I think it was the hardest place I ever saw on the frontier except Cheyenne, Wyoming."

After all that Bat had been through on many a hoof-beaten trail, this town probably seemed like a good place to slap the dust off his clothes, wet his whistle, and enjoy the company of good gamblers and not-so-good women. At that time, Mobeetie was known as Sweetwater. A year earlier, a band of hunters down from Kansas founded a camp near Sweetwater Creek. The camp was nicknamed "Hidetown" because the hunters used buffalo hides to construct rudimentary dwellings.

Bat either arrived in the camp in June 1875 or had arrived earlier and took up buffalo hunting again for quick cash. That month, a contingent of the 4th Cavalry commanded by Major H. C. Bankhead rode into the area to build a fort. With the Red River War over, the government wanted to make sure the Comanche and Kiowa stayed on their reservations and didn't venture north out of Indian Country again.

With soldiers and supplies only a couple of miles away, Hidetown went through a bit of a boom period and was officially named Sweetwater City, and soon simply called Sweetwater. That name would stick until 1878, when the town applied to the U.S. government for its first post office, and with a Sweetwater post office already designated elsewhere, the place became Mobeetie.

As they had at Adobe Walls, several Dodge City merchants — particularly Charles Rath, Robert Wright, and Lee Reynolds — established a trading post to buy buffalo hides and sell supplies in Sweetwater, which bloomed to a population of 150 residents. The merchants later claimed that before the buffalo virtually disappeared from the Panhandle, the outpost had purchased over 150,000 hides. Such brisk business put money in the pockets of the hunters, offering businesses like saloons and brothels the opportunity to be established.

As the summer passed into fall 1875, Bat remained in the town, which was growing by leaps and bounds. The nearby garrison had been officially renamed, becoming Fort Elliott. As a result of all his exertions in tracking down the four German sisters, Bat was on the inactive list of scouts, meaning it was pretty much up to him when or if he wanted to ride out with the army again. With only a few renegades not confined to reservations, and with the army contingent at the fort dissuading the other Indians from straying, scouts were not in demand.

Rath's store was open and thriving. A fellow named Tom O'Loughlin, with his wife, Ellen, had arrived in Sweetwater and opened a restaurant and hotel. When another man, W. H. Weed, pulled into town carting hundreds of barrels of whiskey, the first saloon was founded. There was even a laundry operated by a Chinese immigrant. Another saloon opened, and then others, with names like the Pink Pussy Cat Paradise, the Buffalo Chip Mint, and the White Elephant. (Two miles outside of town was the Ring Town Saloon, which catered only to the black buffalo soldiers at Fort Elliott.) One that also featured dancers and rose quickly to being considered the main saloon was called the Lady Gay. The owners were Henry Fleming and Billy Thompson.

There wasn't any place calling to Bat except the Sweetwater saloons, and the tales of his rescue of the sisters — which grew taller with every telling — resulted in other customers and even barkeeps buying him drinks. Dodge City was another two hundred miles away, and he figured he'd get there eventually, when Sweetwater lost its charm. For now, life was good.

It was about to get even better: Bat fell in love, or something like it. Unfortunately, Bat's first love was about to suffer a fate similar to Wyatt Earp's first love, but under more dramatic circumstances . . . or as Bat would describe it, "Things went lickety-bang."

After his Ellsworth adventures, Ben Thompson, sometimes accompanied by his troublemaking brother Billy, had moved back and forth to Texas and from one Kansas town to another, always willing to relieve cowboys and fellow gamblers of their money. He continued to dress the part of a successful frontier gentleman, with a touch of his native England: "He was what could be called a handsome man," Bat later wrote about him. "He was always neat in his dress but never loud, and wore little if any jewelry at any time. He was often seen on the streets, especially on a Sunday, wearing a silk hat and dressed in a Prince Albert suit of the finest material."

Bat and Ben Thompson may well have crossed trails before, more likely when gambling in saloons rather than in the buffalo hunting grounds. Some friendship may already have developed, but it was in Sweetwater that they became better friends — enough that one saved the other's life.

In the summer of 1875, Thompson had come to Sweetwater to deal faro at his brother's brand-new saloon. Faro is a card game at which Wyatt Earp was already proficient and one that was a lot more well known among the general population on the frontier than it is today. There was even a study done on it in 1882 showing that it was the most popular form of gambling in the United States, with the money wagered being more than all other games combined. The American version was based on a late-seventeenth-century game in France that was called *pharaon.*

The game was played on an oval table covered with a green cloth, with a cutout for the banker. One suit of cards was placed on a board atop the table, with the cards in numerical order — for example, thirteen cards, from the deuce of spades to the ace of spades. Each player put his money on one of the thirteen cards, and he could bet on more than one card. The rules get rather complicated after this, but the goal was, as in most saloon gambling games, to beat the bank by drawing higher cards. Cheating was rampant in saloons across the West, especially by the bank. Some manufacturers practically encouraged this by producing faro equipment in marked boxes that aided cheating. The time came when *Hoyle's Rules of Games* warned readers that there was not one honest faro bank left in the United States.

In addition to the Thompson brothers, the

Lady Gay featured girls who would dance with customers and do a few simple stage routines. This was also true of a saloon down the street owned by a man named Charlie Norton. There, the dancers were known as the Seven Jolly Sisters. One of them was Kate Elder, who would later find fame on the frontier as the consort of Doc Holliday. (She had also been a soiled dove in Wichita, but ever after insisted that she had not known Wyatt Earp.) Another was Mollie Brennan, who had dark hair and blue eyes and a cheerful, lively disposition — much like Bat Masterson was often described at the time.

Mollie was most likely a player in a typical scenario: as a teenager she had traveled west from a city or left a farm behind to seek a more exciting life. What she found in Denison, Texas, was life as a prostitute. In 1872, she was in Ellsworth, Kansas, and she married Joe Brennan, a saloon keeper there. Who knows what the chances were of that marriage working, but they went to zero the following year when Ben and Billy Thompson hit town. Mollie fell for the latter and followed him to Texas after the killing of Sheriff Whitney. Two years later she was in Ellsworth again, and later that year, as the winter of 1875–1876 approached, Mollie was in Sweetwater. She was reported to be a popular performer at Charlie Norton's place. She had the ability to dance with men, make them laugh, and persuade them to keep ordering drinks.

Mollie Brennan may also have still been a prostitute, because in frontier dance halls in the 1870s the line between that profession and singing and dancing was, at best, blurred. Many men who frequented such establishments accepted this without a moral qualm. Everybody had to make a living. Wyatt's second and third "wives" worked as prostitutes, even during the years they considered him their husband. Bat would have had the same tolerant attitude, or none of it mattered: he found Mollie fetching and his heart expanded.

She may well have felt the same way about him, the dark-haired, twinkle-eyed, dashing rescuer of kidnapped girls. They laughed and drank and danced together, and did whatever else together after hours because Bat had been given a key to the Lady Gay by Billy Thompson, implying his relationship with Mollie by then was purely professional, or Bat and his brother Ben being friends trumped everything else. With the key, Bat could come and go at all hours, and it was a better place to be than the poorly constructed boardinghouse that O'Loughlin called a hotel. Mollie had to continue laughing and drinking and dancing with other men to keep her job at Norton's saloon, but it was understood that she was the object of Bat Masterson's affections. What were the chances of a buffalo hunter / scout / gambler and a dance-hall girl / fallen woman making a go of it?

Betting against it was Sergeant Melvin King. He was a member of the 4th Cavalry, and in January 1876 the unit was still stationed at Fort Elliott. King was infatuated with Mollie and jealousy was eating away at him. He was not someone you wanted as an enemy. He had fought in the Union Army during the war and in postwar Indian battles along the frontier, and he fought in bars and saloons, too. He was older than Bat by eight years, and just from having a lot more experience as a brawler, King may have been better with his fists than the lovelorn twenty-two-year-old.

He certainly had been in a lot more trouble. The man who would go down in American frontier lore as Melvin King was born Anthony Cook, in Quebec, as was Bat. He was the oldest of five children and his family farmed in Upstate New York. When he turned eighteen in October 1863, he joined the Union Army. During one battle Cook was taken prisoner, but fortunately it was in March 1865 near Petersburg, and he was free weeks later when the war ended.

He tried farming, didn't take to it well, and in July 1866 he was back in the army. Stationed in Georgia, he was court-martialed for shooting at a dog and hitting another soldier instead. Cook received a light punishment, but a harsher one of hard labor was meted out after he beat up his commanding officer. There were more drunken brawls and the punishments escalated, until Cook was dishonorably discharged in August 1869.

Two months later in New Orleans, as Melvin King he enlisted in the 4th Cavalry. He pretty much kept his nose clean and became one of the unit's best wranglers. For some of 1875, he had served as Colonel Ranald Mackenzie's orderly. King had apparently gotten some control over his drinking, and in any confrontations he brandished only his fists.

However, the confrontation he and Bat had was fought with more than fists. On the night of January 24, a drunken Sergeant King showed up at the Lady Gay. Norton's saloon was closed that night, and Mollie, Kate, and a few other girls decided that they would join their boss and drink and be entertained at Billy's place. Bat was there playing cards with three men, and when one of them dropped out, King took his place. After a few losing hands the sergeant, now even more irritable, left the Lady Gay.

Around midnight, Bat, Mollie, and Norton strolled over to the latter's saloon. The owner went behind the bar and the young couple sat at a table. Suddenly, there was pounding on the front door. When Bat opened it, a drunken Sergeant King burst in shouting and waving a gun. Before Bat could make any attempt to placate him, King fired. The bullet entered Bat's groin and traveled to where it broke his hip. King fired again, but this time Mollie had flung herself in front of Bat and she took the bullet. As both of them fell to the floor, Bat yanked his six-shooter clear and shot King in the chest. He, too, fell to the floor.

Having heard the gunshots echoing in the empty confines, people were piling into the saloon. They were joined by a squad of troopers, who found their sergeant mortally wounded. With Bat on the floor near death, it wouldn't take much to finish him off and avenge King. What happened next has been the subject of much debate over the years.

Ben Thompson, distracted from dealing

faro at the Lady Gay, had gone to Charlie Norton's place to see what the commotion was about. Seeing that the soldiers were about to kill his friend Bat, Thompson drew his pistols and leaped atop a gaming table. Wyatt gave this description many years later to Stuart Lake, which some have considered at the very least embellished: "Blue eyes snapping, legs spread wide, a six-shooter in either hand, he held King's trooper friends at bay until Bat had been moved to safer quarters."

The commotion had also attracted Henry Fleming, Billy Thompson's saloon partner, and he had the presence of mind to send a messenger to Fort Elliott to rouse the 4th Cavalry's commander. He in turn ordered the fort's doctor to hurry to Norton's saloon. He did, accompanied by a contingent of soldiers charged with keeping the peace. When the doctor arrived, he pronounced Mollie dead. But both King and Bat were still alive. After examining the sergeant, the doctor had his comrades prepare to bring him to the fort hospital. Maybe he had a chance to survive.

Bat's prospects were gloomy. Initially, the doctor directed that he be made as comfortable as possible. There was no hospital in Sweetwater to bring him to, and it would not have been too smart to put him up in the surgery at the fort. Bat was brought to his room at O'Loughlin's hotel. Since no bullet could be found, it was assumed that it had exited. The army doctor said that ultimately the only way to be certain was if Bat did not develop blood poisoning. And it wouldn't matter to him at all if Bat simply died, as many men before him had done after being so grievously wounded.

But Bat's strong constitution and youth combined to keep him alive. It was a slow and painful fight, but he survived. Sergeant Melvin King died the morning of January 25 and was buried at the fort the following day.

When Bat was able to get up and move around, he walked with a limp, and would do so for the rest of his life. The walking stick he often used out on the street would erroneously be credited with giving "Bat" his nickname.

A few accounts credit Billy Thompson as the man who jumped up onto a table and faced down the angry soldiers. However, recollecting later in life, it was Ben Thompson whom Bat cited among his personal pantheon of heroes, along with Wyatt, Wild Bill Hickok, Charlie Bassett, and Bill Tilghman. "Those men," he wrote, "all of them, lived and played their part and played it exceedingly well on the lurid edge of our Western frontier at the time Ben Thompson was playing his, and it is safe to assume that not one of them would have declined the gauge of battle with him had he flung it down to any one of their number."

Thompson, alas, did not live to an age when he could spend much time recollecting, though he tried. Later in 1876, when he tired of Sweetwater, Ben returned to Austin and opened his own saloon, called the Iron Front. A man named Mark Wilson owned the Capital Theater and viewed Thompson as a competitor. Apparently, Thompson was not aware of any ill feelings, because on Christmas Eve he took friends there for a drink. A fight erupted involving other patrons, and when Thompson tried to play peacemaker, Wilson appeared with a shotgun and fired. He missed Thompson, who, wasting no time, whipped out his six-shooter and killed Wilson. The bartender fired a rifle, hitting Thompson in the hip, and then he, too, was shot by Thompson. A judge decided both shootings were in self-defense.

Ben Thompson then led a relatively quiet life, until 1881, when he was hired as marshal of Austin. Trouble arrived in the person of another theater owner, Jack Harris, while Thompson was visiting San Antonio. Once again things escalated fast, Thompson and Harris reached for their guns, and moments later the latter was dead. Thompson was tried and acquitted, and he rode back to Austin.

If he had only stayed there. Back in San Antonio in March 1884, Thompson was ambushed. No longer a lawman, he was in San Antonio on private business and ran into King Fisher, a rancher of his acquaintance. They decided to see a show that evening at the Vaudeville Variety Theater. Obviously, it did not bother Thompson that it had been owned by Jack Harris.

At the theater, the friends were invited upstairs to sit with Joe Foster, who had been a friend of Harris's. Also seated in the box were Jacob Coy and Billy Simms, who had also known the dead former owner of the theater. Suddenly, when Coy and Simms moved away, guns blazed in an adjoining box. Fisher, though shot thirteen times, managed to get off a shot, hitting Coy and crippling him for life. Thompson had collapsed to the floor, where Foster finished him off with a shot to the head. Somehow, he'd also managed to shoot himself in the leg. It later had to be amputated, and shortly after the operation, Foster died.

Ben Thompson's body was returned to Austin, and his grave can be found in the Oakwood Cemetery there.

Eight or so weeks after killing Sergeant King, when Bat was able to ride again, he decided to put some distance between himself and Sweetwater. He went home to the family farm outside Wichita and remained there until he felt fully recovered. Then, in the spring of 1876, he traveled to his once and future home, Dodge City.

Eleven

Bat's gun-hand was in working order, so I made him a deputy. He patrolled Front Street with a walking-stick for several weeks and used his cane to crack the heads of several wild men hunting trouble; even as a cripple he was a first-class peace officer.

— WYATT EARP

Dodge City had to pull together a police force that would uphold the law — and do it before Marshal Lawrence Deger wound up like his predecessors. He had the advantage of the support of the new Hoover administration, which wanted an end to the rampant lawlessness. The first appointment, in May 1876, was to make Wyatt Earp the deputy marshal. Another step toward a more civilized city that month was the founding of its own newspaper, the *Dodge*

City Times, by the brothers W. C. and Lloyd Shinn.

Wyatt later claimed that the mayor himself had sent him a telegram in Wichita offering him the marshal's job. Half of this is true. Hoover, not Deger, had the authority to choose Deger's right-hand man, and because of the good reports about Earp that had drifted west from Wichita, the mayor may indeed have sent off the invitation. But Hoover already had a marshal, even though Deger might end up being nothing more than a rather rotund figurehead.

Wyatt, with Mattie, also came to Dodge City because James and Bessie were there, in the brothel business. (A month after Wyatt arrived, they would be joined by Morgan.) This would seem to set up a conflict of interest, with Wyatt charged with enforcing law and order in the city. But prostitution, while not condoned, was not high on the list of sins as long as the soiled doves were not flaunting it on the streets. The killings and other forms of violence, especially by the cowboys — with "cow boy" being a derogatory name given to the trail riders, devoid of the romantic image of today — instilled more fear in the citizens and those businesspeople who did not depend on selling alcohol. It was beginning to get crowded up on Boot Hill, with grave markers informing that recent additions included Horse Thief Pete, Pecos Kid, and Toothless Nell.

Dodge City needed an enforcer who was not going to cross the line into lawlessness himself, as the soon-to-be-lynched Brooks had. And that man had to get to work right away because all indications suggested that the summer of 1876 would be the biggest and busiest and therefore rowdiest cattle-drive season the city had ever seen. That did not bode well. The word "stinker" was first applied to buffalo hunters due to the odor they spread through Dodge City, and another word recently introduced into the American language was "stiff," attributed to dead men found lying in the streets. (A third slang word, "joint," was what the *Dodge City Times* was calling a saloon.) The more civilized element did not want any more of such vocabulary entries.

While Hoover could not appoint Wyatt to the top job, he did allow him to select the deputy marshals. Deger had inherited a man named Joe Mason from what was left of the previous police force, and perhaps for continuity's sake, Wyatt kept him on. His first new hire was Jim Masterson. Bat's brother was three years younger and thus was only twenty in 1876. He could not have had much lawman experience at such a tender age, so most likely he was appointed because of Wyatt's regard for Bat and seeing potential in him — potential that would be well fulfilled. Wyatt said that Bat's brother was "a good, game man who could handle himself in a fracas."

There was one more opening on the force, and that was filled by Bat himself. He was still limping from the gunfight with Sergeant King when he arrived in Dodge City. Bat already had an older brother, so it is probably a stretch that Bat saw Wyatt in that role, but Wyatt was someone he respected as well as being a good friend. However, and as far as other friends went, Bat counted several among members of the Dodge City Gang, given his enjoyment of spirits and gambling during his previous sojourns there. Still, Bat signed on to become a peace officer.

Thus, for the first time, and in the nation's centennial year, Wyatt Earp and Bat Masterson would be frontier lawmen together. One question to be asked: Why do this?

Wyatt had experienced "lawing," as he preferred to call it, in Wichita, so he had some taste for it. And there was the money — many years later, he claimed that in

Dodge City he had been paid more than the marshal. This may have been true because added to the monthly salary was $2.50 for every arrest made by Wyatt, who, unlike the deskbound Deger, spent much of his time out on patrol. Still, what a frontier lawman made paled in comparison to what could be made as a full-time faro dealer or as a saloon enforcer, especially in the most booming cow town in Kansas.

But the better answer probably goes back to Lamar. When he and Aurilla were newly-weds with a baby on the way and Wyatt was working as a peace officer, he was approaching respectability. Maybe he could go places. Maybe of the six Earp brothers he could make a name for himself by upholding the law, especially having a father who some viewed as a restless ne'er-do-well with a reputation as a welsher. That piece of his life had ended tragically and shabbily for Wyatt, but then in Wichita, especially, he had distinguished himself as being a man with more sand than a brothel bouncer. Wyatt didn't necessarily aim to be a saint in Dodge City, but being less of a sinner could be a more satisfying life. There was more of a future in it, and the same for the American frontier. If he didn't get killed upholding the law, the Earp name might mean something more reputable.

For Bat Masterson, there was loyalty to Wyatt and the opportunity to watch over his younger brother. And for an adventurous young man, "lawing" offered a challenge and a different kind of excitement. Bat had already experienced quite a bit of the frontier and its harsh realities. Maybe staying put and trying to build something good in Dodge City would make for a full life in a different, more enriching way . . . as long as he didn't get shot, again, doing it.

Wyatt and Bat were intelligent but not necessarily educated young men, yet they and Charlie Bassett, the Ford County sheriff, were now responsible for enforcing the rudimentary and flawed system of justice trying to take hold on the frontier. If it worked in Dodge City, it could spread to the rest of the Wild West. And Wyatt and Bat were indeed still young men. In early July 1876 — as the nation tried to swallow the astonishing news circulating about the Little Bighorn debacle — Wyatt was twenty-eight and Bat only twenty-two. They could not possibly have had any grand design about how to bring law and order to the wickedest town in the West. If there was any kind of plan, it was to get going with the lawing and see what came of it.

It helped the effort that both men made a good impression on others. Built into Wyatt's lean, six-foot frame was a lot of taut muscle. When he wasn't wearing a hat, people could better see his dark-blond hair and piercing blue eyes. His chin jutted in a determined way under a bushy dark mustache. He didn't scare easily, and according to many who encountered him, he didn't scare at all. As Bat would tell *The Tombstone Prospector* in 1910, "I think it was the distinguishing trait of Wyatt Earp, the leader of the Earp brothers, that more than any man I have ever known, he was devoid of physical fear. He feared the opinion of no one but himself and his self-respect was his creed."

Much of this was true for Bat, too, who had already survived several tough scrapes. His hair was darker than Wyatt's and his shoulders were wider, and he was mostly muscle, too. He appeared a bit dapper with a brown bowler hat and an occasionally twirled cane. Wyatt wore a white shirt, but otherwise his hat, pants, and boots were black. What Wyatt and Bat had come to know about each other included courage, not backing down, and loyalty to friends. For that time and place on the frontier, if any two men could lead a town-taming effort, those men were Wyatt Earp and Bat Masterson.

They would not be alone, of course. There were Joe Mason and Jim Masterson, and Bassett, who now had Bill Tilghman as undersheriff. For him, this was where and when one of the longest and most successful careers as a lawman began.

Tilghman was even younger than Bat, born on Independence Day in 1854 in Fort Dodge — the one in Iowa. He was hunting buffalo on the frontier before he turned sixteen, and it was during the next couple of years that he first encountered Wyatt and Bat. Like the latter, Tilghman was accompanied by an older brother, Richard. They, like other young men in hunting parties, worked long, hard days in difficult conditions and tried to stay away from Indians — but the Tilghman brothers were not successful, in that Richard was killed during a raid on their hunting camp. Bill was finished with hunting after that and went to work in a saloon in Dodge City. The owner didn't have to worry about profits draining down Tilghman's throat, as he was a teetotaler.

Tilghman would hold several significant law-enforcement positions over the years in

Dodge City; then in 1889 he moved to Guthrie, Oklahoma, to become a lawman in Logan County, which was booming thanks to the land rush. Though wounded, he survived the Battle of Cimarron that year — fighting alongside Jim Masterson — the most famous gunfight of the Gray County War. With other colleagues, Tilghman tracked down the Wild Bunch and the Doolin-Dalton Gang, the latter a notorious band of brothers. (Theodore Roosevelt once stated, "Tilghman would charge hell with a bucket.") In 1900 he became sheriff of Lincoln County, also in Oklahoma, and eleven years later he was appointed the chief of police in Oklahoma City.

When he retired, Tilghman became a member of the Oklahoma State Senate, and in 1915 he starred in the Hollywood western *Passing of the Oklahoma Outlaws*. In 1924, at age seventy, Tilghman was persuaded to come out of his second retirement to become marshal of Cromwell, tasked to clean up the city, which was ignoring Prohibition and had some business leaders thriving on prostitution profits. He was in the process of doing that when a drunk and corrupt Prohibition agent killed him in a street shoot-out. No one was ever convicted of the crime. A month after Tilghman died, Cromwell was set afire, its saloons, brothels, and seedy flophouses destroyed.

Wyatt was often described as a dour man who did not talk much and also as pretty sensible. He demonstrated the latter quality when he told the deputies that bounty money would be pooled but paid out only when prisoners were brought to the jail alive. This would not be "wanted, dead or alive": dead prisoners were worth nothing. Each officer carried two six-shooters, and Wyatt placed loaded shotguns at locations only he and the deputies knew about, but shooting at a man would be a last resort. The mayor had told Wyatt of Brooks's failed strategy, and he wasn't about to repeat it. According to Wyatt, "Hoover had hired me to cut down the killings in Dodge, not to increase them."

The assistant marshal could count as well as the next man, and if there was a fight involving gunplay, there were a lot more cowboys than there were lawmen. As Wyatt pointed out, "Any one of the deputies could give the average cowboy the best of a break, then kill him in a gunfight," but the odds would eventually catch up with him. Equally undesirable would be ranch owners and trail bosses looking for other cow towns in which to sell their cattle if, ironically, the law made

Dodge City too dangerous for their employees.

Wyatt imparted to his outgunned team three guidelines: One was to try to politely reason with a man, because he was not as dangerous when in the middle of a conversation. The second was if a deputy had to shoot, do it deliberately and accurately, because often the quickest man was off the mark. Third, don't shoot to kill, because wounding a man usually disabled him enough and he would be worth more money that way.

This policy was fine with Bat and Jim Masterson. They hadn't signed on for a license to kill but to keep the peace and earn decent wages while doing it. They would enforce the new laws, which included no horses or other animals in saloons and no guns allowed north of the "Dead Line," which essentially was the railroad-tracks separation between the respectable section of the city on the north side of Front Street and the "anything-goes" section between Front Street and the Arkansas River.

What went on south of the Dead Line was what the business leader Robert Wright characterized as the "greatest abandon." The prairie historian Odie B. Faulk wrote that there were seemingly moral civic-minded men who "would drink on the north side of the street until the dark of night, when their wives went to bed, and then cross the tracks for uninhibited fun until the early morning hours."

But cowboys and buffalo hunters made up most of the customers, with money in their pockets "and a desire to make up in a single night for all the revelry they had missed during the lonely nights on the plains," wrote Faulk. "They drank the raw, potent whiskey or huge steins of beer, they smoked cigars, they talked loudly, they spent seventy-five cents to dance ten minutes with one of the dark-eyed viragoes or brazen-faced blondes, and all the while the music swirled about in loud profusion." Between dances, the girls "escorted the men to the bar to accept a drink, which usually was tea, or they coaxed them into the back rooms."

The Hays City Sentinel reported, "Gamblers are congregating at Dodge and Larry Deger has his hands full."

The mandate for Wyatt and Bat and the other officers who worked for the city was to contain the chaos that the town had experienced since the railroad had arrived four years earlier. But because they did it, herding many of the troublemakers to be confined to literally the wrong side of the tracks, what ensued was by Dodge City standards a nonviolent summer of 1876. Wyatt helped the deputies sharpen their skills at buffaloing, and that maneuver was often a preamble to a man landing in jail. The bars clanged shut quite a few times, with three hundred arrests a month. This kept the peace and made lawing a profitable occupation.

Some men needed more convincing than others, "but as practically every prisoner heaved into the calaboose was thoroughly buffaloed in the process, we made quite a dent in cowboy conceit," Wyatt reported. "We certainly enforced a change in their ritual."

Based on his experience with Virgil in the freight-hauling and mining camps, Wyatt was the better man with his fists. One day in Dodge City, after a herd had been penned up, the cowboys prepared to begin the same revelry they had enjoyed the last time in town, which had often ended with a midnight ride down Front Street with six-shooters blazing. As they were about to cross the Dead Line, Wyatt halted them and explained there was a new assistant marshal in town.

There was a lot of guffawing and backslapping over that. When Wyatt insisted that the cowboys either stay south of the line or leave their guns at the marshal's office, the biggest of them was chosen to remind the impertinent lawman what Dodge City was really all about. The cowboy was flexing his fingers when Wyatt slugged him twice in the jaw, with a shot to the belly in between. The unconscious man was dragged off by his fellow cowboys as they headed south of the Dead Line.

Another incident tested Bat's patience. He and Wyatt were confronted by a group of cowboys who wanted to air their grievances, and talking with their fists was just as fine. A large man hailed by his friends as the "champion of Texas" (there was probably one with every herd) stepped forward. Bat deferred to Wyatt, who removed and handed him his gun belt, and the bout began. The cowboy must indeed have been one of the better-boxing Texans, because before it was lights-out for him, Wyatt was bruised and bloodied.

Wyatt called out to the others, "Any of you want trouble?" Bat stepped in, offering to fight next. Wyatt refused, saying, "Either I run this town or I don't."

Another cowboy did step forward and put up his fists, but in a few moments the tips of his boots were pointed at the sky. There was no more trouble from this group.

As the eminent biographer Robert DeArment pointed out, "Bat's role at these slugging sessions was more than that of an interested bystander." As more of the cowboys fell to Wyatt's fists, "doubtless they would have liked to catch him with his gun belt down. Bat was there to see that Wyatt did not take a bullet in the back while fighting."

Understandably, Wyatt, Bat, and the other peace officers did not endear themselves to the Texans, who made up most of the cowboy population. Business was booming thanks to the Texas ranchers from as far south as the Rio Grande sending their cattle to Dodge City, where they were purchased for anywhere from ten to twenty-five dollars a head, depending on how fat they were at the end of the journey. In 1876, 250,000 head of cattle hoofed their way to the city, and that number would increase by 50,000 head the following year. Having too many cowboys buffaloed while forking over their wages to saloons, brothels, and the more upstanding businesses could begin slowing that swollen stream of revenue.

Sometimes it wasn't cowboys but their bosses who caused trouble. One night that summer of 1876, Bob Rachals, a cattleman from Texas, was amusing himself by shooting at the feet of a musician — proverbially "making him dance." The gunshots attracted Wyatt's attention, and Rachals learned what being buffaloed meant. Wyatt dragged him off to jail, and the weary musician could finally stand still.

The assistant marshal did not know that Rachals was a friend of Robert Wright's. (The entrepreneur did not include this incident in his memoir, for an obvious reason.) Wright confronted Wyatt, demanding that the cattleman be released immediately. The lawman refused. Wright threatened to have Wyatt fired, and launched into a rant about how arrogant and high-handed the lowly assistant marshal was. Finally, even Wyatt's patience was exhausted. A couple of minutes later, Rachals had company in his jail cell.

A story has persisted for decades that the initial successes of Wyatt, Bat, and the other lawmen in lifting Dodge City up out of chaos attracted the attention of Ned Buntline, whom biographer Jay Monaghan, with justification, called the "great rascal." Among other things, the man was a prolific writer of "dime novels," tales that used few if any facts and were aimed at creating or enhancing the legends of lawmen and outlaws on the frontier. Buntline was credited with composing at least three hundred of them, many written not in a town west of the Missouri River but in his home in Upstate New York. It was reported that in 1876 he traveled to Dodge City to present members of the marshal's and sheriff's teams with custom-made Colt guns that would become known as "Buntline Specials" or "peace keepers."

It is true indeed that the rascal had a very active life. Edward Zane Carroll Judson was born in Stamford, New York, in 1823. He was called Ned, and he later adopted the nautical term "buntline" to become his pseudonym, as he had run away at age eleven to become a cabin boy on a ship. As a midshipman, he participated in the Seminole War in Florida, and during the Civil War he rose to the rank of sergeant in the Union Army before being dishonorably discharged for drunkenness. He always referred to himself as "Colonel" because he was photographed in Mathew Brady's studio wearing such a uniform, which was as close to being an officer as he got.

Somehow, Buntline was able to combine being a heavy drinker with being a serial philanderer and husband. He was paid handsomely for giving lectures on temperance, often delivering them while drunk. He had six wives and committed bigamy at least twice. He had five children that he knew about. In 1846, in Nashville, Tennessee, a man confronted Buntline over having an affair with his wife and fired a gun. He missed, but Buntline didn't. He pleaded self-defense during the hearing, then fled the courtroom, followed by an angry mob. He was chased through the streets and in and out of buildings and was finally caught and taken to jail. That night the impatient mob broke open the jail and hung Buntline. Somehow, he managed to pretend he was dead while staying alive, and when the crowd dispersed, the few friends he had in Nashville cut him down. Over the years, when Buntline displayed his scars, he contended that he had survived an Indian's arrow.

He did travel to the frontier several times, and hit pay dirt in 1869 when the *New York Weekly* published his serial titled "Buffalo Bill: The King of Border Men — the Wildest and Truest Story I Ever Wrote." One of the most surprised readers was Cody himself, upon learning of all his exploits and that he did not drink alcohol. The frontiersman was smart enough to go along rather than object. He met the author in Chicago and starred in a play Buntline had written in only four hours (some critics wondered what took so long), *Scouts of the Prairie,* with the playwright costarring as well as Texas Jack, a friend of Cody's, and an Italian actress playing an Indian maiden with a "weakness for scouts" (and apparently for Texas Jack, as the two wound up married). The play toured other cities, and for a time Wild Bill Hickok was a member of the cast in a rewritten version titled *Scouts of the Plains.* In 1876, Buntline could afford to commission the Colt company to manufacture single-action pistols with twelve-inch-long barrels and detachable shoulder stocks. Buntline traveled to Dodge City to personally present them to Wyatt, Bat, Bill Tilghman, Neal Brown, and Charlie Bassett. Wyatt preferred the long barrel, the better to buffalo miscreants, but the other four cut their barrels down.

Here is one of those temptations to print the legend, but the facts do not support the gifting of the "peace keepers." Colt has no record of the custom-made weapons, and there is no evidence that Buntline was anywhere near Kansas in the summer or fall of 1876. For some historians, the convincing point is that Buntline always exploited and exaggerated adventures he was involved in, yet wrote nothing about meeting the "famous" lawmen and presenting them with unique pistols with "Ned" carved into the stocks. Also, in 1876, though the building of their reputations was under way, Wyatt and Bat were far from famous and no one from the East would make a special trip to honor them.

Buntline continued to write and have trouble with women and money, yet he still found ways to maintain his estate, Eagle's Nest, in the Adirondacks. He occasionally roamed the grounds there wearing buck-skins and carrying a rifle. When he died in July 1886, one New York newspaper, per-haps with some tongue in cheek, credited Buntline with being the "most thoroughly 'American' American of his time." Because of all the debts that lived on after him, his remaining wives had to sell Eagle's Nest.

Bat's first year of lawing didn't last very long. In the aftermath of the Little Bighorn disaster, the army was running down Indi-ans and forcing them onto reservations, or killing them, or frightening them enough to follow Sitting Bull to Canada. (Another shocking piece of news would sweep through the frontier towns that summer: in Deadwood, South Dakota, the seemingly invincible Wild Bill Hickok had been killed, shot in the back by "Crooked Nose" Jack McCall.) That left the Black Hills in southwest South Dakota wide open. Gold had been discovered there.

Like many other men his age, Bat contracted gold fever. The team of Wyatt Earp and Bat Masterson ended — temporarily — when Bat hopped on a horse and headed for what he hoped would be riches ready for the taking.

Wyatt would miss his friend, but he had an able and willing replacement as a deputy marshal. The dust had hardly settled behind Bat when Morgan Earp was appointed to replace him.

TWELVE

Dodge City is bracing herself up for the cattle trade. Places of refreshment are being gorgeously arrayed in new coats of paint and other ornaments to beguile the festive cowboy. — *Dodge City Times,* April 28, 1877

The Earp brothers, Jim Masterson, and the other lawmen were keeping an eye on things during a winter of little activity. Before 1876 was over, the Dodge City Fire Company was established, and the following February the Union Church was organized. Services were held in the same building that had been constructed the year before to hold nondenominational services.

The Victorian custom (or dictate) that a man and woman living together must be married was practiced by those in the middle and upper levels of society, but in the frontier towns everyone else was not concerned about such morality. It was not uncommon in Dodge City for men and women to live as man and wife, even if they were lawmen and brothel operators or their employees. This group included Wyatt and the blond, slightly plump Mattie.

With Sally Haspel having disappeared out of Wyatt's life, Mattie had him to herself. One wonders how unromantic or at least practical a man Wyatt had become by 1876, because Mattie did not leave some of her Wichita ways behind. Mattie, it seems, was Mattie, warts and all. As E. C. Meyers offers in his biography of her, when Wyatt and his "wife" took up residence in Dodge City "real doubt exists that Mattie was even interested in a completely domestic life for she had grown used to the glitter and auditory vibrancy of nightlife. She knew her way around the sporting areas . . . and she felt very much at ease among her peers. She could always make a few dollars hustling drinks in whatever saloon Wyatt was operating his faro game; and if a new-found friend expressed interest in her she could always spare some of her time for him."

It does not sound like Wyatt and Mattie had much of a romantic relationship. Making it worse was that she was flirting with addiction. That she liked whiskey could have been harmful enough, given that Wyatt's preferred drink continued to be coffee, but Mattie was now beginning a relationship with opium. She had to buy it from somewhere, and she had no other marketable skills than being a prostitute. She lived in a small house north of Front Street, which Wyatt had probably bought or rented for her but did not visit very often if it doubled as a brothel. With the lack of any mention of Mattie in the two local newspapers, either she was very discreet or Wyatt's connection to law enforcement kept her out of trouble.

Other than any volatility in his relationship with Mattie, the winter was too peaceful for Wyatt. There weren't even that many dogs to shoot. No, he was not necessarily cruel to animals, but part of the job of a peace officer was to get rid of dogs that were suspected of having rabies. Though it still made him the highest-paid lawman in the city, Wyatt's modest salary was no longer being boosted by earning $2.50 per arrest. With cattle drives done for the year and a prairie winter having arrived with its frigid windy blasts from the western mountains, troublemakers were in short supply. That was good news for the law-and-order faction, but not for Wyatt and Mattie.

They left Dodge City in early March 1877. Wyatt's destination was Deadwood. It shared with several of the Kansas cow towns a reputation for lawlessness, where gambling and violence thrived, with one exception being that the source of income was not cattle but the nearby mining operations. Wyatt went there to make money. Deadwood was fertile ground for a man experienced in dealing faro. (Participating in a game and hoping to beat the dealer was sometimes called "bucking the tiger.") And whatever lawlessness transpired on the streets or behind saloon doorways was not Wyatt's concern.

Given its rowdy reputation, few would have predicted that thanks to mining profits Deadwood would become one of the wealthiest communities west of the Mississippi River. Just two years after Wyatt gambled there, and a year after the new device was installed in the White House, lines were strung to give Deadwood the distinction of being the first community west of the Mississippi River to have telephone service.

Wyatt would later report that he did not end up doing much gambling while in Deadwood because another opportunity to make money was available. Unlike the seasonal cattle drives and buffalo hunts in and around Dodge City, mining operations and thus the building and maintaining of mining camps were year-round. Harking back to his freight-hauling days, Wyatt delivered wood. The demand was such that he did it seven days a week, and the job was made more difficult by the weather conditions in western South Dakota even in March and April. "But I was young and tough," said Wyatt, who was turning twenty-nine, "so were my horses, and we came through into spring in fine shape physically."

As summer approached, Wyatt and Mattie remained in Deadwood. Wyatt took on a side job riding shotgun on stagecoaches. He would have been safer if he were back wearing a badge in Dodge City.

With the mines in the area thriving, gold had to be regularly shipped out of Deadwood. Outlaws and would-be thieves caving in to temptation knew that. And men taking on the job of guarding the shipments knew they knew that. The pay had to be very good, especially for Wyatt, who with every trip was taken away from wood-hauling and some faro dealing. He signed up as a guard with the Cheyenne and Black Hills Stage and Express, a subcontractor working for Wells Fargo.

Legend has it that because Wyatt Earp was on board, his stages traveled unmolested. However, while he had experience lawing in Wichita and Dodge City, Wyatt would not have been well known beyond those cities, where he had not even been the marshal but an assistant. He might have struck some fear in an inebriated cowboy who fired off a shot on Front Street, but not among the larcenous likes of those in the hills surrounding Deadwood. He had to take his chances, just like any other driver and guard.

During a robbery of a stage, a man with the prescient name of John Slaughter was shot dead, becoming the first driver killed along the Cheyenne-Deadwood Trail. On a Monday morning soon after this ominous event, Wyatt rode shotgun on a stage that was to follow the same route. The report that it carried two hundred thousand dollars in gold was most likely an exaggeration, but no doubt the stage still had enough to make any successful self-respecting bandit happy.

Wyatt was armed to the teeth — a short-barreled shotgun, a Winchester rifle, and two Colt revolvers. The stage had gone only two miles when Wyatt noticed movement, and then it became clear that there were several men on horses riding parallel to the road. They worked their way out of the hills and drew closer to the stagecoach. Now the driver saw them, too, but his job was to keep the horses moving in the right direction. Just like with buffaloing a man who could be dangerous, Wyatt didn't wait for the other guy to make his play: He raised the Winchester and fired. He continued to fire until a horse went down. That display of aggression and firepower was enough to persuade the men to wait for easier pickings, and the stagecoach made it to Cheyenne.

The Cheyenne and Black Hills Stage and Express did not want to depend on the bravery or mortality of drivers to safeguard their cargo. They built two new stagecoaches with steel-plated compartments and named one the *USS Monitor* after the ironclad submarine that had fought the CSS *Virginia* to a draw in March 1862. The other special coach was named *Slaughter*. The fortified vehicles dissuaded robbers, except for one gang that attacked the *Monitor* in September 1878 and made off with its treasure. Over time, all of the gang, except for its leader, Charles Carey, were caught. Carey and the ten thousand dollars in his saddlebags were never found.

Wyatt continued to ride shotgun as the days grew longer and the chilliness of spring in western South Dakota softened. Wyatt's absence from Dodge City had made his heart grow fonder for it.

Just in time, too. The town was gearing up for an even more active cattle-drive season. And after the cattle business, the best money in Dodge City was found in gambling and liquor, so no wonder every few months another saloon or dance hall with gambling facilities opened on Front Street or Railroad Avenue or the dicey area across the Dead Line. As Robert Wright noted in his memoir, "Gambling ranges from a game of five-cent chuck-a-luck to a thousand-dollar poker pot. Nothing is secret, but with open doors upon the main streets, the ball rolls on uninterruptedly."

The bigger the game and the players, the better the payoff. One example was Thomas Carney. A wealthy resident of Leavenworth and a former governor of Kansas, in March 1877 he came to Dodge City to buy buffalo hides and, he thought, to make some easy money off the local yokels at the gambling tables. The *Dodge City Times* reported with a touch of glee that Carney thought he was sitting down with three businessmen ripe for the taking, but Robert Gilmore, Charles Ronan, and Charlie Norton (who had relocated from Sweetwater) were actually professional gamblers who were more wolves than hens. As the drinking continued, the stakes in the poker game increased.

Finally, the former governor had what he believed was an unbeatable hand: four kings. He was delighted as the other men kept matching and raising his raises. When he had exhausted his chips but not his excitement, Carney upped the ante again by tossing his watch and gold chain and cuff links on the table. It was showtime. Norton placed his cards on the table. What they revealed to the visitor "caused his eyes to dilate with terror, and a fearful tremor to seize his frame, and his vitals to almost freeze with horror." Norton had four aces.

It was time to bid farewell to the abruptly destitute governor, and "dragging his feet over the floor like balls of lead, he left the room, sadly, tearfully."

When Bat left Dodge City the previous year, he had traveled by train to Cheyenne. Though not adjacent to the Black Hills, where men and women hoped to get rich from gold, it was a place to purchase supplies and get outfitted for exploring. Inflation ran rampant, as the hotels, restaurants, stores, saloons, and other establishments were tripling and quadrupling their prices.

This didn't dissuade more people from coming. The *Wyoming Weekly Leader* had commented rather indelicately that so many "gamblers and sneaks" had arrived from Denver that "the dying town seems to be 'taking a puke.' " Wild Bill Hickok had been in Cheyenne but left right before Bat arrived — for his date with destiny in Deadwood.

Because he was on a winning streak at the gaming tables, Bat stayed in Cheyenne into the fall. It is not known, when he finally did leave, whether it was because his hot hand had turned cold or he was wise enough to quit while he was ahead. Instead of purchasing a pick and a mule to go prospecting, Bat returned to Dodge City, but he did not stay long. It seems that Bill Tilghman and Neal Brown had experienced enough lawing for a while and wanted to see if there were any buffalo herds left to hunt. Bat agreed to accompany them.

The trio were joined by a teenager named Fred Sutton. Tilghman had known the Sutton family during his early days in Atchison, and he promised to look after the boy during his search for adventure. Mostly, it was the adventure of living out on the prairie that they got, because there were far fewer buffalo to hunt, skin, and sell than there had been just a couple of years earlier. Most of Bat's shooting involved rabbits and other game to feed the hunting party as it endured winter. Tilghman told his wife, Zoe, many years later (twenty-six years younger than her husband, she wrote the memoir *Marshal of the Last Frontier,* and died at eighty-four in 1964) that Bat also used his guns to conduct shooting contests, until his companions resisted losing any more money.

Like Wyatt, Bat certainly had an entrepreneurial streak — he was just better at it than his friend was. He apparently had saved some of his winnings at the gaming tables in Cheyenne, because back in Dodge City, after tiring of buffalo hunting, Bat invested in the Lone Star Dance Hall. It was on the south side of the Dead Line and was set up with everything any self-respecting, or nonrespecting, cowboy would want — faro and roulette and other gaming tables, a mahogany bar, a stage wide enough to accommodate dancing girls with an actual orchestra pit in front of it, and rooms upstairs for the girls to provide other forms of entertainment.

Bat was about to offer his saloon, or maybe just a portion of it, as a congenial place for an Earp family reunion.

In the spring of 1877, Nicholas and Virginia Ann Earp, with their two youngest children, Warren and Adelia, were on the move again. This time, it was back to California. Nicholas had not been successful with several ventures, and there had been a few more legal skirmishes, so the promise of California glowed brighter than ever. They were joined by the equally restless Virgil and Allie. On the way west, the group stopped in Dodge City and visited with Wyatt and Morgan. James and Bessie were still in business in Dodge City, and Wyatt had returned from Deadwood. In its July 7 edition, the *Dodge City Times* reported that Wyatt "will accept a position on the force once more." He probably worked at it in some capacity, even if it was as a special deputy during the peak cattle-drive months, but he apparently did not make headlines. For a peace officer in a Kansas cow town in the 1870s, that was a good thing.

According to Allie Earp's reminiscences, as Nicholas drove his wagon through town, he spotted two of his sons, Wyatt and Morgan, walking down Front Street. Virgil hopped off his wagon and the three brothers greeted each other warmly. (Presumably, young Warren squeezed in there, too.) It stands to reason that the Mastersons and

Earps hoisted a few together at the Lone Star. Allie also mentions that one night when Wyatt, Virgil, and Morgan visited the wagons, they brought along a couple of friends: "One of them was a handsome young man I liked right away. His name was Bat Masterson."

Allie and the rest of the Earp family plodded on to a Quaker town in Kansas named Peace. Virgil, who had stayed behind to spend a little more time with his brothers, rejoined them there, and the travelers crossed the Plains and turned south to Arizona. Newton Earp and his wife had already relocated to Prescott in the middle of Arizona Territory from the farm in Kansas. Based on the reports they had mailed back, Virgil and Allie had considered settling there, with Virgil remembering it from the days when he and Wyatt were freight haulers.

The town rested in a small fertile valley and there would be no Kansas-like or midwestern winters. He and Allie did decide to stay when Virgil was offered a job as a hauler of mail and other cargo in and out of Prescott, and Allie found work as a caretaker for a family with five children. By that fall, with Prescott having been designated the capital of Arizona Territory and the town enjoying some prosperity, Virgil and Allie planned to stay indefinitely. Nicholas and the other travelers had continued on to California.

Like Wyatt had experienced, Virgil found that he was not done with lawing, no matter how far west he traveled. The sheriff of Yavapai County was James Dodson, a great-grandson of Daniel Boone, and Virgil became his deputy. Newton Earp, showing as much restlessness as any family member, and his wife tired of Arizona pretty quickly, and they packed up and headed back east, to Missouri. They were not in Prescott, then, to witness Virgil become involved in one of the more famous gunfights in the territory.

On October 16, 1877, a man came running fast into the center of town waving a document. He was Colonel W. H. McCall, and the document was a warrant for the arrest of a fellow named Wilson, wanted in Texas for murder. McCall had just spotted Wilson and another man, John Tallos, on the edge of Prescott. Both were drunk, and they were taking turns trying to shoot a dog, seemingly not concerned that they might also hit the yelping woman who owned the dog. When a constable, Frank Murray, appeared, the two intoxicated men began directing shots at him.

The two men wearing badges, whom Mc-Call had run up to, were William Standefer, a U.S. marshal, and Ed Bowers, the new sheriff of the county. There was a buggy handy, and Standefer and McCall hopped into it. Bowers got on his horse and was soon joined by an unscathed Murray on his. Virgil had heard the commotion and come running, toting a Winchester rifle. Continuing on foot, he hurried after the other men. It is not known if the dog survived its ordeal, but when the five pursuers found Wilson and Tallos, they still held their pistols. With seven men holding weapons, guns began blazing.

Within seconds, Tallos was dead from eight bullet wounds. Wilson had been shot in the head, a cigarette still sticking out of his lips, and he too would be dead within a few days. It was later learned that not only had Wilson been accused in Las Animas County in Colorado of killing a sheriff and deputy there, but in 1875 in Wichita he had defaulted on a debt involving a wagon, and the lawman who had forced Wilson to pay up was Wyatt Earp.

Though all of the lawmen had drawn their guns in the free-for-all, Marshal Standefer was to credit Virgil and his Winchester with hitting both men. As word spread in the ensuing days and weeks, the most famous lawman in the Earp family was not named Wyatt.

THIRTEEN

The man has no future who makes himself round-shouldered stooping over a liquor bar. — *Ford County Globe*

In May 1877, *The Kansas City Times* sent one of its reporters the 335 miles west to give readers a glimpse of the young city on the edge of the frontier that the people to the east were hearing more and more about. He stepped off the train at 8:30 A.M. "in the tranquil stillness of the morning. In this respect Dodge is peculiar. She awakens from her slumbers about eleven A.M., takes her sugar and lemon at twelve, a square meal at one P.M., commences biz at two o'clock, gets lively at four, and at ten it is hip-liiphurrali till five in the morning."

After having breakfast at the Dodge House, the correspondent clambered up to the top of the recently constructed courthouse. "A lovely prairie landscape was here spread out before us," he informed readers. "As far as the eye could reach, for miles up the [Arkansas] river and past the city, the bright green velvety carpet was dotted by thousands of long-horns which have, in the last few days, arrived, after months of travel, some of them from beyond the Rio Grande."

As the summer of 1877 began, Bat was enjoying being back in Dodge City and the profits of his saloon, and leaving the lawing to his brother Jim or Ed, whichever one sported a badge at any given time. But his peace of mind was disrupted one day when he wound up on the wrong side of the law, even if it was for the right reason.

In a rare display of authority, Larry Deger had pushed himself up from behind his desk to make the rounds. On Front Street he encountered a young and rambunctious cowboy. As the June 9 edition of the *Dodge City Times* described it, "Bobby Gill done it again. Last Wednesday was a lively day for Dodge. Two hundred cattle men in the city; the gang in good shape for business; merchants happy, and money flooding the city, is a condition of affairs that could not continue in Dodge very long without an eruption, and that is the way it was last Wednesday. Robert Gilmore was making a talk for himself in a rather emphatic manner, to which Marshal L. E. Deger took exception."

Finding Gill a tad too lively at that particular moment, Deger arrested him. Gill taunted the marshal by walking slowly, and the response was a boot in the butt, then another one. Bat and his cane were sauntering along the sidewalk, and he observed this. Thinking the cowboy was being treated too roughly, he went up to Deger and wrapped one arm around him. His ability to restrain a three-hundred-pound man is an indication of how strong Bat was. While Deger was occupied trying to separate himself from Bat, Bobby Gill saw his opportunity and took it, fleeing down the street.

Deger shouted for help. Ed Masterson was a deputy marshal then, but understandably he took one look at the melee and changed direction. The other deputy, Joe Mason, did respond, and with the help of a couple of alarmed citizens he took Bat's gun and freed Deger. The next chore was getting Bat to the jail, which took some doing, including the two lawmen bashing Bat with their pistols "over the head until the blood flowed. Bat Masterson seemed possessed of extraordinary strength, and every inch of the way was closely contested, but the city dungeon was reached at last, and in he went."

Bat was a man who did not anger easily, but he must have been pretty furious with Deger and his deputy, because the *Dodge City Times* concluded, "Had he got hold of his gun, before going in, there would have been a general killing." Probably trying to keep his job, later in the day Ed found and arrested Gill, who became Bat's cell mate.

Fortunately, Bat had friends in high places. That April, James "Dog" Kelley, a prominent member of the Dodge City Gang, had replaced Hoover as mayor. He was forty-four years old and a veteran of the Confederate Army. After the war, he served as a scout for the 7th Cavalry Regiment commanded by Colonel George Custer. While the regiment was stationed at Fort Dodge in 1872, Kelley saw an emerging city with potential and decided to stay put. As a good-bye gift, Custer gave him some of his own greyhounds, and thus, a nickname. He and P. L. Beatty went into a partnership to open the Alhambra Saloon and soon opened a restaurant next door to it. Kelley would also operate an opera house, and in addition to becoming mayor, his political career would include serving in the Kansas House of Representatives.

After Bat was tried, found guilty, and fined twenty-five dollars, Kelley made him an offer. Charlie Bassett, who in November 1875 had been reelected as Ford County's first sheriff, was looking for a deputy. If Bat signed up, Kelley would cancel the fine. This seemed like a profitable direction to take, so Bat went to find Bassett.

As a result, he became Undersheriff Masterson. Bat wasn't done with Deger, however. It is not known what transpired between the two men, but a few weeks later the *Dodge City Times* reported that at Masterson's request, Deger had resigned his side job as one of Bassett's deputies.

Bat didn't put all his eggs in the lawman basket. As undersheriff, he wasn't making Wyatt Earp money, so he continued as a partner in the Lone Star Dance Hall and Saloon. As such, he wouldn't have to wait to get a seat at any of the games, and he probably imbibed discounted drinks.

Bat soon became a familiar and distinctive figure on the streets of Dodge City while on patrol, alternating shifts with Bassett and Bill Tilghman. Though he limped, he was described as a dashing figure with a red neckerchief and Mexican sash and a gray sombrero sometimes replacing the bowler hat. Bat wore two six-shooters and both had ivory handles. Given that he rarely was involved in gunplay during this time, his eye-catching appearance alone may have had a pacifying impact on potential law-breakers.

And there were plenty of those. In the 1877 cattle-driving season, over two hundred thousand longhorns were brought to Dodge City from Texas, requiring a steady stream of cowboys to escort them. Though Bat may not necessarily have intended to be a lawman again, he would do his part to make sure that the law enforcement of the previous year was not an aberration but the way Dodge City would operate from then on. Fortunately, to help keep the peace going, that summer of 1877, Wyatt Earp was back to lawing.

The *Dodge City Times* informed readers that Wyatt "had a quiet way of taking the most desperate characters into custody, which invariably gave one the impression that the city was able to enforce or mandate and preserve her dignity. It wasn't considered policy to draw a gun on Wyatt unless you got the drop and meant to burn powder without any preliminary talk."

However, on July 21, his "quiet way" uncharacteristically left him. He was accosted by a woman named Frankie Bell, a prostitute. What their relationship was beyond acquaintance is not known, but apparently it was not a happy one. The newspaper reported that Miss Bell "heaped epithets" on Wyatt, and his goat was gotten to such an extent that he slapped her. The woman was the one hauled off to jail, and she was fined twenty dollars for disturbing the peace. For the slap, Wyatt was assessed a one-dollar fine.

A couple of weeks earlier, farther south, in Breckenridge, Texas, there had been a different confrontation that would have an impact on Wyatt, though this one was decidedly more serious.

Doc Holliday had been having a restless year thus far. The dentist-turned-gambler had spent time in Cheyenne and in Denver. Then, though never to be mistaken for a family man, he had visited an aunt in Kansas. The next stop was Texas. In Breckenridge, he resumed gambling. There were fireworks on July 4, but not to celebrate the country's independence. Doc and another man, Henry Kahn, also a gambler and a member of a Dallas clothing family, got into an argument. Instead of going for his gun, Doc, reverting to his southern roots, used his walking stick on the other man. Local peace officers interrupted the fight and arrested both men, who were later fined and released.

John Henry Holliday had been born in Griffin, Georgia, in August 1851 to Henry Burroughs Holliday and Alice Jane Holliday. Griffin was surrounded by fertile farm fields, and the Holliday family had come there from South Carolina. His father, like Wyatt's, served in the army during the Mexican-American War. His contingent was called Fannin's Avengers, after the hero of Goliad who had been murdered. Carrying a banner that read YOUNG HICKORY and DALLAS AND VICTORY, the outfit helped to chase the Mexican Army out of Vera Cruz. Second Lieutenant Henry Holliday must have participated in plenty of action, because of the eighteen thousand men in the Georgia and Alabama regiments who had been sent off to fight, six thousand were killed, wounded, or declared missing.

Back home in Georgia, Holliday tended to his business interests and his son John Henry and to Francisco, whom he had brought home from Mexico and adopted. But he was back in uniform when the Civil War began, as a captain in the 27th Georgia Regiment. Once again, in 1862, he was in the thick of battle, with his regiment fighting at Seven Pines, Mechanicsville, Cold

Harbor, and in other bloody conflicts. Every day, John Henry feared notification of his father's death. What was left of the regiment was sent to Richmond, the survivors wounded, sick, and worn-out. Whatever afflicted Holliday, now a major, was serious enough that his resignation was accepted. He traveled south, to Georgia, while the 27th Regiment marched north, to Maryland, to fight its next battle, at Antietam.

The Hollidays picked up and moved farther south, away from the war, to Valdosta near the Florida border. It was there in 1866, right after the Civil War, that Alice Holliday died of tuberculosis. According to Pat Jahns in *The Frontier World of Doc Holliday,* John Henry "was completely stunned right after it happened . . . a rift that once made would deepen and widen under the smallest of blows until the house of morality collapsed and 'Doc' Holliday escaped from the wreckage of 'John' Holliday."

Three months later, in December, John's adopted brother, Francisco, was taken by the same disease. And only three months after that his father remarried, to a woman named Rachel, a twenty-four-year-old war widow.

Until he was eighteen, John Henry had been given an academic education appropriate for a young southern gentleman, or as much of one as was possible in the small town, at the Valdosta Institute, which had been founded by local parents. He studied Latin, Greek, French, rhetoric, mathematics, history, and other subjects. He appeared to be a bright young man with a lot of promise. Life took another turn, though, when he fell in love with Mattie Holliday, his Catholic first cousin.

When her parents objected, John Henry was sent north, to Philadelphia to study dentistry. He was not yet twenty-one when he graduated from the Pennsylvania College of Dental Surgery. He had won awards during his dentistry studies for his skills, and when he moved to St. Louis to begin practicing with a partner, the future was promising. He was a handsome-enough man from a good Georgia family, and he was addressed as Dr. Holliday. In July 1872, he moved to Atlanta, where he opened a private practice. Though he did not stay in Atlanta long, he would always be associated with it in a subtle way, as a cousin by marriage to Margaret Mitchell, author of *Gone with the Wind*.

In Atlanta, Holliday was diagnosed with tuberculosis and informed he had only a few months left to live. Having seen how easily the disease killed his mother and brother, he had no trouble believing this. Instead of giving up, though, he followed his doctor's suggestion that the drier fresh air of the Southwest might extend his life. First he detoured home. Mattie had vowed to wait for him. Once he was twenty-one and a dentist, they could go wherever they pleased and be together. But there was no chance for John Henry now. He couldn't be romantically involved with any woman, especially one who would wind up being a young widow.

He packed his dentist tools and grabbed his guns — his father had made a keen marksman out of him — and visited Florida with a few friends before heading west. It was in Florida that he killed his first man, if conflicting accounts are to be believed.

When the Holliday group arrived at a popular bathing spot on the Withlacoochee River (which originates in Valdosta, Georgia), it was occupied by several young black men. A dispute began, which escalated to a point at which those present reached for their guns. Holliday, with a shotgun, killed one of the men and possibly two or three, depending on the account. Further motivated to travel, Holliday departed for Dallas.

There in Texas he and a partner, a fellow

Georgian, John Seegar, opened a dental office. In his free time, Holliday frequented several Dallas saloons, where he took up gambling to go along with his increasing intake of whiskey. He was good at doing both. Soon, he was making more money from gambling than from pulling teeth. (Plus, a persistent cough made it difficult to retain patients.) But this was a risky sideline. In May 1874, he was arrested for being a gambler, and in the first month of 1875 Holliday was again carted off to jail, this time for a shoot-out with a saloon owner. He was acquitted of that charge, but when he was arrested again for gambling, Holliday decided to make his way to Denver.

He went by stagecoach from town to town, staying a few days in one or another if the gambling pickings looked good. Once he arrived in Denver in the summer of 1875, he assumed the name Tom Mackey and worked as a faro dealer at the Theater Comique on Blake Street. Holliday did not last long in Denver. An argument with another gambler, Bud Ryan, got out of control, and Holliday used a knife to carve him up. Wyoming seemed like a good place to visit, even in winter, and in February 1876 he was there working as a faro dealer again, this time in Cheyenne at a saloon named the Bella Union. When it was relocated to Deadwood that fall, Holliday went with it, where he may have been one of the observers when cowardly Jack McCall was hung for shooting Wild Bill Hickok in the back the previous August. Much of 1876 was a relatively stable period in Doc Holliday's life on the frontier.

The following year, however, he took to wandering again. He left Deadwood to go back to Cheyenne, then to Denver, then took a side trip to Kansas to visit an aunt before heading to Breckenridge in Texas.

Later on the same day as the confrontation with Kahn, Doc made a mistake — rather, two mistakes. One was not fully appreciating Kahn's continuing anger at being beaten. The second mistake was going out without his guns. When confronted, even though Doc was unarmed, Kahn shot him. Three days later *The Dallas Weekly Herald* reported that Doc Holliday had died.

He hadn't, but the serious wound combined with his worsening tuberculosis made it a close call. A cousin from Georgia, George Henry Holliday, moved to Breckenridge to help Doc recover. When he was finally up and about, he was arrested again, this time for gambling. A change of scenery seemed like a good idea, though he was to remain in Texas. His next stop was in Fort Griffin, and it was there he met the two people who would be the closest to him for the rest of his life — Mary Katharine Horoney, known as Kate Elder, and Wyatt Earp.

FOURTEEN

Dodge City is a wicked little town. Indeed, its character is so clearly and egregiously bad that one might conclude, were the evidence in these latter times positive of its possibility, that it was marked for special Providential punishment. Truly, the more demonstrative portion of humanity at Dodge City gives now no hopeful sign of moral improvement, no bright prospect of human exaltation; but with Dodge City itself, it will not always be as now. — *Washington (D.C.) Evening Star*

In his book on Wyatt, Allen Barra writes, "However much Earp later exaggerated his position in Dodge, he did exactly what he was hired to do. In effect, after Wyatt Earp's arrival Dodge City ceased to be Dodge City."

This in itself is a bit of an exaggeration. In late summer 1877, it was still a wild and woolly city. With sixteen such watering holes, the city had reached the highest number of saloons it would have during the golden decade. However well the lawmen carried out their responsibilities and whatever steps toward a safer civilization had been taken, there were plenty of strange and sometimes violent characters in Dodge City, and from time to time they encountered each other.

Bat was kept busier than Wyatt. He was co-owner of the Lone Star at the most profitable time of year, and no doubt he had to act as bouncer on many a night. But when duty called, as undersheriff he had to drop everything and become a lawman. And if it can be confusing as to who held what position when on the Dodge City and Ford County police forces — the marshal and sheriff routinely deputized each other's deputies and former deputies when extra manpower was needed — it could get confusing for citizens, too.

It was also confusing to keep them all straight — the cowboys, outlaws, and others who passed through the city. At one point in 1877, Robert Wright recorded the names of those he had recently encountered. They included Dirty Face Charlie, The Off Wheeler, The Near Wheeler, Eat 'Em Up Jake,

Shoot 'Em Up Mike, Stink Finger Jim, Frosty, The Whitey Kid, Light Fingered Jack, Black Kelley, Bull Whack Joe, Conch Jones, Black Warrior, Hurricane Bill, Shoot His Eye Out Jack, Rowdy Joe, and The Stuttering Kid.

In September, a horse theft was reported to Sheriff Bassett, and he dispatched Bat to trail and apprehend the culprit. He did. No rest awaited Bat, though, because as soon as he returned, his next mission was to track down three thieves, which almost resulted in a deadly shoot-out.

Though the buffalo population continued to decline, enough of the beasts could still be found in late summer to make a living, albeit still a harsh and unsavory one. One day three hunters pulled their wagon to a stop in front of Robert Wright's store and were allowed to pile supplies in it. They needed a Sharps rifle, too, but explained to the owner that they had enough money for the supplies but not the gun. However, they could pay for the latter with a gold watch and chain. After examining the twinkling timepiece, Wright agreed, and he requested that the men let him know when they were ready to settle up. The merchant was uncharacteristically naïve as well as distracted, because next time he looked out his front window, the wagon was gone.

It was probably Bassett's jurisdiction, not Deger's, because it was very unlikely the hunters had remained in Dodge City, but were somewhere else in Ford County. Bat saddled his horse, and because he was an experienced tracker — plus he deduced the thieves would not head north or east but south to the nearest hunting grounds — the wagon soon came into sight. Bat confronted the hunters. It was three against one out in the prairie, and the hunters had a new and loaded Sharps rifle, but most of the time Bat had a way of persuading people that gunplay was not the healthiest option.

This was one of those times. The hunters ponied up twenty-five dollars in cash and a gold watch and chain. A look at the supplies and quick figuring convinced Bat that would cover the bill. But then there was the rifle. It was hard for Bat to make enemies because he was a fair man, and accepting that the hunters really did need the rifle to kill buffalo, he let them keep it. That dumb Robert Wright should be happy enough with the cash and gold, he thought.

Bat rode back to Dodge City feeling pretty pleased with himself — unaware that he was carrying stolen property. Bob McCanse, the sheriff of nearby Edwards County, and two deputies were closing in on the three men who had made off with a gold watch and chain. At the same time, a rancher named J. E. Van Voorhis was as angry as a swarm of bees that some of his horses had disappeared. Obviously, they had been stolen. He couldn't abide anyone getting away with his good horseflesh, and when he saw three armed men riding away from his ranch, that was it. Van Voorhis hopped on a horse and hurried to Dodge City to report the theft and the thieving varmints who had done it. This he did at the sheriff's office, to the just-returned Bat and the deputy marshal Joe Mason.

Before Bat could hit the trail again, the three men whom the rancher had described rode into town. He and Mason must have suspected the thieves had hidden the stolen horses and were confident enough to come in for a drink, because otherwise it made no sense they would be coming *into* Dodge City instead of riding rapidly *away* from it. As the men were unsaddling their horses at the livery stable on the southwest side of Front Street, Bat and Mason were waiting for them. They emerged from the shadows with six-shooters in their hands.

McCanse and his deputies must have thought that everything bad they had heard about the "wicked little town" was true, because here they were chasing thieves to Dodge City and getting robbed for their trouble. Quickly, Bat snatched the pistol out of the holster of one deputy while Mason did the same for the other. He then got the sheriff's gun — or tried to. It had been a long, hot, frustrating day, and McCanse had had enough. He held on to his pistol, prompting a tug of war. When he jerked it loose he backed up against the wall, ready to pull the trigger.

At that pivotal moment, the sheriff's face was spotlit in the flare of a lantern. Bat had ridden with McCanse before on a couple of cases, and he recognized the Edwards County lawman. Bat put up his hands and announced himself. Mason was pretty confused, but after McCanse let out a big exhale of relief, explanations were traded. Bat escorted everyone to the nearest saloon, where the drinks were on him.

The gold chain and watch were handed over to McCanse, and Bat described where he had last seen the three buffalo hunters. The sheriff and deputies set off in that direction the next morning, and within a few days the hunters had traded the wide-open prairie for a small jail cell in Edwards County.

■ ■ ■ ■

As would be emphasized to Wyatt the following year when the notorious bad guy
Clay Allison came to town looking for him,
there were those, especially the Texans, who
were unhappy about the attempts by him
and Bat and others to impose law and order
on Dodge City. The cowboys could be
angered by being buffaloed and otherwise
subdued and jailed, but they were cowboys,
mostly anonymous men who were here
today, gone tomorrow, and city officials
weren't worried about them. However, they
continued to be concerned that the cattle-
ranch owners would listen to the complaints
of their hungover and hurting employees
and decide to take their herds to the next
town on the railroad line.

An instance of this occurred toward the
end of the summer of 1877 — the second
and last confrontation Wyatt was to have
with Robert Wright.

One evening in one of the Front Street
saloons, a cowboy was not fond of a tune a
fiddler was playing. His musical criticism
came in the form of taking his gun and
smacking the man's head with it, opening a
gash. The terrified and bloodied fiddler fled.

Wyatt had been eating dinner in the restaurant section of the saloon and witnessed the attack. He braced the cowboy at the bar, telling him to turn over his gun and that he was under arrest for assault. The young drover said words to the effect that he was as fond of the local lawmen as he was of music. He may not have finished his sentence when Wyatt buffaloed him. By this time another assistant marshal, Neil Brown, alerted by the fast-moving fiddler, arrived, and he and Wyatt dragged the unconscious cowboy to the jail.

Wright got there just as they did. He pointed out to Wyatt that the man's employer had previously complained about his cowboys winding up behind bars, and this new arrest might be one too many. Wright further explained about the wealthy rancher, "His business is worth half a million dollars a year to Dodge."

Wyatt responded that he recognized the man's value to the local economy . . . and while saying that, he opened the jail cell and pushed the prisoner inside it. This act of defiance infuriated Wright, who warned, "You'll let him go, if you know what's good for you."

That approach hadn't worked the first time, and it wouldn't work this time either.

Wyatt shut and locked the cell door. Wright grabbed his arm and tried to wrest the key away from the assistant marshal. Wyatt could have become furious himself, and perhaps he was, but his way of lawing was to be efficient and effective. Wright stopped wrestling with Wyatt when he unlocked the cell door and swung it open. But instead of taking the wobbly cowboy out, he put the apoplectic Wright in and shut the door again.

When a subdued Wright was let out of what was often called the "calaboose" and complained to the mayor, Dog Kelley backed his lawman. Change indeed was afoot in Dodge City.

FIFTEEN

City Marshal Masterson contemplates the organizing of a tramp brigade for the purpose of clearing the streets and alleys of the filth and rubbish that has been accumulating for a year or so. There are about thirty tramps now sojourning among us, all of whom have no visible means of support and are liable to arrest under the vagrant act. — *Dodge City Times*

In November 1877, Wyatt again left Dodge City. As usual, he wanted to make more money than off-season lawing offered, but instead of returning to Deadwood to deal faro, Wyatt wound up in Texas. That is where the trail of a gang of train robbers took him, men he had been hired to find.

While Wyatt was hunting outlaws, there was a rearrangement (as often happened) of the local law-enforcement personnel. Ed Masterson was named Dodge City marshal.

Even though he did not have a reputation equal to Bat's, he had been a capable assistant. According to Robert Wright — who certainly had a better relationship with the Masterson brothers than he did with the Earps — Ed was "in every way well qualified to fill this position. He was a natural gentleman, a man of good judgment, cool, and considerate. He had another very important qualification, that of bravery. In those days, a man with any streaks of yellow in him could have accomplished nothing as such officer in Dodge."

Ed had courage and, like his brothers, he was good with a gun. But only a few days after Ed's appointment there was a demonstration of the different approaches to lawing that he and his brother had.

On a chilly mid-autumn evening, shortly after sundown, the two older Masterson brothers were standing outside the saloon owned by P. L. Beatty and Dog Kelley. They weren't expecting trouble, because there were few cowboys in town. One of them, though, a Texan named A. C. Jackson, thought it was too dull a night, even after spending some of it drinking whiskey. As the cowboy staggered toward his horse, he pulled out his pistol and fired five shots. He either intended to shoot in the air or was too drunk to hit anything.

Whatever Jackson's intent, he had just committed a crime. Both Bat and Ed went to arrest him, but the cowboy had managed to climb up onto his horse and was not inclined to climb back down. He was not impressed by the sudden appearance of so much law on an otherwise calm evening, and, in defiance, he fired off another shot, then turned and galloped away. Ed essentially said, "Let him go," pointing out that no one had been hurt and the drover couldn't cause any damage except maybe to himself on the trip to his outfit's camp on the other side of the Arkansas River.

But Bat was of a different bent on such matters. It rubbed him wrong to be flaunted. He jumped on a horse and gave chase. He fired until one of his six-shooters was empty, but the elusive Mr. Jackson made it safely across the bridge. With full night descending, a red-faced Bat returned to the downtown area. He was more worried about Ed and his mild disposition than he was angry at his older brother. For good reason, as it turned out.

Bat soon had another opportunity to get his man. A telegram was received from Big Springs, Nebraska, informing that a Union Pacific train had been held up near there.

The robbers were believed to be riding southwest, perhaps heading to the Panhandle or Indian Territory. The leader of the five-man gang was Sam Bass. It was anticipated that the outlaws would cross the Atchison, Topeka & Santa Fe tracks near Lakin, Kansas.

Instead of climbing on their horses, Charlie Bassett, Bat, and a deputy sheriff, John Joshua Webb, caught the next westbound train out of Dodge City. They wanted to catch Bass so badly they could taste it. In the annals of frontier villains, he was an all-star bad guy.

Samuel Bass had been born in Indiana in 1851. When he was a young child, both his parents died, perhaps from exhaustion after having ten children. Bass was given to a mean-spirited uncle, who treated him like an indentured servant, forcing the boy to spend long days out in his fields. The farm was right by the Mississippi, and Bass took advantage of this when he was eighteen by building a raft and escaping down the river. He stayed first in St. Louis, then Mississippi, and eventually Denton, Texas. There he made good money racing horses, but drinking up most of the proceeds seemed to erode whatever moral fiber Bass may have acquired during an abusive upbringing.

After a fight in Denton and a warrant for his arrest in the summer of 1875, Bass fled to San Antonio.

He met Joe Collins there, a fellow who liked to raise hell and had a penchant for taking instead of earning money. They teamed up and recruited a gang. (Some accounts say a member was the buffalo hunter Tom Nixon, but this is unlikely.) They headed north to South Dakota. The Black Hills area was no longer defended by the Oglala leader Red Cloud and his warriors, but it became a dangerous place all over again when the Bass-Collins Gang robbed seven stagecoaches going to and from Deadwood. Armed men were concealed in the seventh stage, and they opened up when the bandits rode down on it. During the gun battle the stage driver was killed. With a murder charge hanging over their heads, the gang decided it was time to relocate. This time they headed south, to Nebraska.

One of the outlaws, Jack Davis, shared his belief that Union Pacific trains carried gold shipments that would wind up in banks back east, and the best way to find out was to rob one. One night he, Bass, Collins, and three others (one more than the five reported) boarded the train that was stopped at a water station near Big Springs. Davis was right in a big way. As passengers cowered in fear, facing six-shooters with the hammers cocked, Bass broke into the mail car and found a gold shipment — sixty thousand dollars in twenty-dollar coins, a jaw-dropping jackpot. They had been lucky enough to find a shipment that was being sent east from the U.S. Mint in Denver.

On their way back through the train, the gang took a total of thirteen hundred dollars from the petrified passengers. Splitting up in pairs, and with ten thousand dollars in gold coins in each man's two saddlebags, they hurried off.

Bassett, Bat, and Webb arrived in Lakin in plenty of time, their guns loaded and ready. But Sam Bass and his gang didn't cooperate by showing up. After a day of fruitless waiting, the lawmen returned to Dodge City, where a telegram notified them of five men who had been seen thirty miles west of the city, heading south. This time the three lawmen did saddle up, and Ed Masterson and a deputy were sent west by train. Once again, all were thwarted.

Whoever those five men were, they weren't the six outlaws, who were still traveling in pairs in different directions. While the subsequent adventures of the cowboy A. C. Jackson, after eluding Bat, have been lost to history, that is not true about the larcenous life of Sam Bass.

First, though, about his outfit of outlaws. A week after the robbery, Joe Collins and one of his criminal colleagues, Bill Heffridge, were found near Buffalo Station on the Kansas Pacific line by a posse led by George Bardsley, the sheriff of Ellis County, Kansas. With the prospect of jail and probably a hanging not all that appealing, Collins and Heffridge tried to shoot their way free. They failed. Both men were killed, and the posse recovered the thieves' share of the gold coins. Another of the outlaws, James Berry, obviously not having planned ahead very well, returned home to Mexico, Missouri. Lawmen found him there in October. He, too, put up a fight but was not killed, just wounded. Hoping for leniency, he gave authorities the names of the other gang members and details about the robbery. Davis apparently got away, as did one other outlaw.

Bass wound up deep in Texas, where he formed a new gang and returned to robbing trains, beginning with one on the Houston & Texas Central line in February 1878. They took on another train on the same line in March, then had some bad luck in April. Bass and the gang boarded a Texas and

Pacific Railway Company train unaware that it contained convicts and armed guards escorting them to prison. Passengers dove for cover as shotguns and six-shooters blasted away. The gang managed to escape, and Bass, with a growing reputation of being untouchable by the law, lay low in a remote hideout in Denton County.

June Peak, who had once served as a deputy sheriff in that county, was appointed a captain in the Texas Rangers. He formed a company of thirty men under his command, with one purpose: bring in Sam Bass, dead or alive. In June, they found the Bass gang's camp at a place called Salt Creek. After Peak had sent men to the other side of the camp to secure the gang's horses, he and his men attacked just before dawn. In the gunfight three deputies and one outlaw were killed. Incredibly, though vastly outnumbered, Bass and the rest of his gang escaped on foot and made their way to a nearby ranch, where they stole horses and fled as the sun rose.

Authorities and surrounding residents were apoplectic that the Bass gang got away. The outlaws stayed hidden; then in July they planned to rob a bank in the Texas town of Round Rock. Bass was unaware that the newest member of his gang, James Murphy, was about to betray him. Murphy and his father had been arrested months earlier for helping Bass hide out, and the authorities said the charges would be dropped if the younger Murphy could deliver the gang leader. He got word to lawmen about the Round Rock raid.

However, they were not alert and waiting on July 19, when Bass, Murphy, and two others rode into town, because the thieves had moved their plans up a day. Instead of a company of Texas Rangers spotting the outlaws, that fell to Sheriff Hoke Grimes and a deputy, Morris Moore. They approached the gang members as they tied up their horses next to the bank. A word was barely spoken before Bass, Seaborn Barnes, and Frank Jackson jerked out their guns and started shooting. Filled with lead, Grimes died immediately. Moore was hit twice in the chest but managed to get off one shot, hitting Bass in the hand.

Suddenly called into action, from every corner Rangers converged. The outlaws took off on foot, with a petrified Murphy separating himself to hide in a doorway. During the running gun battle, one of the lawmen giving chase was Dick Ware. The Ranger had been in the barbershop, and after hearing gunshots he had emerged from it with shaving cream on his face and a striped bib around his neck. But he had a six-shooter in each hand, and when he found Barnes mounting a horse, Ware pulled the triggers. Barnes was struck in the head and killed. When he saw Sam Bass on a horse, Ware fired again. A bullet got Bass in the back, and another got him in the arm. Jackson, though wounded in the shoulder, began firing at Ware and the Rangers hurrying up behind him, then grabbed the reins of Bass's horse, and they rode away, out of Round Rock.

When the pain and loss of blood became too much to bear, Bass begged Jackson to stop. He got off the horse and slumped down against a tree. He urged Jackson to go on without him. After some resistance, Jackson did and was never heard from again. Sam Bass was soon found by Texas Rangers, who carted him back to Round Rock, where he died on July 21, his twenty-seventh birthday.

James Murphy, though relatively rich thanks to the generous reward, was not viewed as a hero, rather he was vilified as a traitor, with even the Texas Rangers calling him "Judas." He became a Round Rock recluse, expecting that friends of Bass would avenge his death. He endured a lonely, paranoid existence until the following June, when he poisoned himself.

There had been a different outcome for Bat when he encountered train robbers, thanks to Wyatt Earp and the new acquaintance he made, Doc Holliday.

In October 1877, a gang of thieves had robbed a Santa Fe Railroad construction camp. The gang was led by Dirty Dave Rudabaugh, a twenty-three-year-old Illinois native. As a youngster, his family had moved to Kansas and to Colorado, and then he had struck out on his own for Texas, turning to a life of crime while still a teenager. He earned the nickname naturally, by bathing infrequently and wearing clothes that even by frontier standards were quite filthy.

The October robbery had taken place in Kansas, and it was believed the thieves had escaped into Texas, so a U.S. deputy marshal was required to do the chasing. That job was given to Wyatt. This would be lonely, dangerous, and exhausting work. Certainly, Wyatt could have made more money at the gaming tables. It can only be conjectured that the challenge appealed to him. If there wasn't enough action in Dodge City to make lawing worthwhile there, Wyatt would bring it with him on the road.

Day after day, for four hundred miles, he

tracked Dirty Dave and his gang through Kansas and the Panhandle and deeper into Texas. Along the way he was buffeted by the late-autumn winds, his face swept by sand and grit, traveling from one watering hole to the next, being told tales of the gang having passed through, some of them being true.

When Wyatt arrived in Fort Griffin, he came to a different sort of watering hole, the Bee Hive Saloon. A honeysuckle-bordered sign out front offered, WITHIN THIS HIVE WE'RE ALL ALIVE, GOOD WHISKEY MAKES US FUNNY, SO IF YOU'RE DRY COME UP AND TRY, THE FLAVOR OF OUR HONEY. Wyatt would have enjoyed the faro games inside more than the whiskey, but the reason he entered the saloon was that he knew it was owned by John Shanssey, whom he had met before during a detour to Wyoming.

Shanssey revealed that Rudabaugh had been in his establishment several days earlier but was gone, destination unknown. He suggested that Wyatt ask the man sitting by himself at the table in the back corner, because the man had somehow managed to hold his breath long enough to play a few hands of cards with Dirty Dave.

Doc Holliday invited Wyatt Earp to sit

down. When Wyatt declined, Doc poured a shot of whiskey just for himself. Holliday, though only twenty-six years old, had a haggard face and a chronic cough. He dressed well, and his face showed some spark thanks to his deep-set blue eyes and neatly trimmed mustache.

Sitting at the table idly dealing cards, Doc couldn't say for sure where Dirty Dave Rudabaugh and his fellow outlaws were, but he suspected from a few comments made that they had doubled back to Kansas. Word had traveled faster than Wyatt's horse that the former Dodge City lawman was trailing the gang into Texas, and doing what was not expected might enhance their escape.

This made sense enough to Wyatt that he headed over to the telegraph office and sent a message to the sheriff of Ford County that the gang of thieves might be back in the area. Upon receiving the telegram, Bat Masterson put together a posse.

It was his responsibility now because Bat had become the top lawman in southwest Kansas.

Sixteen

Bat Masterson was Dodge's favorite, a calm, well-dressed, blue-eyed man, an artist with a Colt forty-five and a veteran buffalo hunter. — DEE BROWN, *Trail Driving Days*

The previous November, soon after Wyatt left Dodge City, there was an election for a new sheriff. Charlie Bassett could not run for reelection as the sheriff of Ford County because the Kansas Constitution allowed for only two consecutive terms. One would think county voters would turn to his undersheriff to take his place, and indeed Bat wanted the job. But if he ran, he would have stiff competition from a familiar face in Dodge City: Larry Deger, the man Ed Masterson had replaced as marshal.

"At the earnest request of many citizens of Ford county, I have consented to run for the office of sheriff," Bat wrote in a letter published in the *Dodge City Times,* announcing his candidacy. "While earnestly soliciting the sufferages of the people, I have no pledges to make, as pledges are usually considered, before election, to be mere claptrap."

Several Dodge City officials and businessmen endorsed him, as did the newspaper's editors. They opined that Bat "is well known as a young man of nerve and coolness in cases of danger" — he was still three weeks from his twenty-fourth birthday — and that he "knows just how to gather in the sinners, and if elected will never shrink from danger."

Deger was not nearly as eloquent, and perhaps that made a razor-sharp difference, because after short but vigorous campaigns conducted by both men, Bat won by only three votes. He was set to be sworn in as sheriff on January 14, 1878, and his territory would include not just Ford County but all the unincorporated territory between it and the Colorado line. Reporting on the election outcome, the *Dodge City Times* noted that "Bat Masterson is said to be cool, decisive, and a bad man with a pistol."

His first decision had been to fill out his staff. He appointed Charlie Bassett as undersheriff, meaning that he and Bat had simply switched offices. At various times when he needed them, Bat deputized his brother Jim, Bill Tilghman, John Joshua Webb, "Prairie Dog" Dave Morrow (he had acquired the nickname thanks to his pointy ears), and Wyatt, after he returned to Dodge City. The two top lawmen in Dodge City and Ford County were now Ed Masterson and Bat Masterson.

When Ed had become the marshal, Robert Wright had referred to his bravery. It is not clear how he had previously demonstrated the lack of a yellow streak, but he made Wright's comment prescient in an incident in November, right around the time that Bat was being elected sheriff. But in doing so, the Mastersons almost lost a lawman brother.

An argument had erupted at the Lone Star Dance Hall that Monday afternoon. Having drinks there was Bob Shaw, who accused another imbiber, Texas Dick Moore, of stealing forty dollars from him. As the insults and threats escalated, one of the employees was dispatched to go find a peace officer. Marshal Ed Masterson was the first to arrive at his brother's saloon.

Entering the Lone Star, he saw Shaw bleeding from a head wound, holding a pistol on Moore, and looking furious enough to fire. A hot-headed lawman might have tried to fire first, but Ed was no hothead, and the law-enforcement culture had changed since the days of Bully Brooks. Ed told Shaw to put the gun away. Even better, Ed suggested as he stepped toward the bar, would be for Shaw to hand the six-shooter over. Shaw did not agree. When he turned his attention back to the trembling Texas Dick, Ed whipped out his gun and, by applying it to the top of Shaw's head, buffaloed him.

Though this was seemingly the second blow to his head, Shaw remained upright. He turned toward Ed and pulled the trigger.

The bullet entered his side, broke one of his ribs, bounced off it, and emerged from the back of his right shoulder. Ed felt his gun hand going dead. His legs buckled, and as he fell, he pushed his pistol into his left hand and opened fire. He struck Shaw in the left arm and leg, and while Ed was at it, he shot Texas Dick in the groin. One citizen observed that "for a time, it looked as though the undertaker and coroner would have something to do."

A doctor was quickly located, and when he pushed his way through the lingering gunsmoke, he found Ed Masterson propped up against the bar, the gun still in his left hand and pointed at the two wounded men he had just arrested.

Ed recovered from his painful injury, and as had happened to the Earps, for a while the most well regarded lawman in the Masterson family was not named Bat. Dodge City officials showed their appreciation by voting to give him twenty-three dollars to cover medical expenses. Charlie Bassett was appointed interim marshal while Ed convalesced.

Though swearing-in day in January 1878 hadn't arrived yet, with Bassett covering for his brother as marshal, Bat was the de facto acting sheriff. He went to work right away when he received Wyatt's telegram from Fort Griffin. If this had been a year or even a few months later, Bat might have tossed it aside if he'd known that the deputy U.S. marshal's hunch had been helped along by Doc Holliday. The two men quickly came to dislike each other and observed an uneasy truce only because they were Wyatt's best friends. One indication of how generally unlikable Doc was could be summed up this way: if the gregarious and often cheerful Bat wanted to have as little to do with you as possible, you must have been rather unappealing company.

Another indication was what Bat wrote about him. One of the magazine essays he wrote thirty years later was on Doc Holliday. All of the essays are complimentary, even admiring, of their subjects, especially those about Wyatt and Ben Thompson — with one exception. Bat begins in an evenhanded way: "While he never did anything to entitle him to a Statue in the Hall of Fame, Doc Holliday was nevertheless a most picturesque character on the western border in those days when the pistol instead of law determined issues."

Then, even though Bat had to consider that Wyatt might read what was written about his old friend who was long in the grave, Bat could not resist: "Holliday had a mean disposition and an ungovernable temper, and under the influence of liquor was a most dangerous man. . . . Physically, Doc Holliday was a weakling who could not have whipped a healthy fifteen-year-old boy in a go-as-you-please fist fight," he wrote, pointing out that this was why Doc was quick to go for his gun when threatened. "He was hot-headed and impetuous and very much given to both drinking and quarrelling, and, among men who did not fear him, was very much disliked."

However, that January such judgments

were ahead of him, plus Bat doubted that Wyatt could be hoodwinked with false information. Thus, he acted on the belief that Dirty Dave and his gang were back in Kansas. And Bat was probably aware that a couple of previous efforts north of Fort Griffin had failed. His old "friend" Bob Mc-Canse had led a posse that followed the gang's trail to the town of Kinsley. The former sheriff crossed the Arkansas River after them, thinking he was closing in, but a dense fog closed in instead and the posse lost the trail. Back in Kinsley, they drowned their sorrows of having ridden 115 miles with nothing but dusty clothes and tired horses to show for it. J. W. Fuller, who had replaced McCanse as the Edwards County sheriff, had also led a search, accompanied by army cavalry. He too came up empty.

Undeterred, Bat put together a posse that consisted of Prairie Dog Morrow, John Joshua Webb, and his former boss, Bassett. The third week in January, having by then been duly sworn in, and braving the risk of blizzards, Sheriff Masterson and his posse set off for the territory between Dodge City and the Texas Panhandle, which included the Cherokee Strip. They picked up signs on the trail that made them think the Ruda-baugh group was in the area. Nasty winter

304

weather caused Bat and his deputies to seek shelter at a ranch owned by cattleman Henry Lovell.

As the storm worsened, many travelers would have been content to wait it out at the ranch. But Bat had another idea: if those outlaws were in the area, they would be looking for shelter themselves, and Lovell's ranch was known to all. Bat suggested that they abandon the ranch but stay near it, at least for one night. They bedded down within sight of the compound, and the four men took turns as lookout. The night ended but the storm didn't, making for a cold and miserable posse. But Bat wasn't a quitter and neither were his deputies.

Late the next afternoon, as the wan light was fading from the western sky and Bat debated whether another night spent in the snow was merited, the lawmen saw four riders approach the ranch. The sighs of relief of Dirty Dave and his desperadoes turned to groans as Bat, Morrow, Webb, and Bassett appeared out of the driving snow with their hands full of shotguns and six-shooters. Bat ordered them to throw down their guns and throw up their hands.

Though heavily armed themselves, the outlaws were too flummoxed to fire a shot. The next morning, Bat led his party back to Dodge City, where the lawmen were lauded and the outlaws were taken by train east to await trial.

"The successful efforts of Sheriff W. B. Masterson in this capture entitle him to the unanimous accord of praise given him, and in which I join," offered an approving Robert Wright.

Two postscripts to this story are warranted. One is that after the robbers had been questioned, a judge, based on a claim by one of the crooks, ordered the arrest of Bill Tilghman as being an accomplice. Bat knew this was ridiculous but realized that to avoid violence he had better put the cuffs on Tilghman himself, which he did. Bat promised his falsely accused friend to get the matter straightened out. Tilghman was put on the same train as the outlaws, but three days later, with the accusation proven to be a complete fabrication, Bat went and got Tilghman and brought him back to Dodge City.

The second postscript is that the saga of Rudabaugh's life of crime had more chapters to it. Dirty Dave was a low-down scoundrel to the rest of his gang. He informed on them, probably heaping most of the blame on his former comrades. They wound up in prison. Rudabaugh, after promising to go straight, was released and allowed to ride off to New Mexico.

After some time in the territory, he returned to his thieving ways. By 1879, he had put together a fresh (except for him) band of outlaws, and a crime spree commenced. Because there were several fellows from Kansas in his new gang — including Hoodoo Brown, and, of all people, former lawman John Joshua Webb — Rudabaugh's outfit was known as the Dodge City Gang. During a six-month reign of terror they robbed stagecoaches and trains. One of the more sensational attacks on a train in New Mexico took place on October 14 of that year, when a group of masked men led by Dirty Dave held up a train outside of Las Vegas in New Mexico. They rode off with not only over two thousand dollars in cash but every lantern on the train.

Not long into the new year, Webb was found and arrested. He waited in jail to be tried. Rudabaugh led the effort to free him, and in the ensuing melee he killed Deputy Sheriff Lino Valdez. Breaking off the attack, Rudabaugh fled, soon finding himself in Fort Sumner. There he joined up with another gang, this one led by William Bonney, known throughout the frontier as Billy the Kid.

On the night of November 30, 1880, Dirty Dave and the Kid and a third outlaw rode into White Oaks, New Mexico. There was a gunfight with local lawmen, and another one at dawn, resulting in the death of a deputy sheriff, James Carlyle. After their escape, Sheriff Pat Garrett set off after them. For almost three weeks the relentless pursuit continued. When Billy the Kid's gang arrived in Fort Sumner on December 19, Garrett and his posse were waiting for them. Guns blazed, men and horses were hit, one outlaw was killed, but Billy the Kid, Rudabaugh, and three others who had joined the gang got away. They holed up in a cabin near Stinking Springs, which had earned its name naturally, not thanks to Dirty Dave.

In the morning, when one of the gang stepped outside the cabin, he was shot dead. During the night, Garrett and his men had tracked them to Stinking Springs. As the other four ran toward their horses, Garrett killed another one. Rudabaugh and the Kid and a third man hurried back into the cabin and for much of the day shot it out with the posse. Finally, low on bullets and water, Rudabaugh fluttered a piece of white cloth out a window and the outlaws surrendered. Billy the Kid was jailed in Lincoln, New

Mexico. (On April 28, 1881, he escaped, as will be detailed.)

This would seem to be the end of Dirty Dave's days as a desperado, but he was not finished yet. He was tried and convicted of murder. He was put in the same Las Vegas prison as Webb, which turned out to be unwise. Somehow, on September 19, 1881, they and two other men obtained guns and attempted to shoot their way out of prison. They failed, but one man was killed. In the first week in December, Rudabaugh and Webb had better luck when they dug a hole through one wall, crawled out, and fled. Webb made his way east, where for several months under the name Samuel King he worked as a teamster in Kansas and Nebraska, and ended up in Arkansas, where he died of small-pox. Dirty Dave escaped to Mexico.

For years there, he apparently found ways to stay out of trouble . . . until the night of February 18, 1886. He was involved in a card game at a cantina in Parral when Rudabaugh and a local man accused each other of cheating. They jumped up and jerked their guns. The gringo was faster, with the Mexican man taking a bullet in the head. His friend went for his gun and Rudabaugh shot him through the heart. He went outside, couldn't locate his horse, and returned to the cantina. By this time, angry friends of the dead men had gathered inside and they had put out the lights. Rudabaugh, encountering the darkness, tried to turn and leave but he was seized. Knives went to work. For the next few days, Dirty Dave's severed head was paraded through the town. He had lived a full life of villainy in only thirty-two years.

Virginia and Nicholas Earp.
(COURTESY OF KANSAS STATE
HISTORICAL SOCIETY)

Thomas Sr. and Catherine Masterson. (COURTESY OF DENVER PUBLIC LIBRARY)

Virgil Earp. (COURTESY OF ARIZONA HISTORICAL SOCIETY)

Morgan Earp. (COURTESY OF BOOT HILL MUSEUM)

Ed Masterson. (COURTESY OF BOOT HILL MUSEUM)

James Masterson. (COURTESY OF BOOT HILL MUSEUM)

Kit Carson, who fought in the first Battle of Adobe Walls. (Courtesy of Kansas State Historical Society)

The city was most likely named after General Grenville Dodge. (Courtesy of Kansas State Historical Society)

This sod house is believed to be the first Dodge City structure. (Courtesy of Kansas State Historical Society)

Front Street in Dodge City, as it was in the 1870s. (Courtesy of Kansas State Historical Society)

An illustration depicting cattle being hurried through the city toward their holding pens. (Courtesy of Kansas State Historical Society)

For cowboys, Dodge City was a welcome end of the trail. (COURTESY OF KANSAS STATE HISTORICAL SOCIETY)

Buffalo Bill Cody did his share in the eradication of the buffalo herds. (COURTESY OF KANSAS STATE HISTORICAL SOCIETY)

The prominent businessman Robert Wright sits atop a pile of buffalo hides. (COURTESY OF KANSAS STATE HISTORICAL SOCIETY)

Wild Bill Hickok set the standard for frontier lawmen. (COURTESY OF KANSAS STATE HISTORICAL SOCIETY)

The only known photograph of Billy the Kid. (COURTESY OF NATIONAL ARCHIVES AND RECORDS ADMINISTRATION)

The death of Jesse James symbolized the taming of the "Wild West." (COURTESY OF BOOT HILL MUSEUM)

Until his death, Frank James corresponded with old friend Bat Masterson. (COURTESY OF BOOT HILL MUSEUM)

Two 1870s Dodge City lawmen, Wyatt Earp and Bat Masterson. (COURTESY OF ARIZONA HISTORICAL SOCIETY)

Top Left: Doc Holliday was a thirsty man with a bad temper, but ever loyal to Wyatt Earp. (Courtesy of Kansas State Historical Society)

Top Right: No one in Dodge City was more colorful than the entertainer Eddie Foy. (Courtesy of Library of Congress)

Bottom Left: Bill Tilghman (right) with Jim Elder (left) during their buffalo-hunting days. (Courtesy of Kansas State Historical Society)

The dapper Ben Thompson, a friend of Bat's and a fellow gambler. (Courtesy of Denver Public Library)

Top Left: Clay Allison came to Dodge City gunning for Wyatt Earp. (COURTESY OF DENVER PUBLIC LIBRARY)

Top Right: Larry Deger was a lawman and later mayor of Dodge City. (COURTESY OF KANSAS STATE HISTORICAL SOCIETY)

Bottom Right: Mysterious Dave Mather was one of the frontier's more curious characters. (COURTESY OF KANSAS STATE HISTORICAL SOCIETY)

It is clear how James "Dog" Kelley earned his nickname. (COURTESY OF KANSAS STATE HISTORICAL SOCIETY)

No one served longer as a lawman than Ham Bell. (Courtesy of Kansas Heritage Center)

Bat's brother George Masterson was a bartender at the Varieties saloon. (Courtesy of Kansas State Historical Society)

Dull Knife and his followers and two interpreters on the steps of the Ford County courthouse. (COURTESY OF BOOT HILL MUSEUM)

Mattie Earp was Wyatt's third "wife." (COURTESY OF BOOT HILL MUSEUM)

Allie Earp and her husband, Virgil, were devoted to each other. (COURTESY OF ARIZONA HISTORICAL SOCIETY)

"Big Nose" Kate Elder and Doc Holliday were a volatile couple. (COURTESY OF ARIZONA HISTORICAL SOCIETY)

Bottom Left: Josephine Marcus Earp and Wyatt remained together until his death. (COURTESY OF TOMBSTONE WESTERN HERITAGE MUSEUM)

Bottom Right: Emma Walters, Bat Masterson's one and only wife. (COURTESY OF AMON CARTER MUSEUM)

A post–Dodge City Bat Masterson and his friend Charlie Mitchell on a Colorado outing.

An elderly Wyatt Earp in the 1920s, in the house he and Josephine shared in Los Angeles. (COURTESY OF ARIZONA HISTORICAL SOCIETY)

An older Bat Masterson, when he was a newspaper columnist in New York City. (COURTESY OF KANSAS STATE HISTORICAL SOCIETY)

SEVENTEEN

Such, then, was the beginning of my acquaintance with Doc Holliday, the mad, merry scamp with heart of gold and nerves of steel; who, in the dark years that followed stood at my elbow in many a battle to the death. — WYATT EARP

With Bat and his posse taking care of Rudabaugh and his gang after they had doubled back from Texas, Wyatt returned early to Dodge City in January 1878. Around this time, his new acquaintance, Doc Holliday, began the flight that would eventually bring him to Dodge City. It was Kate Elder who got him out of a serious jam. It wouldn't be the last time.

Mary Katharine Haroney was born in Hungary in November 1850. The family then lived in Mexico because her father was the personal physician of that country's emperor, Maximilian. But after only three years, in 1865, Maximilian was ousted and the Haroneys fled Mexico, winding up in Davenport, Iowa. Within months, Kate's displaced parents were dead and she and her siblings were sent to live in foster homes. Kate tolerated this until she was sixteen, when she stowed away on a steamship that landed her in St. Louis. She enrolled in a school there, changing her last name to Fisher, after the ship's captain.

The first dentist she fell in love with was Silas Melvin. The two married and had a child. But in less than a year, Kate had lost her child and become a widow. She headed west and wound up in Wichita, working as a prostitute in the brothel run by James and Bessie Earp. It would seem highly unlikely that she did not encounter Wyatt. (Some have speculated that she knew him all too well but both denied it out of respect for Holliday.) The following year, in 1875, she went by the name of Kate Elder and was performing in a Dodge City dance hall and was probably a part-time prostitute. Though an attractive woman, her nose was a tad prominent, and both men and women began referring to her as Big Nose Kate. Some of those same people were afraid of her because she had a terrible temper, especially when drinking, which was often.

Why she was in Fort Griffin, Texas, in January 1878 is not known. It may simply have been a place to find work at a time of year when saloon jobs were scarce in Dodge City. It was there that she met Doc Holliday. They had quick tempers, alcohol, independence, restlessness, and a low regard for life in common. All that and more would be enough to keep them together despite the knock-down, drag-out fights that would impress those who knew them.

Soon after Wyatt left Fort Griffin to head north, Doc was playing cards with Ed Bailey, a man whose reputation included being a bit of a bully. Doc was the one dealing, and Bailey picked up the discarded cards and looked at them. The former dentist must have been in a mellow mood because he let slide what was a clear violation of western poker. But when Bailey continued to do it, Doc warned him, and after a couple of unheeded warnings, he simply raked in the pot without revealing to Bailey if his hand was a winner or not.

For Bailey, this was like waving a red flag in front of a bull. Immediately furious, he reached for his gun. Just as it was coming visible above the table, Doc slashed a knife across his stomach. Bailey lurched to his feet, then pitched forward, his blood drooling out across the poker table. There were witnesses to the incident, so when lawmen arrived, Doc surrendered the knife and co-operated with his arrest. It was clearly a case of self-defense, as the others in the saloon would testify. Because there was not a jail in Fort Griffin, Doc was kept in a hotel room until the judge could be found.

But Bailey had friends who didn't take kindly to him being filleted like a fish. They gathered and began heading toward the hotel with a long length of rope. Fortunately for Doc, Big Nose Kate got wind of what was going on, and thinking fast, she set fire to an old shed filled with hay. The sudden conflagration and the hectic activity involved in trying to douse the fire slowed the lynch mob enough that Kate arrived at the hotel first, a pistol in each hand. This surely intimidated the guard, who ran off. Kate and Doc commandeered a couple of horses and left town while the fire continued to be fought.

Their destination was Dodge City. The reason may have been to seek the protec-tion of Wyatt Earp in case some people in Fort Griffin went on being agitated about Bailey's bloody demise. In any event, when the two fugitives arrived they checked into Deacon Cox's Boarding House, with Doc signing the register as Dr. and Mrs. J. H. Holliday. They were so relieved by their escape from the mob that Doc vowed to give up gambling and return to dentistry, and Big Nose Kate reciprocated by vowing to give up the whoring saloon life. For a time, both were sincere.

Once Bat could get settled in as sheriff of Ford County, he added the recently exonerated Bill Tilghman to his staff. He was good with a gun, people trusted him, like Wyatt he shunned alcohol, and he kept a cool head. Bat had thought well of him since their buffalo-hunting adventures.

Tilghman and his new wife, Flora, had been trying to make a go of it as ranchers in Bluff Creek. They had 160 acres on the prairie west of Dodge City, and they worked from dawn to dusk despite having a baby, and during the winter of 1877–1878 another one was on the way. Flora was quite pleased with the ranching and domestic life. Her husband grew increasingly restless. So it was that on the day when Tilghman had seen a lone rider approaching from the east and it turned out to be Bat Masterson, the would-be rancher was more receptive to what was offered to him. Flora could have dug her heels in but recognized that holding her husband back would not do the marriage or the ranch any good.

During his first day on the job as deputy, Tilghman encountered Luke Short being shot in the head several times, which had to make him think that this job was going to be a lot tougher than he'd anticipated.

In the annals of Dodge City and the lives of Wyatt Earp and Bat Masterson, Short would be a familiar figure, popping up here and there. He did not save Bat's life, like Ben Thompson had done in Sweetwater, nor was he a steady badge-wearing man like Tilghman, but Wyatt and especially Bat considered him a friend, and as such he deserved their loyalty.

Luke Short was only a couple of months older than Bat and hailed from Polk County, Arkansas, but when he was six the family relocated to Montague County in Texas. That would suit him just fine because Luke took to being a cowboy, and beginning when he was sixteen, in 1869, as the cattle-driving business began to boom, he regularly went on the trail north, steering cattle to the Kansas cow towns, especially Dodge City. His lifelong enjoyment of — many might say addiction to — gambling commenced early on, when he got to the end of the Chisholm Trail and the gaming tables of Abilene.

Wyatt later claimed that was where he set eyes on him: "First time I saw Luke he was selling red likker to the hide hunters. He'd quit working as a cowhand already, didn't cotton to it. That little fella never did hanker for lifting and straining."

He hadn't quite quit being a cattle driver yet, but in the cow-town saloons, he watched and listened as the experienced gamblers plied their trade. He learned the tricks and how to cheat only enough to not get killed and how to read in the eyes of other men what they were holding. When he won, he improved the way he dressed. The ladies in the saloons took notice of that and of his easy grin behind the fashionable brown mustache.

When Lady Luck was against him, Luke found other ways to raise a stake. One example was during the Great Sioux War of 1876, when he was a scout for General George Crook. Another was heading out to the buffalo camps with a wagon full of whiskey. He had the reputation of being reliable and of offering fine-tasting whiskey. No one knew he stacked the bottom of his barrels with rattlesnake heads. Luke liked to partake himself, but never touched his own supply. When he'd made enough money, he exchanged his dusty duds for his successful frontier gambler outfits and returned to the tables.

Along the way at those gaming tables he had met Bat Masterson, and inevitably Luke gravitated toward Dodge City, where Bat and Wyatt were. There he won at faro and other games more than he lost, and when he asserted that he was good with a gun, no one tried to disprove him. Luke had done pretty well in either Texas or Deadwood over the winter, and in spring 1878 he was on Front Street in Dodge City, though seemingly in a bad way.

Bill Tilghman's inaugural patrol through the streets of Dodge City had been a pleasant one. Most people greeted him with courtesy, welcoming him to the sheriff's department. Gamblers and prostitutes mingled on Front Street with dust-covered cowboys and farmers and ranchers, some accompanied by wives who wore ankle-length calico dresses. When Tilghman arrived at the train station, he sat down to rest and chat with the freight agent, recalling how on any given day the area adjacent to the station was once piled high with buffalo hides and behind that were the piles of sun-bleached buffalo bones.

Suddenly, there were gunshots. Tilghman jumped up and ran for Front Street. Having not met Luke Short before, Tilghman did not recognize him; he simply saw a man walking down the middle of the street, his boots covered with mud, wearing a tall black plug hat. A man crossed over from the sidewalk, aimed a gun at the head of the man in the street, and pulled the trigger. The sound of the shot was still echoing when another man appeared and also shot the victim in the head.

Tilghman took out his gun and the two men fled. The deputy should have gone after at least one of them, but he was too amazed that the man who had been shot at least twice was still on his feet. Luke Short grinned, took off his hat, and showed the gaping Tilghman the holes in it. "I made a bet with the boys back at the Red Dog that I could walk down the street without my plug hat being shot off," he explained, returning the hat to the top of his head. "Well, it ain't shot off, so I win the bet."

Tilghman noticed several men had gathered on the sidewalk, and they appeared to be trying not to laugh. Catching on, he made tracks to the sheriff's office. Bat sat with his boots perched up on his desk. He asked his deputy if there had been any trouble.

"None worth mentioning," Tilghman replied.

"No arrests for Luke's hat being shot full of holes?"

That and the sheriff's big grin told the story. For Tilghman, it was "welcome to lawing in Ford County," Bat Masterson style.

In addition to having an irrepressible personality, Bat enjoyed practical jokes because he knew that having fun endeared him to many of the city's citizens, yet his past accomplishments meant he wasn't thought of any less as a lawman. And sometimes what Bat concocted could have a practical purpose.

Cowboys were not the only ones who got drunk in Dodge City. There were men in other occupations who could not resist whiskey, and lots of it. Sometimes they got into a bit of trouble, while other times for the local lawmen it was a routine task to find a fellow passed out in the street, haul him to the calaboose, and let him out when sobriety was regained.

Bat and a few of his like-minded acquaintances had an idea of how to cure these unfortunates, and they invented what came to be called the Dodge City Keeley Cure. With many "patients," it worked. (This can be considered the first "intervention," long before there was Alcoholics Anonymous or group therapy.) A chronic drunk was approached at the bar in a saloon and actually encouraged to have more whiskey. Rarely was there any resistance, with the rounds being bought for him. When he passed out, he was taken to the sheriff's jail as usual. But instead of being locked up, his face was powdered white, he was dressed in black, and he was laid out in a coffin with a mirror above his head. It had been arranged ahead of time that his friends who had hoped the man would see the light would gather.

Finally, when the man awoke from his stupor, he opened his eyes to his reflection in the mirror, which showed him laid out in a coffin and his friends standing around him murmuring prayers. The man was terrified at first; then, discovering that he was alive again and had been given a Scrooge-like second chance, he tearfully vowed never to touch another drop of liquor.

This time when Wyatt had returned to Dodge City, it was the new *Ford County Globe* that made note of it, telling readers he had arrived from Fort Clarke, Texas. If he did any lawing, it was not until the middle of May, when *The Wichita Eagle* reported that Wyatt was to be paid two hundred dollars a month to be the new Dodge City marshal.

This was a handsome sum, and the report could well have been true. It was not true, though, that he would be the new marshal. Charlie Bassett had the job. (Ed Masterson had recovered and returned as marshal in April, but for a reason to be detailed, it was Bassett's post once more.) Wyatt willingly signed on as his assistant, as he had been to Larry Deger two years earlier. *The Eagle* continued to pay attention to activities of its former peace officer, informing readers that Wyatt was "adding new laurels to his splendid record every day." He was even credited with putting out a fire on the outskirts of town.

Unless one of them was out of town, Bat's and Wyatt's paths crossed on a daily basis. But they managed to get into plenty of scrapes while on separate paths.

Unlike the quiet and laconic Wyatt, the more gregarious Bat continued to enjoy a practical joke. Thus, some believed that he was really behind an incident that took place around this time at the Lady Gay Saloon. A man calling himself Dr. Meredith arrived in Dodge City offering to lecture on phrenology and its use in diagnosing diseases. The "doctor" approached the sheriff asking for his protection, explaining that some towns along the frontier, especially ones filled with cowboys, had not received his lectures with anything approaching courtesy. Intrigued, Bat agreed and went so far as to persuade the owners of the Lady Gay Saloon to suspend their usual entertainment long enough for the visitor to give his lecture.

On that evening the saloon was almost full, and the regular patrons were at least puzzled when, instead of singing and dancing girls taking to the stage, a stranger appeared. Even Bat's introduction wasn't placating enough. Dr. Meredith was only a few words into his lecture when a member of the audience shouted, "You lie!" Bat stood, turned to the audience, and declared, "I'll shoot the first man that interrupts this gentleman again."

Again, Dr. Meredith began his lecture, and again a man in the audience blurted out, "You lie!" Bat was back on his feet, saying, "I meant what I said. The next time this gentleman is interrupted, I'll begin shooting."

The third time was not a charm. Bat produced his pistol and shot out the lights. The crowd went crazy, fighting each other to get through the front door, and a few audience members jumped out the windows, one man not bothering to open it first. When Bat lit a lamp, the distressed "doctor" was found cowering behind the lecture podium. Dr. Meredith was done as far as Dodge City was concerned, and he was on the next train out. Town wags believed that Bat either planned the mischief from the moment he met Dr. Meredith, or after only a few words realized anything would be more fun than the lecture.

Of course, Bat could not lollygag around Ford County playing practical jokes. There were outlaws to be caught, and one adventure was a postscript to the arrest of the Rudabaugh gang. When word came to the sheriff that not all of the men who had ridden with Dirty Dave were behind bars and that in fact one of them, Mike Rorke, had put together a new gang to bedevil banks and trains, Bat gathered a posse and hit the trail.

Riding with him were Charlie Bassett, Miles Mix, John Joshua Webb (apparently, before he fell under Dirty Dave's spell), and Red Clarke, a respected local rancher. With the *Ford County Globe* declaring, "No better posse ever undertook such a duty," the pressure was on to deliver. Bat had a pretty good idea of the direction the bandits had taken, and he turned out to be right when ranch hands and settlers reported Rorke and several other men having passed by a few hours earlier.

For thirteen days the posse stayed close behind the outlaws. They continued south, past the Cimarron River, then southeast, finally getting to the Staked Plains in Texas. There the trail ended. There was no sign of Rorke and his men. After a pursuit of three hundred miles, Bat and the posse had to backtrack to Dodge City. Even with no one to toss in the calaboose, the lawmen were cheered for what had been a valiant effort when they returned.

Rorke did not remain a free man very long. Later in 1878, in October, he and a companion, Dan Dement, were spotted in Ellsworth. The attempted arrest turned into a gun battle. Dement would die from his wounds, and Rorke was tried, convicted, and sentenced to ten years in prison. Perhaps to gain some satisfaction, Bat paid him a visit.

EIGHTEEN

What fools some young cowboys were after long drives "up the Chisholm trail," and after filling their hides full of the poison liquors manufactured to put the red-shirted Irish rail-road builders to sleep, so that the toughs could "roll" them, and get their "wads." Instead of putting a cowboy to sleep it stirred up the devil in his make-up, and made him a wide-awake hyena.

— CHARLES SIRINGO

It did not look too good for the future of Dodge City that death took a high toll in 1878. The fatalities would include women and lawmen, illustrating the risks both faced in their respective professions. But the year would prove to be a turning point.

A couple of names on wooden signs above their graves implied that women were buried at Boot Hill, but the only confirmed female buried there by then was named Alice

Chambers. She was known to acquaintances and customers as Squirrel Tooth Alice — not because of her teeth, but for a fondness for the rodent. She was a prostitute who fronted as a dance-hall girl. In frontier towns, especially growing ones like Dodge City, there could be more than one or even several working women named Jane, Mary, and Alice (with only a few of the names being real ones), so even a minor physical characteristic inspired a nickname that distinguished one Alice from another. The story of the one nicknamed "Squirrel Tooth" pretty well represented the perils and often the fate of the soiled doves of Dodge City.

It was estimated at the time by the *Ford County Globe* that of Dodge City's seven hundred residents there were forty-seven prostitutes. Some were tough, imposing women in the Big Nose Kate mold. According to Odie Faulk, "Most were as crude as their customers." Even those hailing from Ohio, Illinois, or even New York often took on names like Belle, Dixie, and other ones with a southern flavor that were more appealing to their clientele, most of whom were Texas cowboys. The rest were hunters, gamblers, and the occasional Ford County citizen who had ridden in for a night on the town. Between the drinking, long hours, physical abuse, and sexually transmitted diseases, few frontier women in this profession lived to middle age. Old age was miraculous, with the odds much more in favor of an early demise, sometimes in unexpected ways.

That happened to a prostitute named Lizzie Adams. She had made a romantic conquest of George Palmer, who owned a ranch quite a way outside the city limits and brought her there as his bride. One would think that being a housewife and perhaps a mother would be a preferred existence, but apparently Lizzie missed the old life, because she began to entertain former clients in a room at a Dodge City boardinghouse. One night the building burned to the ground, with Lizzie in it. Palmer was the prime suspect but he was nowhere to be found, until his lifeless body was discovered some weeks later. One of Lizzie's old clients, apparently another romantic conquest, was arrested, and he confessed to the revenge killing.

Squirrel Tooth Alice's turn as headline fodder came one day in March 1878, but for a benign reason. The *Dodge City Times* reported that as she was walking down the street, a sudden blast of late-winter wind tugged seven dollar bills out of her stocking. The reporter contended that a six-hour search was undertaken "by all the tramps in town," yet when it was called off, only one of the dollars had been recovered. The article concluded, "We did not suppose that the Kansas wind was of a higher order and did not stoop to such larceny."

Sadly, during that spring Alice lost more than six dollars. She spent her last days and nights in a small room above the Lady Gay Saloon. It was not reported what her fatal ailment was, but prostitutes were easy prey for consumption, infections, botched abortions, and the like. The pastor of the new Presbyterian church visited to offer some comfort, which got him in hot water with his congregation for spending time with a woman of ill repute. Squirrel Tooth Alice Chambers soon took up residence in the Boot Hill cemetery.

About this time another woman caught everyone's attention, though just for a single visit, and she came out of it in fine health. She had been born Myra Maybelle Shirley in a log cabin outside of Carthage, Missouri, and had just turned thirty when she made an appearance in Dodge City. Her tempestuous personality could be attributed to her mother being a member of the Hatfield family that wound up feuding with the

McCoys.

The Shirleys became a prosperous family, and Myra and her four brothers were given good schooling. She attended the Carthage Female Academy, where she excelled at classical languages and music. How did a cultured girl destined for matrimony to a man well placed in southern society become a notorious outlaw? As with many other members of that generation, it began with the Civil War, and specifically for the Shirley family, it began with the Missouri-Kansas Conflict. The oldest son, Bud, joined Quantrill's Raiders, riding with Jesse James, and was killed in June 1864. Devastated financially as well as emotionally, the Shirleys left Missouri, relocating to Scyene, Texas. That by itself did not transform Maybelle Shirley into Belle Starr — her brother's bandit friend did that.

After the end of the Civil War, when Jesse and Frank James had teamed up with the Younger brothers to rob banks, their first successful attempt was in Liberty, Missouri. They made off with six thousand dollars and kept riding, all the way to Texas. Taking advantage of the Missouri connection and having known Bud, Jesse and his gang hid out at the Shirley farm. Myra fell in love with Cole Younger; however, it was Jim

Reed, a member of another gang seeking shelter with the Shirleys, whom Myra married in November 1866. They moved to Missouri, and for a time the Reeds enjoyed a peaceful domestic life with their two children, Pearl and Edward.

That life came to a sudden end when Reed murdered a man named Shannon and the family fled to California. Embarking on her own life of crime, the woman who would be dubbed the Bandit Queen made up for lost time. While in North Canadian River country, she and Reed and two other men tortured a Creek Indian into revealing where he had accumulated thirty thousand dollars in gold. The gang returned to Texas with Myra, then known as Belle Reed. They rode hard and evaded capture until August 1874, when Reed was killed in a gun battle. Unpersuaded by this to go straight, Belle deposited her children at the Shirley farm and set off for Indian Territory. There she took up with an Indian desperado called Blue Duck, who may have been the inspiration for the renegade half Comanche in Larry McMurtry's *Lonesome Dove*.

Belle and Blue would be acquainted, romantically and otherwise, for the rest of her life (he died of tuberculosis in 1895), but it was another Indian, the Cherokee

Sam Starr, whom she married. She and her new husband and Blue Duck and several others became an outlaw band, using a sixty-two-acre ranch north of the Canadian River, which Belle named Younger's Bend, as their hideaway. One of their visitors there was an old friend, Jesse James. Led by Belle Starr, the gang committed robberies and other crimes.

It was on one of their side trips, perhaps needing to leave the Panhandle in the dust for a few days, that, according to the recollections of several residents, Belle and her husband came to Dodge City. They checked into a boardinghouse run by Dog Kelley's wife. Their "vacation" was cut short by an incident at the Long Branch Saloon. Sam Starr walked in and became involved in a faro game — so involved and so unlucky or so unenlightened about the odds favoring the bank that he lost two thousand dollars. Back at the boardinghouse, the news did not amuse his wife.

Belle had Sam saddle their horses and she trailed him back to the saloon. Once inside, the action picked up. She marched in and yanked out her pistols. Her eyes darting here and there, she moved from table to table, collecting the cash on the players and pocketing about seven thousand dollars.

The men at the bar and tables were slack-jawed, too astonished at the sight of a female robber expertly wielding a pair of six-shooters and covering the room to offer any resistance. Belle backed out to where the horses were waiting, and she and Sam were on their way.

Remarkably, for four more years Belle and her gang continued to leave their sanctuary of Younger's Bend to conduct more raids and elude the law. But in 1882, she and Sam were convicted of horse theft, and Judge Isaac Parker in Fort Smith, Arkansas, sentenced them to a year in prison. (He had earned the nickname the "Hanging Judge" in September 1875, when Parker had the necks of six men stretched in the same day.) After serving their sentences, Belle and Sam returned to Younger's Bend. Belle had become something of a folk hero along the frontier — aided by the inevitable dime-store novels easterners devoured — and for a time she acted roles (usually outlaws, of course) in a traveling Wild West show, in between ongoing robbing and stealing adventures.

During a Christmas party in 1886, Sam got into an argument with another man that escalated to the point of him being shot to death. Belle continued with her gang, and she married one of its younger members, Jim July. He quickly became enraged by his bride's demanding and mercurial ways, and he offered other gang members two hundred dollars to kill her. When there were no takers, July announced, "I'll kill the old hag myself." He did just that, shooting the forty-year-old Belle to death on February 3, 1889.

Her children did not have the opportunity or inclination to honor her memory. Edward Reed was sent to prison for horse theft by Judge Parker the same year his mother died. After his release, he received a presidential pardon and became a deputy in Fort Smith. One day in 1895, when two outlaws tried to escape, Edward killed them both. He in turn was shot to death a year later in an Oklahoma saloon. Pearl Starr became a prostitute and a madam, operating brothels in Arkansas up to World War I.

By April 1878, though Ed Masterson had been officially the marshal for six months, he had spent most of that time recovering from the gunshot wounds suffered the previous November. It was much too soon to become involved in more gunplay, yet after he took the marshal's badge back from Charlie Bassett, almost immediately there was another confrontation.

Even in so short a tenure and on limited

duty, Ed had proven to be a popular peace officer. With Bat as sheriff of Ford County and Jim on and off the peace-officer rolls, the Masterson brothers were the most responsible for keeping order in and around Dodge City. The knock on Ed continued to be what had been said about him since childhood, that he was a gentle sort, soft-spoken and slow to take offense, especially compared to the more direct and dynamic Bat Masterson. After Ed's fight with Bob Shaw, Bat was, of course, greatly relieved to find Ed alive, but he also threatened to run his own brother out of town — after he was back on his feet, of course — if he again allowed another gunman similar leeway in a showdown. Ed promised he wouldn't.

When Ed was up and around enough to resume his duties as marshal, Bat figured that just like when they were kids he would keep an eye on him and be prepared to protect him if necessary. But on April 9, 1878, Bat wasn't there. Or at least, not in time.

Around ten that night, Ed was on patrol along Front Street, accompanied by an assistant marshal, Nat Haywood. As they passed the sheriff's office, Ed may well have waved at his younger brother seated inside, unless they had already passed each other while patrolling on the street. From across the Dead Line could be heard loud shouting and laughter, which was not unusual. Then there was a more disturbing sound — a quick series of gunshots. With luck, it was just an exuberant cowboy having a hurrah. Just in case, though, Ed and Nat hurried south.

More shots were heard coming from inside the Lady Gay Saloon. The season had begun early that year, with a herd of cattle having just been delivered to Dodge City from a ranch in Texas. Alf Walker was the trail boss. He and his dusty and dry-mouthed drovers had been lubricating their throats with whiskey most of the evening. One of the cowboys was Jack Wagner. It was clear he was very drunk, and with a pistol in hand, he had been the one blasting away.

Entering the saloon, Ed glanced around. No one appeared to be hurt, but there were a bunch of holes in the ceiling. He approached Wagner. Most likely, Wyatt or Bat would have buffaloed the cowboy right then and there, but Ed said in an even tone, "You better check that gun with me." It probably surprised most of the men in the smoke-filled room "sweetened" with kerosene fumes from the stove when, without hesitation, Wagner turned the six-shooter around and handed it to Ed.

Learning that Walker was the trail boss, Ed turned the gun over to him and suggested that he leave it with the bartender for safekeeping. His man Wagner could collect it when the Texans were ready to head back to camp. Walker agreed, and with the Lady Gay much quieter and the routine gambling and drinking resuming, Ed and Nat Haywood left.

But only a few moments later, the two lawmen heard footsteps behind them. They turned to find Walker and Wagner on the wooden walkway outside the dance hall. Ed saw that Wagner's shoulder holster had his gun in it. Irritated that Walker had returned it to the drunken drover so quickly, Ed advanced on Wagner and demanded it. "Come down to the marshal's office in the morning and you can have it back," he instructed.

Wagner responded, "You ain't got no business taking my gun. Who do you think you are?"

"Marshal Ed Masterson of the Dodge City police," Ed said, putting out his hand for the weapon.

Wagner wouldn't give it up, and that led to a fight for the pistol. The saloon door swung open and more cowboys spilled out.

When Haywood went to help Ed, Walker pulled his gun out. He told the assistant marshal to mind his own business and aimed the pistol at his head. Haywood saw that Walker's men were holding six-shooters on him, too. Somehow, Haywood had the courage to go for his own gun. Walker pulled the trigger. His pistol did not fire. However, just hearing the hammer strike metal was enough for Haywood, who took off down the street, shouting for help.

Wagner managed to drag his gun out of the holster. He pressed the barrel against Ed and pulled the trigger. The bullet went through the abdomen of the eldest Masterson brother, a mortal wound. In addition, the muzzle blast right up against him set Ed's vest on fire. Smoke overcoming his senses and knowing he was hurt badly, Ed staggered away.

Nat Haywood would subsequently be criticized for leaving the marshal behind to alone face six armed men, but to be fair, most likely he just would have gotten himself killed. His fast feet were more effective. Bat heard the assistant marshal's shouts and stepped out of his office. He listened to the breathless mentions of Ed being in trouble with a bunch of armed cowboys. Without hesitating, Bat checked that his ivory-handled pistols were loaded, and he quickly followed where Nat was leading him.

He rounded a corner and was within sight of the Lady Gay when he heard the gunshot and saw his brother lurch away. Moments later, with Ed out of the line of fire, Bat jerked his guns and they spit bullets. According to one witness, "It was the fastest gun work I ever saw and so quick it sounded like a Gatling."

Wagner took one of those bullets in the abdomen. Three of them found Walker, one piercing a lung. Both men collapsed in a heap.

As Ed staggered down the street, people ran past him — some away from the gun battle, others to see what all the commotion was about. The *Ford County Globe* would report in a special edition published the next day that Ed's gunshot wound was "large enough for the introduction of the whole pistol." As he continued to will himself down the street, smoke was wafting off his burning clothes. Hoover's Saloon, owned by the former mayor, was two hundred yards to the north, across the Dead Line, and on sheer determination Ed got that far. With slow, pain-filled steps he approached the bar and told George Hinkle, "I'm shot," then slid down to the dirt-covered floor.

That is where Bat found his brother. Ed lived in a room above the saloon, and Bat and a couple of men brought him there, blood leaving a trail up the boot-worn steps. Soon after a doctor arrived, he informed Bat that there was nothing to be done for Ed. In an anguished whisper, Bat said, "This will just about kill Mother," recalling all the times he had been told to watch out for his mild-mannered brother. "She'll never forgive me for letting him get killed in this town." Bat was already certain he would never forgive himself.

Down on the street, the severely wounded Jack Wagner, too, was on the move. After climbing to his feet, he crossed to the saloon owned by A. J. Peacock and fell into the arms of Ham Bell. "Catch me, I'm dying," Wagner sighed, slipping through Bell's arms to the floor. Bell realized that what the cowboy said was true, and murmured, "I can't help you now."

A minute later, Alf Walker also wobbled into the saloon. Because of the punctured lung, blood dripped out of his mouth. He offered his gun, but Bell wouldn't take it, saying, "Throw it on the floor if you don't want it," which Walker did. He turned and tried to leave but made it only a few steps before he, too, was on the floor.

Bat sat beside his brother, holding Ed's hand. During the next thirty minutes, what was left of the young marshal's life ebbed away. Then, without regaining consciousness and thus unaware of his brother's tears, Ed Masterson died.

Bat stood up and checked his guns once more. He had been told that there were several other of Walker's cowboys in the Lady Gay and that they, too, had guns. Bat was prepared to go kill them all. But the problem was that he was the duly elected and sworn Ford County sheriff. As John Wesley Hardin had asserted, some men needed killing, and that was true of the cowboys who had killed Ed, but Dodge City didn't need backsliding to the days of Bully Brooks. What Bat did next would have an impact on the present and future of Dodge City and law and order across the frontier.

Spectators held their breath when Bat emerged from Hoover's Saloon, eyes blazing, his strong hands hovering above his holstered six-shooters. A few gestured to direct him to Peacock's place across the Dead Line. There he found Walker and Wagner. Before the latter took his last breath, he confessed to shooting Ed Masterson. With Walker being treated by a doctor, Bat went to have warrants sworn out for the arrest of the four other cowboys.

Within an hour, Bat had found them, arrested them, and put them in jail. They would later be released when it was determined they had no direct role in the marshal's death. A grieving, hotheaded brother might have then gone after them, but Bat accepted the finding.

Walker managed to survive his wounds, barely. He was bedridden into May, when his father arrived to make sure he was receiving the proper care. Because of his condition and Wagner's confession, Walker was never arrested. When he was able to travel later that month, his father took him home to Texas. It was later reported that Walker contracted pneumonia from the lung wound and died from it.

Wyatt had not yet returned to Dodge City from the trail of outlaws. He was still in Texas, probably doing some gambling, too, and perhaps keeping clear from Mattie Blaylock and her problems for as long as he could. But the death of Ed Masterson changed that. A telegram from Mayor Kelley found him and informed him of the death of Bat's brother and that he was needed immediately back in Dodge City. Charlie Bassett would once again become the marshal, and he and the other leaders of Dodge City wanted Wyatt to return to being assistant marshal. Especially with Bat badly shaken by the shootings, a steady hand wearing a badge was needed, one citizens trusted and potential troublemakers feared.

Wyatt rode north, most likely with a troubled mind. Perhaps if he had been assistant to Ed, Ed might not have died. And he had to be thinking about Bat and his loss. Probably, too, Wyatt was thinking about how awful it would be to lose one of his brothers to a bullet, especially Virgil or Morgan, the ones he was closest to, as Bat had been close to Ed.

He also may have pondered that he was returning to lawing sooner than he expected. "Wyatt Earp," the *Ford County Globe* would soon report, "one of the most efficient officers Dodge ever had, has just returned from Fort Worth, Texas. He was immediately appointed Asst. Marshal, by our city dads," and in its account, *The Wichita Eagle* added, "with all its dangers and responsibilities."

ACT III

Bat Masterson as sheriff of Ford County. **Courtesy of Denver Public Library**

NINETEEN

The sun was shining so clear and sweet you wanted to run out and breathe the brilliant freshness. Father must have felt that way because he jumped up and fairly shouted, "Come on, Shane. I'll show you what this hop-scotch climate does to my alfalfa. You can almost see the stuff growing." — JACK SCHAEFER, *Shane*

Despite the ongoing deaths from violence and disease, in 1878, only six years since it had been the very rough-hewn Buffalo City, Dodge City was much changed. Whether it was for the better depended on how you made your money and what your hopes were for the city's future. To some extent, many of the changes to Dodge City reflected those under way in the United States, coursing across the country from east to west. They previewed what would be the progress in twentieth-century America that would eventually include much of the West.

The reputation of Dodge City had not changed to many people back east. To them, seeing the occasional breathless headline in the newspapers, it remained the center of dangerous hedonism of biblical proportions. Even in Kansas, Dodge was looked upon with awe for its perceived decadence. A Hays City editor expostulated, "Her principal business is polygamy without the sanction of religion, her code of morals is the honor of thieves, and decency she knows not." Another Kansas weekly concluded that Dodge City was "a den of thieves and cut throats."

But the frontier would not be immune to the social, political, scientific, and cultural changes under way in 1878. That year the U.S. Senate first proposed women's suffrage (though women would not actually be given the right to vote until 1920). Also in 1878, the first college daily, the *Yale Daily News,* made its debut, and Joseph Pulitzer bought the *St. Louis Dispatch* and began the process of turning it into a modern major newspaper. A mask for baseball catchers behind the plate was patented. Also in sports, the fourth Kentucky Derby and twelfth Belmont Stakes were held. Thomas Edison patented the gramophone and he incorporated the Edison Electric Light Company, which began to provide electricity to households. A phone was installed in the White House, where Rutherford B. Hayes resided, and the first female phone operator was hired, in Boston. The first typewriter with a shift key enabling lower- as well as uppercase characters was introduced by Remington, and at Johns Hopkins in Baltimore the first university press was established. And perhaps the most low-tech innovation was the first firehouse pole, in New York City. The so-called Gilded Age was still under way and would be through 1896, and only one year was left to the national depression that had begun in 1873.

A sure sign of a more civilized society on the frontier was the proliferation of churches. In Dodge City there had been small congregations as early as November 1872, and two years later a building was used for services by various denominations. In June 1878, the *Dodge City Times* reported, "The wicked city of Dodge can at last boast of a Christian organization. We would have mentioned the matter last week but we thought it best to break the news gently to the outside world."

The gently broken news was that plans had been initiated by the Presbyterian congregation to construct its own house of worship. The Gothic-windowed frame church would be completed two years later. Also in 1878, the Methodist congregation was officially organized and began the process that would lead to building a church. The congregation of Baptists would follow suit. Alas, it would seem that part of being more civilized was less mingling of the different faiths.

Catholicism made its way to Dodge City, too, which included the founding in nearby Clark County of a monastery known as the "Christian Fort." In Windhorts, Ford County, was a church, and Bishop Louis Fink designated Reverend Ferdinand Wolf to man it. The priest ventured forth from time to time to conduct services, such as celebrating Mass for the first time in Dodge City in August 1878. Efforts to build a house of worship got under way, which would result in the opening of the Sacred Heart Catholic Church four years later. Not far behind with their own church would be the Episcopalians. Of course, all houses of worship would be north of the Dead Line.

The children of parents in an environment moving toward peace and prosperity needed to be educated. A schoolhouse had been built in 1873, anchoring the intersection of

Walnut Street (two blocks north of Front Street) and First Avenue. This served the youngsters well enough for several years, but then it was obvious that a bigger building was required to house an expanding student body. This would result in the end of Boot Hill.

Dodge City needed a bigger cemetery, too. That fact plus the location being more desirable for a new school added up to those interred at Boot Hill being dug up and transported to a new and less centrally located cemetery. In their place went a two-story brick building that served elementary through high school students. The first teacher hired when the new schoolhouse opened in September 1880 was Margaret Walker, who, typical of teachers in those times, was unmarried.

Within the city limits more homes and commercial buildings were being constructed, and with better materials to withstand the wind-driven prairie storms. The city in southwest Kansas was maturing in 1878 — so much so that it rated a visit from the commander in chief. But the visit of President Hayes also illustrated that Dodge City was indeed still a cow town on the frontier. The president desired to visit Dodge City to see firsthand what a Chicago newspaper editor had dubbed the "beautiful, bibulous Babylon of the West," which now shipped almost all of the longhorn cattle driven up from Texas.

On that exciting day in late September, the presidential train arrived and Hayes emerged from his private car, accompanied by the Civil War hero William Tecumseh Sherman and the Kansas governor, John St. John. It was probably bad enough that summer hadn't completely loosened its grasp, and the hot wind coming off the flat prairie carried with it clouds of dust. The wooden buildings and horses and the people waiting in the street as music blared were covered with the yellow, gritty powder. But the wind carried something else, too. During Mayor Dog Kelley's flowery speech of welcome, the presidential nose began to twitch. The wind had picked up and brought along the unique scents of the cattle pens, and Hayes, though an Ohioan, had never been acclimated to that particular fragrance. The president returned to the less-aromatic confines of his car, leaving General Sherman and the governor to soldier on as the speech continued.

Most likely, Wyatt Earp looked on with a taut smile, while Bat Masterson repaired to one of the saloons for a rueful shake of his head and a beer. Though in Casey Tefertiller's biography his focus was on Wyatt, the author pointed out that Bat "always had an air about him, a blend of cockiness and charisma that charmed just about everyone he met, and a style that seemed to invite good times."

Loud tunes to welcome the twitchy-nosed chief executive were probably provided by another sign of civilization, a musical ensemble. It had begun as the pet project of Chalk Beeson, who was one of the more familiar and forward-thinking members of Dodge City society.

Chalkley McArtor Beeson had been born in Salem, Ohio, in 1848. As the youngest of seven children, he may have realized there would not be much opportunity left over for him in Albion, Iowa, where the family had moved, so at nineteen, like thousands of other young men soon after the Civil War, he set out for the West, landing in Denver. There he drove a stagecoach, and when he had enough for a stake, he became a rancher near a Colorado town named for Kit Carson.

By this time, Chalk could play violin pretty well. In January 1872, Denver hosted three distinguished visitors, the Union cavalry heroes Philip Sheridan and George

Armstrong Custer, and the Russian noble-man they had just taken buffalo hunting, Grand Duke Alexei Romanov. At a ball in their honor, Chalk was one of the featured performers, and subsequently he served as a guide on the trio's next hunt, which resulted in forty buffalo being shot and skinned.

He sold his ranch and began another one near Dodge City. Chalk's timing was excellent, and he prospered. He and Ida Gause married and had three sons. His next investment was in a saloon — the Long Branch, which was named after a sportsmen's resort in the East. Beeson wanted less of a haven for rowdy cowboys and more of a high-class tavern, so instead of prostitutes and the cheapest whiskey, the Long Branch offered top-shelf liquor, bartenders adorned with silk vests, walls festooned with artwork, and a long, carved-wood bar. By 1878, another incentive was a five-piece house band whose members were actually good musicians.

That same year, Chalk Beeson raised funds among members of polite society to match his own to underwrite what became the Dodge City Silver Cornet Band. It would expand and evolve into the Dodge City Brass Band, and by 1880 it was the Dodge City Cowboy Band. There were no actual Texas trail riders in it, but the musicians dressed the part with broad-brimmed hats, leather chaps, and unloaded six-shooters. Chalk boasted that one of his "cowboys" could "throw a steer over a horse." The only loaded gun was brandished by the band's director, a man known as Professor Eastman, who used it as a baton. When asked why a gun, Eastman replied, "To kill the first man who strikes a false note."

The Cowboy Band played at holiday events and other celebrations, and its popularity spread enough that it would be invited to play in such major mid-American cities as St. Louis, Chicago, and Kansas City. It would even get to perform before another U.S. president, in March 1889 in Washington at the inauguration of Benjamin Harrison, "and my what a swath the bunch did cut," commented Robert Wright, who had accompanied the troupe. "People just went wild over them, I expect because many of them had never seen a cowboy before and their uniforms were a wonder to them."

The Washington visit was the proudest event in Chalk Beeson's musical career. He later went into lawing, serving as the sheriff of Ford County in the 1890s, and in the decade after that he was a member of the

Kansas legislature. He died at sixty-four in 1912 as one of Dodge City's most respected citizens for having guided it into the new century.

Also in 1878, the city's residents would no longer have to depend on buckets and willing neighbors when one of their wooden structures turned into a tinderbox, especially during the tail end of a typical bone-dry prairie summer. The Dodge City Fire Company was formed. The young men who volunteered for it had been born elsewhere, but by 1878 they must have believed that their future and that of their families lay in a growing Dodge City.

Surrounding Dodge City were more ranches and farms, yet western Kansas was still a largely unsettled expanse of land on the frontier. Men and women and children still shuddered along in prairie schooners, heading west on trips that had originated in Kansas City or St. Louis. Whether they were searching for a site to stake out and build a homestead or had dreams of California, they confronted hundreds of miles of flat land carpeted with tall grass being tossed by the warm winds coming up from the south. Above was a seemingly endless blue sky.

As Laura Ingalls Wilder recalled from her

family's travels west, "In a perfect circle the sky curved down to the level land, and the wagon was in the circle's exact middle." No matter how far her family drove their wagon during the day "they couldn't get out of the middle of that circle. When the sun went down, the circle was still around them and the edge of the sky was pink."

Travelers through Kansas had to be careful when they camped not to start a fire that would rush across the prairie, burning everything in its path. Before getting a campfire going, one had to clear a circle by pulling grass out by the roots. Drier grass could be mixed with twigs to begin the fire, then larger sticks of wood were laid on top. During the night the fire would keep away coyotes and most other animals.

In the morning the migrants would be woken by the songs of hundreds of meadowlarks, and after drawing water from the stream they had camped near and having a simple breakfast, the journey deeper into Kansas would resume. As the wagon trundled along, its occupants observed deer lying under trees on the low, rounded hills, and the pink, blue, and white blossoms of wild larkspur; and slithering along the ground were a variety of snakes making sure to keep clear of the horses and the rolling wheels. There was a scent in the air that reminded the travelers of bread being baked, which was really grass seeds parching in the heat.

Thankfully for those entranced by history, there remained in Dodge City and its surroundings characters drawn to frontier life who made an indelible impression. One was Mysterious Dave Mather, and a good illustration of him is his experience with Bill Tilghman and a petrified preacher.

David Allen Mather, born in 1851, was another adventurous man from New England — specifically, Connecticut. He claimed to be descended from the Pilgrim leader Cotton Mather, which probably did not mean a darn thing on the frontier. His father, Ulysses Mather, had been a ship's captain who sailed away in 1856 and never sailed back. He was found murdered in Shanghai eight years later.

When he was nineteen, Mather and a younger brother boarded a ship, and this one brought them to New Orleans, where they worked as laborers. They took on jobs that kept them going west, and Dave's first venture into Dodge City was in 1872 when he and his brother, Josiah, gave buffalo hunting a try. Not much is known of his activities after that, until 1878 when he was back in Dodge City.

Somewhere along the way Dave acquired his nickname. His personality was so taciturn that he made Wyatt Earp seem giddy. He rarely spoke, and even those who considered themselves friends could not discern what he was thinking. There was rarely an expression on his face. The curling of his thin lips was a dramatic outburst. Whatever went on in Dave Mather's head was a perpetual mystery.

One evening, the last place Bill Tilghman, Bat Masterson's deputy, expected to find him was at a revival meeting, but that is what happened at around nine. A preacher who had been dubbed "Salvation Sam" had come to Dodge City with a few male and female followers and had been given permission by Luke Short to hold a soul-saving service at the Red Dog Saloon, which had Luke as a silent partner. Tilghman was alone in the Ford County sheriff's office when he heard shots fired. He hurried down the street, having been told that whatever was going on, it was happening inside the Red Dog.

Entering the saloon, Tilghman saw Salvation Sam and his followers cowering behind a lectern that stood before several rows of wooden benches. Mysterious Dave stood to the side, a gun in one hand. Tilghman did not know which way this situation was going to go, but his future suddenly got a lot shorter when Mather turned the gun on him.

As usual, whatever was on the gunman's mind could not be gleaned. Hoping these were not the last words he would utter, Tilghman calmly said, "Dave, I need you to give me your gun."

No response. Mather stared at him. In case the man was indeed mad, Tilghman kept his voice low and calm as he walked forward, assuring Mather that he would not hurt him and that he wanted the gun "so that you don't hurt anybody either." He could hear the preacher and his followers panting. Finally, he stood before Mather and extended his hand. After a few more moments of quiet, the gun was relinquished.

The others in the saloon stood up and spread out, still eyeing the unarmed Mather fearfully. The deputy sheriff looked them over. No one appeared injured. He asked Salvation Sam to accompany him to the sheriff's office to swear out a complaint against Mather. But the preacher pointed toward the ceiling and said, "Charges against this sinner have been made in heaven. God will punish him as he sees fit."

Good enough. Now to get Mysterious Dave out of the saloon so it could go back to being a church for one night. Once they were out on the street, Mather finally spoke: "Hypocrites." Wondering if there was more, Tilghman waited patiently. In what for him was the equivalent of a Shakespearean soliloquy, Dave continued, "The preacher asked them to come forward and confess their sins, and after they did the preacher said they could go straight to heaven. I figured to help them take advantage of that opportunity right away, before sinning again and ruining things. But they really didn't want to go, so they're a bunch of hypocrites."

Tilghman chewed that over while he escorted him to the bridge that crossed the Arkansas River. Handing back the gun, he told Mysterious Dave, "It's best you stay out of Dodge City for a while." Dave got on his horse and rode across the bridge — without a word, of course.

While characters like Mysterious Dave reminded folks that Dodge City was still very much a frontier town, another clear sign that civilization was encroaching was the ongoing efforts of its peace officers. A specific example was Bat Masterson not avenging his brother by gunning down the other cowboys who rode for Alf Walker and who had been present when Ed Masterson was killed.

Few would have blamed Bat for allowing his ivory-handled pistols to settle the score. As a county sheriff he had the power and opportunity, and he had watched his brother die from a grievous wound. Then, being still only twenty-four years of age, Bat could have put Ford County and its troubles behind him and gone elsewhere to start over. But he did not. He was surrounded by people he knew; there was his friendship with fellow lawmen, especially Wyatt; and he had a job to do, which included upholding the law and demonstrating a belief in the justice system, as faulty and arbitrary as it could be. Bat was emerging as a new kind of frontiersman, one who attempted to elevate law and order in the West, not ignore or repudiate it.

This was mostly true of Wyatt, too. Like the system he represented when he wore a badge, Wyatt was flawed, too, and he had a past that included being on the wrong side of that system. He did not envision spending the rest of his life as a lawman but as a businessman, and just having turned thirty, he had little time to waste in an era when for many men of that age, life was more than half over. But whatever other motivations he had, in the spring of 1878, Wyatt returned to Dodge City and the marshal's office out of loyalty to Bat and to the citizens of the city. He probably did not have lofty thoughts about creating a peaceful environment for when he became a family man, because he was usually looking west for opportunity, and, in fact, Wyatt would never have children. (The same would be true for Bat.) But the job of taming Dodge City and by extension the American frontier was incomplete that April. There was much more to be done so that other people could raise families there.

That month saw the first public and certainly the biggest funeral in the brief history of Dodge City. The combination of a marshal being gunned down and the affection many of the population felt for Ed Masterson resulted in most residents turning out for it. The funeral began at two on the afternoon of the tenth. All businesses had closed at 10 A.M., and those that reopened would not do so until 6 P.M. Doors and windows were draped with black crepe paper. When the account of the funeral was published the following week in the *Ford County Globe,* the paper's front page was bordered in black. Attending the funeral was

Bat, the only Masterson brother there. He followed on foot, his eyes fixed on the wagon bearing Ed's body as it trundled slowly out of town.

According to the newspaper's coverage, "Everyone in the city knew Ed Masterson and liked him. They liked him as a boy, they liked him as a man, and they liked him as their marshal. The marshal died nobly in the discharge of duty; we drop a tear upon his grave." It then offered a poem:

Whether on the scaffold high,
Or in the battle's van,
The fittest place for man to die
Is when he dies for man.

The day after the funeral, Bat and a friend, Mike Sutton, journeyed to Sedgwick to give the news to his mother and father, Thomas and Catherine Masterson, and the three children still living with them on the farm, George, Minnie, and Thomas Jr. Yet to be told were Nellie, who was living in Wichita after marrying a lawman there, and Jim Masterson, who was off buffalo hunting and did not yet know of his brother's death. After the trip to Sedgwick, Bat would track Jim down and tell him the details.

Because Boot Hill was not a cemetery for

solid citizens like Ed Masterson, he was buried at Fort Dodge. In 1879, when the Prairie Grove Cemetery opened, members of the Dodge City Fire Company took care of moving Ed's body to be reburied in it. Sadly, years later when the Prairie Grove graves were transferred to the larger Maple Grove Cemetery, the remains were lost, and there is no longer a grave in Dodge City bearing the remains of Edward Masterson.

TWENTY

Then the town's peace officers were called to restore order, although many of those wearing badges little understood — or believed in — the laws they swore to uphold when they took their oaths of office. — ODIE B. FAULK

After the funeral, Charlie Bassett resumed the role of marshal while remaining Bat Masterson's undersheriff. Shaken by his close brush with death and the shame of having fled the fight, Nat Haywood had resigned as assistant marshal, so Bassett was indeed free to appoint Wyatt Earp to the position. With the cattle-driving season fast approaching, Bassett was quick to fill out his staff by appointing John Brown and Charles Trask as peace officers, and he would soon select Jim Masterson to replace Trask when Bat's grieving brother was back from the buffalo hunt.

Steady lawmen with experience would be needed like never before in Dodge City in 1878. That year would go down as the one that saw the most cattle arrive from Texas, accompanied by well over a thousand drovers. That would mean the saloons would operate at full capacity, constantly populated by gamblers and dancing girls and prostitutes and an excess of customers. Drinking and carousing and hurrahing would be a nightly revelry, and not all of it stayed confined to the south side of the Dead Line. How the peace officers handled all this activity would determine whether the city could continue to progress or would descend into chaos.

Dodge City was as ready as it was going to get with Bassett's team in place, and on the Ford County side of the ledger, Bat had Bassett — part-time, anyway — and the redoubtable Bill Tilghman as deputy. The *Dodge City Times* reported that the "far-famed 'wicked city' is decked out in gorgeous attire in preparation for the long horn" and the "Mary Magdaleens" were about to be "selling their souls to whoever'll buy." The saloons were well stocked with alcohol and "there is a great ado, for soon the vast plains will be covered with the long horn," and Dodge City "is the source from which the great army of herder and drover is fed. The season promises to be a remarkable one." Indeed: by just the second week in June, 110,000 head of cattle had enjoyed the hospitality of the cow pens near the railroad station.

It was as good a time as any for a confident gambler like Doc Holliday to pull into town. This would be the beginning of people puzzling over Wyatt's devoted friendship with a man whom others disdained and whose sometimes appalling behavior they, with some justification, objected to. Some years later, reflecting on Doc, whom he described as "long, lean, and ash-blond and the quickest man with a six-shooter I ever knew," Wyatt recalled that not long after Doc and Big Nose Kate Elder arrived in Dodge City "his quickness saved my life."

Without identifying who the assailant was, Wyatt told of a man drawing a gun on him while his back was turned. Doc shouted, "Look out, Wyatt!" Before Wyatt could completely turn around, Doc had jerked his pistol out and shot the man. In his recollection, Wyatt commented, "On such incidents as that are built the friendships of the frontier." This incident could have been invented years afterward to justify the odd friendship, but it was not out of character for Doc to have Wyatt's back, and it would not be the only time.

Upon arrival that spring, Doc and Kate Elder settled into the Dodge House. The bursting-at-the-seams environment of Dodge City as the summer approached boded well for a skilled gambler — and con man. One story implies that Doc was still a bit short of cash or enjoyed practical jokes, or both. Wearing shabby clothes, Doc entered the Alhambra Saloon. He attracted the attention of a group of cowboys leaning against the bar, who decided to have some sport with the poor, thin, sallow fellow who obviously had seen better days.

They invited the man to have a drink. Doc refused. This wasn't the expected response, so one of the cowboys called Doc over, poured a whiskey, handed him the glass, pointed a pistol at him, and ordered Doc to drink. Doc did, made a face, and coughed a few times (which did not take much pretending). The trail riders guffawed over this, and wanting to see that reaction again, insisted that the man have another whiskey. Finally, after the fourth drink and with Doc licking his lips and grinning, the cowboys got it. It is not known if the gathering ended in more laughter or with Doc making a quick exit.

With his gambling and carousing in fine fettle, it was odd, then, that Doc decided to resume his dental practice. He sent a telegram to Dallas, asking that John Seegar, his former partner, ship his old dental chair north. Doc then placed an ad in the *Dodge City Times* advertising his "professional services," and set up shop in Dodge House. He was not giving up gambling, but perhaps Doc saw himself as gaining some respectability as a dentist in a city vying to become a bastion of civilization on the frontier.

And what could be more a sign of an emerging cosmopolitan civilization in Dodge City than the introduction of the cancan? And it was done by a man who would wind up being one of the most well known and, he claimed, the longest-living lawman of the West.

Ham Bell, into whose arms Alf Walker had fallen at A. J. Peacock's saloon after the Ed Masterson shooting, had been born Hannibal Boettler Beltz in Washington County, Maryland. When he was nine, he and two siblings became orphans. Five years later, after living with an uncle, he set off on his own. When he was nineteen, he was a restless jewelry-store salesman in Pennsylvania. In 1865, the newspaper editor Horace Greeley had exhorted, "Go west, young man" — borrowing from an earlier editorial in an Indiana newspaper, which had suggested, "Go west, young man, and grow up with the country" — and in 1872, the year Greeley was unsuccessfully running for president against the incumbent Ulysses S. Grant, here was another young man taking that advice. One of the skills Bell had acquired was cleaning clocks, and doing so paid his way to Kansas.

En route, he changed his name to Hamilton Butler Bell. His first stop, a brief one, was in Lawrence; then he moved on to Abilene and Ellsworth and Great Bend. He worked several jobs, including driving freight wagons and delivering ice. Not surprisingly, given the heat of west Kansas summers, there was a great demand for ice on the frontier, and by the summer of 1874, Bell had a contract to deliver ice, railroad ties, and other material to the Atchison, Topeka & Santa Fe Railroad as it steadily worked its way through Kansas and into Colorado. He made Dodge City his headquarters, and it would be home for the rest of his life. His future there was confirmed that summer when he married Josephine Dugan, the daughter of a local farmer.

Bell's first stationary business was a livery stable, and it would become the biggest in

Dodge City. Other endeavors included operating a furniture store and mortuary business (he made sure every casket was adorned with a bouquet of flowers), and he constructed the first women's restroom on the Santa Fe Trail. The industrious and farsighted Bell would go on to own the first car dealership in southwest Kansas, and as proprietor of an ambulance service he introduced the first motorized ambulance in Dodge City. And in case that transportation had not always gone swiftly enough, Bell also introduced the first motorized hearse. When he died, in 1947 at ninety-four, he was operating a pet shop. (During World War II, an Army Air Corps plane featuring his handprint was named for Ham Bell.)

Ida Rath, daughter-in-law of the businessman Charles Rath, once reminisced about Bell that he "had the bluest of blue eyes and brown hair, was spare of build but broad shouldered. He had a decided Roman nose and a very determined chin." His distinctive looks had to help him during forays into politics, which included two terms as mayor of Dodge City and two terms as a Ford County commissioner.

But it was as a lawman that many people came to know Ham Bell, considering he spent thirty-six years at it. In Great Bend he had served as a deputy. There was a lengthy break while he established himself in Dodge City, and in 1880 he would be appointed deputy U.S. marshal there, a position he would hold for twelve years. (More than a few Dodge City residents insist it was Bell, not Wyatt Earp, who was the model for Matt Dillon on the popular TV show *Gunsmoke.*) He also would be the sheriff of Ford County, first elected in 1888 and continuing to be reelected despite being a Democrat in a heavily Republican county. Bell left the office in 1910 to become the head of Dodge City's police department. At various other times he pitched in as deputy marshal and deputy sheriff. During the decades as a police officer he never shot a man, because he was so quick on the draw that the other man froze before he could clear leather. Bell once explained, "If I'd never drawn a gun, I wouldn't have lived a week."

About the cancan: Another of Ham Bell's ventures was a dance hall on Front Street. He had read about the dance that was the rage in Europe and had learned that a troupe performing it was touring the western half of the United States. He thought the citizens of and visitors to Dodge City were ready for such exotic entertainment, so he booked the dance company. The first performance of the lovely high-kicking ladies was on July 4, 1878. Suddenly, the frontier did not seem as far from the sophisticated East Coast and Chicago.

Another sign that Dodge City was more on the map to the folks back east is that well-known entertainers began to include it on their tours. There would be enough of an audience to make it worth the effort, and the presumption — or at least the hope — was that by the summer of 1878 the entertainers would be safe there, that the frontier represented by Dodge City was no longer Wild West enough to put their lives in jeopardy.

The most famous entertainer yet arrived in July, when Eddie Foy, Sr., first set foot on the dry streets that the wind turned into tiny tornadoes of dust. He found it was true that there were plenty of people willing to buy tickets to see him perform. He found it was false that he would be completely safe.

The future father of the Seven Little Foys (who would be portrayed by Bob Hope in the 1955 film with that title) had been born Edwin Fitzgerald in 1856 to Irish immigrants in New York City. He was only six when his father died in an insane asylum, and his mother took her four children to Chicago, where she found work that years later included caring for the mentally ill Mary Todd Lincoln, the president's widow. Right away, to help put food on the table, Eddie began singing and dancing in Chicago saloons and on street corners. At fifteen, he began touring with various stage partners, one of whom was Edwin Booth, brother of the man who assassinated Abraham Lincoln.

In 1878, beginning when the weather allowed, the twenty-two-year-old Foy and performing partner Jim Thompson offered song-and-dance shows in the larger cow towns and mining camps on the western frontier, and that brought them to Dodge City. Perhaps Foy had not been sufficiently reassured about the more effective law enforcement, because when he looked out the window as the train entered the station and saw a large pile of buffalo bones nearby, he thought that men were being killed in the city faster than proper graves could be dug. He had to think this was not a promising place to be for the next few weeks.

Once off the train, Eddie Foy was an odd duck to both Dodge City citizens and cowboys alike. There was little difference between his on- and offstage behavior and appearance — cracking jokes, mugging, a sudden dance step, loud clothes. His partner, Thompson, figured out right away that not being noticed when out and about was best, but Foy was a relentless performer.

And, fortunately, he was quick-witted. In his autobiography, *Clowning Through Life,* Foy recounted that his second day in Dodge City was almost his last — or at least for a few moments it looked that way. Foy was strolling along the Front Street sidewalk, conspicuous in a colorful outfit. Suddenly, a group of rough-looking men cornered him, tied his hands behind him, and dragged him across the street. They pushed the petrified performer up onto a horse, which happened to be under a tree, and he noticed that from one of the thick branches a rope dangled. Once that rope was around his neck, Foy was asked, "Any last words?"

Where was the marshal? Anyone with a badge? Foy found one standing just a few feet away. It turned out to be Sheriff Bat Masterson, who was grinning. Then it dawned on the newcomer, who called out, "Anything I have to say can better be said at the Long Branch Saloon." Bat nodded his approval, the group of men hurrahed, and a relieved Foy bought everyone a round. There would be a few other times that chuckling citizens roped and tied him to a railing or post until Wyatt or Bat helped him get free. (In his autobiography, Foy described Bat as a "trim, good-looking young man with a pleasant face and carefully barbered mustache," who wore a hat "with a rakish tilt and [who had] two big silver-mounted, ivory-handled pistols.") The entertainer treated such actions as being all in good fun.

Foy was fascinated by Dodge City, and his eyes soaked in as much as they could. He noted that the rear ends of the buildings on the south side of Front Street "were not far from the bank of the Arkansas River — a shallow, quiet stream which went on a tear once in a while and did some damage. Spanning the river was a ramshackle wooden bridge. That way the cattle men crossed when they rode back toward Texas. When they were coming in with their herds and the river was low, they rode with them right through the stream."

As he strolled down Front Street, Foy observed that every few yards there "was a whiskey barrel which it was the duty of the police force to keep filled with water for fire protection. Many a boozer put them to similar use by sticking his head into one here and there and cooling his own superheated interior. Most of the stores had wooden awnings or porches extending across the sidewalk. Between the posts at their outer edge was a seat for loafers, and just outside that was usually a horse trough. Of course, there were plenty of hitching posts, usually with horses stamping or dozing beside them."

If his demeanor was part of a strategy to win over his new hosts, it worked. Foy and Thompson were booked to play the Theatre Comique and right away their combination of dancing, jokes, impressions, poems, and songs, especially Foy's signature "Kalamazoo in Michigan," was a smash. The packed house included many cowboys, seeing a show they could not even have imagined during lonely nights on the trail, and they laughed and clapped for a man who was a pure entertainer onstage and showed gumption when off.

Shows could last until well after midnight. The Theatre Comique had a first floor filled with chairs and above it a mezzanine of private boxes, where those who could afford it looked down through the haze of cigar smoke at the stage while eating and drinking. A hallway led to the gaming room, which was full of men drinking and smoking at the tables, and from time to time the audience watching the show could hear the sounds of poker chips, dice, and shouts of joy as well as arguments coming from the room. After a show was over, chairs on the first floor would be pushed aside to clear enough space for dancing, with a local fiddler and other musicians playing for tips. Some nights, the last note wasn't played until the pink light of impending dawn layered the edge of the eastern prairie.

Though the effervescent Foy won over the theater audiences in Dodge City and the citizens in general, every so often he was reminded that this was a frontier cow town and anything could happen — especially when someone like Ben Thompson was involved. Because of his friendship with Bat Masterson, while in Dodge City Thompson was on his best behavior, content to gamble and not wanting a confrontation with the county sheriff or his fellow lawmen. But one night proper decorum failed him, and Foy almost paid the penalty.

Who knew where the drunk Thompson was heading when he left the gaming room, but he wound up backstage at the Comique during a background-scenery change between acts. It suddenly seemed like a good idea to shoot out one of the lights. The problem was that where Foy stood, his head was between it and Ben's six-shooter. Swaying and trying to sight his gun, Thompson told the actor to get out of the way. Foy, "suddenly seized with a sudden foolish obstinacy," refused.

Thompson told him again. When Foy still didn't move, he added, "If you want it through yer head, too, all right."

Thompson pointed his pistol at the comedian, who by then was so filled with fear that he couldn't have moved even if he'd wanted to. Would the drunken gambler have pulled the trigger? We'll never know, because it was Bat Masterson to the rescue. He suddenly burst in backstage, sized up the situation, and pushed the pistol up so it pointed at the ceiling. If it had been any other man, even a lawman, who had interfered in his fun, Thompson might have reacted angrily. But it was his friend Bat, who by now had a good hold of Thompson and was leading him stage left and eventually out of the theater.

"When they had gone, I found my hands shaking so hard that I couldn't put on my makeup," Foy recalled. "I was limp for the rest of the evening." (In a fun and authentic bit of casting, in the 1939 film *Frontier Marshal,* with Randolph Scott playing Wyatt Earp and Cesar Romero as Doc Holliday,

Foy is transported to Tombstone and is played by his son Eddie Jr.)

Ultimately, where did those Seven Little Foys come from? A year after his first appearance in Dodge City, Foy married another entertainer, Rose Howland. Sadly, in 1882 she died while giving birth, as did the baby. Two years later, he met Lola Sefton in San Francisco, and they were together for a decade, until her death in 1894. Two years later, and while becoming a star on Broadway and in other major cities, Foy married a dancer, Madeline Morando. Until her death in 1918, they produced eleven children, and the seven who survived childhood formed the vaudeville act with their father. Foy, ever the relentless song-and-dance man, died in 1928 at seventy-one while performing in Kansas City. The last of the Seven Little Foys was Irving, who died at ninety-four in 2003.

TWENTY-ONE

There is none so brave as he who stands in front of what belongs to him. — LOREN D. ESTLEMAN, "Stuart Lake: Frontier Mythmaker"

Dodge City took a step back in its progress when another peace officer was killed that same year. Harry T. McCarty would not go down in the annals of the American frontier as a legendary lawman, but his death from gunplay was a reminder that despite the efforts of Wyatt Earp, Bat Masterson, and the others sworn to uphold law and order, there was still plenty of wild left in the West.

Ben Simpson was the U.S. marshal for the district that included Dodge City, and in April he had arranged the appointment of McCarty to the post of deputy U.S. marshal. As a surveyor, McCarty knew the surrounding area well, and like Ed Masterson had been, he was well liked. And as with Ed, this did not do him any favors.

Given that July 13 was in the middle of summer and thus the peak of the cattle-drive season, the Long Branch Saloon was still open at four in the morning, serving the last few cowboys who hadn't yet reached their saturation point. One of them was Thomas O'Haran, who also answered to the name Thomas Roach or even Limping Tom. He was a cook for an outfit that had just brought a herd up from Texas. He was known for unpredictable behavior, and he tended to be a tad more unhinged when he had a lot to drink — like on that night.

McCarty, assigned by Simpson to help local law enforcement at its busiest time, had been making the rounds, and he stopped in at the Long Branch to check in with the regular late-night barkeep, Adam Jackson. Suddenly, O'Haran got up from a table and lurched toward the bar. Engaged in conversation, McCarty had his back to him and wasn't aware of the cowboy's approach until he felt his six-shooter leave its holster.

McCarty turned to find O'Haran weaving from side to side with one arm in the air waving the pistol. Maybe he was about to hand it back when he lowered his arm, but he jerked the trigger and the gun went off. Hit, the federal peace officer fell to the floor.

Someone in the saloon fired at O'Haran, striking him in the head, though not a fatal blow. "I am shot!" he cried out, and fell beside the other man.

McCarty, leaking blood, was brought to an adjacent room. The bullet had struck him in the right groin and come out the other side of him, later to be found in the floor. Worse, though, was that during its passage it had severed the femoral artery. A doctor was dragged out of bed, but he could not prevent McCarty from bleeding to death.

The top priority later that morning for Marshal Charlie Bassett and his assistant, Wyatt, and Sheriff Masterson and his deputy, Bill Tilghman, was to prevent a lynching. O'Haran, with a powerful headache (though the bullet had only creased his skull), was in the city jail. As the morning went on, crowds continued to form outside of it, with a few angry citizens brandishing lengths of rope. McCarty had been murdered, and for that crowd, the wheels of justice would grind too slowly. But with the lawmen standing firm with shotguns resting on their crooked arms, no one made a move toward the jail. Onlookers came and went, a few looking more threatening than others, coughing on the dust kicked up by passing wagons on what was turning out to be another blistering hot summer day on the prairie.

They were further dissuaded from mob violence when Doc Holliday arrived and was deputized. Wyatt, perhaps, had sent him a message that got him out of bed, because otherwise Doc's morning was everyone else's afternoon. He had no desire to wear a badge, and he certainly had no interest in being *that* respectable, but he wouldn't refuse a request from Wyatt to help in a tight spot. And maybe not from Bat, either. Biographer Gary L. Roberts writes that as the year went on, Doc "deepened his sense of belonging with the gambling and saloon crowd. . . . Bat Masterson and their associates accepted him in a way he had never known in Dallas, Fort Griffin, Denver, or any of the other places he had traveled. He had found a congenial place, and he apparently had decided to stay."

That same day a coroner's inquest was held, and before a judge O'Haran was bound over for trial on the charge of first-degree murder. Ford County District Court eventually held the trial. O'Haran managed to save his life by pleading guilty to manslaughter and was taken east to serve twelve years in the Kansas State Penitentiary.

That Bat became an expert practitioner of buffaloing implies that he and Wyatt were quick to crack skulls, and that constituted most of their peacekeeping. But both were bright men, more intelligent than most, certainly those who ran afoul of the law. Sometimes, effective policing was simply being smarter. Bat's reputation for cleverness expanded when the story made the rounds of how he captured an escaped prisoner without leaving Dodge City.

A man named Davis had been in jail in Fort Lyon, almost two hundred miles to the west in Colorado. He escaped and managed to elude the local authorities. Thinking that Davis was on an eastbound train, they telegraphed marshals and sheriffs along the route, one of whom was Bat. There was no description of what Davis looked like, so it was rather discouraging to read that the fugitive was carrying weapons and was prepared to use them if cornered.

When the next eastbound train steamed into Dodge City, Bat was waiting at the station. He climbed aboard at the rear of the train so that he could walk through the cars glancing at the passengers, all of whom faced away from him. By this time Bat had developed a pretty good lawman's instinct; when he observed a man who appeared a tad jittery, Bat thought it worthwhile to pull his coat closed over his badge and stop by the man's seat. With a grin and a twinkle in his blue eyes, he greeted the man: "Hello, Davis. How are you?"

Though he was a crook of some kind, at that moment Davis was more concerned about being polite and that his memory was not adequate enough to recall what must be an old acquaintance. He grinned back, and when Bat offered his hand, he shook it. Next thing Davis knew, he was on his feet and his wrists sported a pair of handcuffs. The next day, Bat welcomed a deputy from Fort Lyon, who escorted the dumbfounded Davis back to jail.

As bright a man as Bat was, the fact was that he had been forced to kill a man in the line of duty. In July 1878, it was Wyatt's turn.

George Hoy was a familiar face in town. He was an experienced drover, and when a cattle drive from Texas was done, he was as enthusiastic as anyone in enjoying Dodge City's pleasures. On this particular night, July 26, with the first glimpse of "rosy-fingered dawn," as Homer described it, still hours away, Hoy and his pals were a tad too enthusiastic. They left a saloon, got on their horses, guns raised in the air, and, reeling around, they began firing. The few people left on the street dove for cover, and above the street, windows shattered and occupants screamed.

Even being indoors didn't insure safety from a good hurrahing. The tireless Eddie Foy was wrapping up his last performance of the night, which meant reciting "Kalamazoo in Michigan." Bat, not on duty, was sitting at one of the tables inside the Theatre Comique. According to Foy's recollection, Sheriff Masterson was playing cards with Doc Holliday. As both were night owls, this is not far-fetched, but most of the time Bat and Doc kept their distance from each other. Wyatt and Jim Masterson had been on patrol, and before all the fireworks began they had paused outside the Comique, perhaps trying to hear Foy's big finale. One of the cowboys took the hurrahing to a dangerous level by firing three shots at the lawmen as he galloped by.

A brief pause: There have been accounts, including one by Wyatt himself in later years, that Hoy or all of the cowboys deliberately fired at Jim Masterson and Wyatt, especially the latter. The claim was that there was a bounty on Wyatt's head. Because he had made life so difficult for cowboys in Dodge City, cattle-herd owners and possibly local businessmen conspired to put the assistant marshal out of the way, permanently. But this does not make a lot of sense. Essentially, assassinating Wyatt Earp would still have left Bat and Jim Masterson, Bassett, and Tilghman to toss troublemaking cowboys into the calaboose, no doubt in a more vengeful manner. And there would have been more effective ways to get a good shot at Wyatt, without other peace officers around. The story adds to the legend of Wyatt Earp but does not fit with the reality of the summer of 1878, when he was not the top lawman in Dodge City. Possibly, from the viewpoint of later years, Wyatt believed he was the only peace officer in the city who deserved a bounty.

As Bat later told the tale, the bullets from the cowboy's Colt .45 pierced the wooden walls of the theater and sent the people inside diving for the dirt-strewn floor. Foy was one of them, and he reported that he was impressed "by the instantaneous manner in which [the audience] flattened out like pancakes on the floor. I had thought I was pretty agile myself, but those fellows had me beaten by seconds."

Outside, there was more shooting, and Wyatt and Jim yanked their six-shooters out. The cowboys controlled their horses enough that they could direct them south and get out of town rather than wind up in the jail. The one who had just missed hitting the two lawmen outside the theater was among them. Whether to encourage their departure or actually wound one of the hell-raisers, Wyatt and Jim fired after them. While crossing the bridge over the Arkansas River, Hoy, wounded, fell from his horse.

Wyatt contended that he most likely hit Hoy because he had sighted him against the star-filled night sky. It may well have been his bullet, but other ones were fired in a flurry as the drovers left town. None of this mattered to poor George Hoy: he may or may not have been the one who fired at Wyatt, but he was the one who ended up with lead in his arm. And, it turned out, there was a price on his head. Marshal Bassett learned that Hoy was wanted in Texas for cattle theft.

The wound in his arm was a very bad one, and doctoring being what it was in the 1870s, gangrene began to eat away at it. A surgeon from Fort Dodge amputated the arm, but the damage to Hoy's system had been done, and after suffering for weeks, he died on August 21.

Bat always believed that the escapade of the cowboys was no more than drunken fun that ended badly for the unfortunate George Hoy. He did not consider Wyatt a target because of his vigorous policing. He thought differently, though, a few weeks later when Clay Allison came to town.

A postscript to the shooting of George Hoy was that, deserved or not, Wyatt received his first exposure in the press beyond the frontier and the Midwest. *The National Police Gazette,* which could be found in every barbershop, offered an account to its readers, most of whom lived east of the Mississippi River. Wyatt Earp, it contended, was a marshal to be reckoned with in the Wild West. But Clay Allison did not care about what was in newspapers.

TWENTY-TWO

Upon the sidewalks ran streams of the blood of brave men, and the dead and wounded wrestled with each other like butchered whales on harpooning day. The "finest work" and neatest polishes were said to have been executed by Mr. Wyatt Earp. It was not until towards morning that the smoke cleared away, the din of battle subsided and the bibulous city found a little repose. — *Ford County Globe*

It was expected that cowboys would cause trouble but not the soldiers stationed at nearby Fort Dodge. They did their share of off-duty drinking and whoring, but their superiors expected them to return in one piece. Any friction with Marshal Bassett and Sheriff Masterson was best avoided. And the Bluebellies were treated with extra tolerance by the lawmen and the saloon keepers because one never knew when they might be called upon for help with an Indian uprising (as would soon happen) or some other calamity.

This mostly peaceful relationship broke down one night in early August 1878. A group of off-duty soldiers had ventured to one of the saloons south of the Dead Line. The gamblers there were not as respectful of the uniform, and they took the soldiers for just about everything they had. The soldiers in turn expressed doubts about the integrity of the games and the gamblers. When a fight broke out, other occupants of the saloon backed the gamblers. The soldiers were on the losing end of the brawl, and they ended up out on the street.

They could have simply licked their wounds and resumed routine life back at the fort, but this particular outcome to a Dodge City outing rankled. They complained to their commanding officer. Instead of saying, "I told you so," the officer decided the gamblers and comrades who had sided with them in the fight deserved a lesson.

The next night, the officer marched a contingent of armed men across the Dead Line to the same saloon, which once again was doing a brisk business even without customers wearing uniforms. The soldiers lined up in formation outside one side of the saloon, raised their rifles, and at the officer's command they fired. They did this twice more, then marched back to Front Street. Wyatt or Bat or maybe both came running when they heard the shots but knew better than to interfere, especially after learning the shots were aimed high enough up the side wall to harm no one inside. The message had been delivered, and when the gamblers picked themselves up off the floor, their feelings toward the residents of Fort Dodge had warmed considerably.

During this time, Wyatt saw little of his brothers other than James. Newton, the oldest of Nicholas's sons, lived in California. Nicholas and Virginia Ann had lived in Temescal, California, for a time, then pushed on to Colton, also in California. There the Earp patriarch operated the Gem Saloon, advertising in the local newspaper that it offered "Fancy Cocktails, Tom and Jerry, at all times whenever called for. Call on N.P. Earp and test his superb Tom & Jerry. He is always on hand and ready to wait on customers."

Morgan spent most of his time in Montana and had fallen for a woman he had met. The youngest, Warren, was also out west, wandering in and out of Colton, trying to figure out what to do in life. Virgil was still in Arizona, and it did not seem like he was coming back anytime soon.

Despite the blistering heat and the arid landscape, Virgil and Allie were happy enough in the territory that they had no intention of leaving. Virgil missed his brothers, of course, especially Wyatt, but his idea was not to return east but to get them to come farther west.

He was making a good living. He had a sawmill on his property, and he sold the lumber he produced. People felt safe on the stagecoaches he drove, including John Gosper, who, according to the territorial laws, served as acting governor of Arizona when John Frémont was away. This happened frequently, because the former explorer found his territory and his duties rather dull. On September 3, Virgil's income ticked up a few notches when he was appointed the night watchman of Prescott. Two months later, Virgil was elected as one of the town's two constables. In this role he often worked alongside Crawley Dake, who had replaced William Standefer as U.S. marshal the previous June.

For the next year, life continued to go well for Virgil and Allie. Though it would mean more responsibility, in November 1879, he would not be able to resist the offer to become deputy U.S. marshal for the area that included Tombstone. That would mean picking up and moving again, from the middle of Arizona Territory south and east to the booming town of short adobe buildings that was between Tucson and the border with Mexico.

The new job evidently did not mean Virgil had to arrest every person exhibiting bad behavior. One day in December when he was driving his wagon toward Tombstone, a stagecoach rushed past, so close that one of Virgil's horses was injured. When he arrived at the station the stagecoach was still there. Instead of offering the driver a night in jail, Virgil, as he later reported, "thumped the pudding" out of him. No one messed with Virgil Earp. And he had taught Wyatt well.

Too much alcohol again contributed to an ongoing deadly year in Dodge City. Perhaps the peace officers could not prevent every confrontation, but they could make sure the consequences didn't become worse.

On September 8, two citizens, Arista Webb and Barney Martin, went from drinking buddies to brawlers. Webb punched the smaller Martin, and the latter, once he picked himself up off the floor, apologized for whatever he had done to rile his friend and left the saloon. When Webb left, he may not have noticed his former friend sitting on a bench in front of his shop (he was a tailor), rubbing his swelling jaw. When Webb got home he still hadn't sobered up or cooled off. He got on his horse carrying a Winchester and returned to downtown. Martin was still on the bench, and Webb brought the barrel of the rifle down on the top of his skull with such force that Martin was killed.

Maybe he was appalled by what he did, because by the time it occurred to Webb to turn his horse and attempt a getaway, several men who had witnessed the crime had hold of him. In a minute Charlie Bassett was on the scene, and he handcuffed Webb. The crowd around the marshal and his prisoner kept growing, and the angry citizens demanded that Webb be strung up on the nearest lantern pole. The situation could get out of hand quick, so, smartly, Bassett called out to whoever would listen to "get Bat Masterson."

When the sheriff showed up he shouldered his way through the crowd to put Webb between him and Bassett. There were still only two lawmen in the middle of the angry mob, but they were two of the best. Bat and Bassett each kept a hand on a six-shooter as they led Webb through the crowd and to jail. They had resisted mob rule and saved Webb's life — though that only postponed the inevitable. Four months later he was convicted of cold-blooded murder and was hauled off to be executed at the Kansas State Penitentiary.

That same September, Clay Allison arrived.

In his book *Wild West Characters,* Dale Pierce offers a typical appraisal of the man born in 1841 in Wayne County, Tennessee: "Robert 'Clay' Allison was no romantic hero of the West, but a strange, unpredictable psychopath who drank heavily and enjoyed the company of ladies of the evening, when he wasn't shooting people for illogical reasons." What better man to get rid of the meddlesome assistant marshal and return Dodge City to its rambunctious roots?

Allison had served in the Confederate Army twice. His first hitch began six months after the siege of Fort Sumter in South Carolina started the Civil War, but after only three months he was given a medical discharge. A doctor who examined him reported that because of a blow to the head several years earlier "emotional or physical excitement produces paroxysms of a mixed character, partly epileptic and partly maniacal." In September 1862, Allison managed to join the 9th Tennessee Cavalry, serving with this unit, at one time under the command of General Nathan Bedford Forrest, until it surrendered in May 1865.

After the war, he was a member of the burgeoning Ku Klux Klan until he made his way to Texas. While crossing the Red River on a ferry, Allison got into a dispute with the man operating the boat. It was settled with knives, and the boatman was left lying in a ditch on the other side of the river. For unknown reasons, but no doubt unsavory ones, while employed as a cowhand in the Panhandle, Allison was referred to as the Wolf of the Washita. Into the early 1870s, he was involved in a string of violent incidents, including shooting himself in the foot while trying to steal army mules. The resulting limp made him more surly and confrontational, if that was possible.

In the fall of 1875, Allison had busied himself terrorizing the area around Cimarron, New Mexico. He and two brothers had established a ranch there. Because of political upheavals throughout the territory, which he believed threatened his ranch, Allison lashed out in every direction, and a number of killings and maulings were attributed to him. People scattered and hid under counters and behind bars when Allison rode into town. One day, rather incautiously, Francisco "Pancho" Griego did not. He and Allison had previously had a couple of standoffs. In early November 1875, Griego accepted an invitation from Allison to have a drink at Lambert's bar in the St. James Hotel in Cimarron, thinking the gunman wanted to settle their differences.

Poor Francisco was wrong. After the bartender had served them and gone back into the kitchen, Allison's six-shooter fired three times. The next day, Allison was back at Lambert's. It was reported that he performed a "war dance" where he had killed Griego. Then he took his clothes off and continued cavorting, with a ribbon tied to his penis. A cowed court ruled on November 10 that the death was justifiable homicide — the justifiable part being if Griego was stupid enough to think Allison would make peace with a handshake, he deserved to die.

Wearing a badge did not impress Allison. Late in 1876, he and a brother, John, were drinking at the Olympic Dance Hall in Las Animas, Colorado. Their behavior went from bad to worse, and close to midnight Constable Charles Faber and two deputies entered to arrest the Allison brothers. When John turned to the lawmen, Faber did not hesitate: he pulled the trigger of his 10-

gauge shotgun, hitting John in the chest. Clay jerked his pistol and killed the constable. He then dragged the body over to his brother, bleeding on the floor, and witnesses reported he shouted, "Here's the man who shot you, John, and I killed the son of a bitch!" John Allison survived, and a grand jury refused to indict Clay.

Allison spent much of the next two years ranching and terrorizing; then during the last week of the summer of 1878 he rode into Dodge City. Several accounts contend that he was looking specifically for Wyatt Earp because he meant to collect the rumored bounty, or because George Hoy had been a friend of his and he wanted to avenge his death. If anyone could put the town back on the road to lawless perdition, Clay Allison could. Often described as a "shootist," when he arrived it did seem too much of a coincidence that the notorious gunman happened upon Dodge City.

The day after Allison rode in, it was reported to Wyatt that the shootist was walking the streets wearing a pair of pistols and uttering "a mouth full of threats." The assistant marshal strapped his own guns on and sent someone to find Bat. It made sense that with trouble brewing, Wyatt would call upon a friend known for a cool head under pressure — and one wearing a badge.

More than a few citizens of the city had heard that Allison was in town, so a crowd had gathered to witness the expected gunplay. Wyatt approached the dangerous visitor, who was standing on a sidewalk on Front Street, outside the Long Branch Saloon. Meanwhile, Bat, carrying a shotgun, made a more discreet approach. He would be next up if Allison got to Wyatt, and word was that a band of cowboys from Texas had quietly entered the city to support Allison's play.

Some members of the crowd had to be holding their breath as Wyatt drew close and a conversation began. The only account of that discussion was the one Wyatt gave the *San Francisco Examiner* eighteen years later: "His right hand was stealing round to his pistol pocket, but I made no move. Only I watched him narrowly. With my own right hand I had a firm grip on my six-shooter, and with my left I was ready to grab Allison's gun the moment he jerked it out. He studied the situation in all its bearings for the space of a second or two."

What Allison saw he didn't like. Wyatt might be faster on the draw, and there had to be other lawmen nearby. "I guess I'll go round the corner," he said, and Wyatt agreed.

But the assistant marshal was not out of danger. That band of men with a grudge against Wyatt — he referred to them as "ten or a dozen of the worst Texans in town" — was hiding in a store owned by Bob Wright. In their hands were Winchester rifles, and their intention was to help Allison escape after he killed Wyatt or, if he failed, to kill Wyatt themselves. As Wyatt walked down the street he was about to walk past Wright's store when he saw a signal from Bat, who had spotted the men. As Wyatt backed away, Allison reappeared, this time on his horse. He beckoned to Wyatt, who responded, "I can hear you all right here. I think you came here to fight me, and if you did you can have it right now."

But before they could go for their guns, Wright ran up between them. Bat believed that Wright was part of the plot to kill Wyatt, so Bat had quickly found him, and with the shotgun aimed at him Bat warned, "If this fight comes up, Wright, you're the first man I'm going to kill." With this as motivation, Wright pleaded with Allison to leave town and not provoke a battle.

After considering, Allison said, "Earp, I believe you're a pretty good man from what I've seen of you. Do you know that these coyotes sent for me to make a fight with you and kill you? Well, I'm going to ride out of town, and I wish you good luck." And ride out of Dodge City he did.

A few days after the confrontation, Bat retrieved the same shotgun he had carried to back up Wyatt and went to the outskirts of town, after telling a deputy he was going to do some target practice. There, he discovered that the shotgun was loaded not with buckshot but with birdshot — ammunition very unlikely to have done much to deter attacking cowboys or a psychopathic shootist.

For the next several years, Allison was involved in more violent incidents, including men getting killed, but he always escaped punishment. And then he changed. In 1881, soon before turning forty, Allison married Dora McCulloch, the sister of a sister-in-law. Their first daughter was born in 1885. Two years later Dora was pregnant with their second daughter and the ranching and farming family was living peacefully in Pecos, Texas. Driving a wagon on July 3, Allison was going too fast approaching a draw, and while trying to halt his horses he was flung from the wagon and died of a broken neck — the same neck that many a time had escaped the hangman's noose.

TWENTY-THREE

Of the many Indian raids in Kansas, none was ever characterized with such brutal and ferocious crimes, and none ever excited such horror and indignation as the Cheyenne raid of 1878.

— CLARA HAZELRIGG,
A New History of Kansas

By September 1878, the edge of the frontier had moved west and south of Dodge City and the last of the Indian tribes had been forced into exile in South Dakota or in Oklahoma / Indian Territory. In South Dakota, Red Cloud had transitioned from war general to semiretired statesman; Sitting Bull had fled to Canada rather than face the army units seeking to avenge the Little Bighorn disaster; and Crazy Horse had been murdered the year before at Fort Robinson in Nebraska. Dodge City, continuing its evolution from a wicked city to a somewhat cosmopolitan one, had no time or patience for an old-fashioned Indian attack.

But when Dull Knife came calling, women and children quaked under their beds, and even timid dry-goods clerks stuck pistols in their belts.

Dull Knife — also known as Morning Star — was sixty-eight, well past the life span of a man in 1878, especially an Indian, yet he was still an active and very respected leader of the Northern Cheyenne. He had led warriors in the Cheyenne-Arapaho War in Colorado during the last two years of the Civil War; had joined the Lakota Sioux in the battles in Wyoming in 1866–1868 known as Red Cloud's War, which had included wiping out Captain William Fetterman's entire command; and had been part of the coalition formed by Sitting Bull and Crazy Horse that had sent Colonel George Armstrong Custer to his doom in 1876.

It was a devastating defeat for Dull Knife in November 1876, five months after Little Bighorn, when a vengeful General George Crook, thrashing about the High Plains to kill or capture Crazy Horse, found Dull Knife's camp on the Powder River in Wyoming. The attack decimated the Cheyenne there, and the survivors, with winter taking hold, fled with what little they could carry. Before they reached a welcoming band of Sioux, eleven children died of exposure and starvation, despite the Cheyenne having killed and eaten almost all their horses during the journey. Dull Knife and his followers barely survived the winter, and in the spring of 1877 they surrendered to the army.

The Northern Cheyenne were forced to join other tribes and bands on reservations in Indian Territory. Among the trials and tribulations they endured that year were hunger from an inadequate amount of buffalo and deer to hunt and various illnesses including malaria. Repeated requests by Dull Knife and another Indian leader, Little Wolf, to be allowed to return to their hunting grounds in Montana were rejected. When conditions did not improve by September 1878, the two leaders with three hundred followers left the reservation and began the trek to their home one thousand miles away. They had to get through Kansas first.

As settlements in southwest Kansas were attacked by Indians foraging for food, word spread like a prairie fire. On the seventeenth, several cattle camps near Fort Dodge were attacked, with men killed and cows butchered. Word also spread that a mail carrier had been slain and two ranches, both less than twenty miles from Dodge City, had been attacked and robbed of horses, food, and weapons. This was close enough that people boarded up their houses. Loaded rifles and shotguns were kept right behind the doors and windows. The proximity of Fort Dodge was of less comfort than predicted when it turned out that the entire complement posted there consisted of nineteen Bluebellies. Reportedly, reinforcements from Fort Leavenworth were on the way, but the large force of Cheyenne — and with every hair-raising report, the force grew larger — could attack a defenseless Dodge City at any moment.

Fanning fears were the breathless accounts in the *Dodge City Times,* such as "news brought almost hourly of murder and depredations by the straggling bands of Northern Cheyenne," and that messengers arrived from the prairie "bringing accounts of the Cheyenne murder and stealing." Citizens were thrown "into the wildest tremor when it was reported that the Indians were seen within a few miles of the city."

Wyatt Earp was one of a group of men dispatched to a homestead four miles to the west to put out a blaze believed to have been started by the marauding members of Dull

Knife and Little Wolf's band. Patrolling Ford County, Bat Masterson was reminded of his confrontations with Indians during his and Ed's buffalo-hunting days. He would prefer not to repeat them now.

As the crisis escalated, Wyatt became the one in charge of the civilian guardians of the city. As luck would have it, Bat and Charlie Bassett took on the task of accompanying Robert Wright and other Dodge City businessmen on a trip to Kansas City. Bill Tilghman and John Joshua Webb were not on the city or county police force then, but they volunteered to man the barricades; plans were in place to block the entrances to the city at the first sign of a so-called savage. In addition, to protect the townsfolk, trail bosses sent some of their Texans to Dodge City to stand with Wyatt, Jim Masterson, and the other peace officers as armed guards. Even Doc Holliday brandished a shotgun between hands of poker.

But the Northern Cheyenne bypassed these defenses by moving away from Dodge City, intent on their goal of Montana. The army was in hot pursuit. On September 27, at a place that would come to be called Battle Canyon, on Punished Woman's Fork in Scott County, the Indians were caught by an expanded contingent of troops from

Fort Dodge under the command of Lieutenant Colonel William Lewis. The Indians realized that if they could not outrun the soldiers, they had no choice but to turn and fight. Dull Knife, Little Wolf, and their warriors hid the women, children, and elderly in a cave and then went out to meet the Bluebellies.

It was a victory of sorts, in that during the battle Colonel Lewis was wounded and his troops were daunted by the desperation of the Indians' fighting. (Lewis would become the last military man to die in Kansas in a battle with Indians.) The Cheyenne kept pushing on, but more skirmishes resulted in more casualties. New army and mobilized civilian units appeared, like wolves attacking a wounded buffalo. Finally, after traveling through Kansas into Nebraska, the Indians under Dull Knife once more surrendered. The threat to the frontier towns ended.

Though there are several conflicting accounts, it appears that the Cheyenne uprising in September produced an incident that further cemented the friendship between Wyatt and Doc. While Dull Knife's band was in the area and tales abounded of plundered homesteads, fifty-five head of cattle belonging to the ranch owned by the brothers Tobe and Bud Driskill and Ed

Morrison were taken. Either for the adventure or the reward offered, Doc joined the ranch owners, several ranch hands, and cavalry commanded by Captain William Hemphill to catch the thieving Indians.

On the eighteenth, there was a skirmish between the searchers and Northern Cheyenne, and some of the cows were recaptured. All returned to Dodge City to re-supply for what could be a longer follow-up chase. The next day, filled with too much as-yet-unspent adrenaline, the civilians and soldiers began to fight each other. Guns were drawn, and one soldier was shot in the leg. Doc had no interest in such doings and was seated inside of a saloon at a monte table.

However, he became more attentive to events in the street when Wyatt and other peace officers arrived to quiet the would-be cattle rescuers. They were having a tough time of it, and from the other side of the window Doc could see more guns being jerked out of their holsters. A man named Frank Loving was the monte dealer (we'll soon hear more about him), and Doc asked him for a gun. Loving produced one from under the table. Doc came out of the saloon with that gun and the one he kept tucked behind him for emergencies.

As Wyatt recalled it, after Doc emerged, he stood on the sidewalk "and throwing both guns down on the crowd, said, 'Throw up your hands!' This rather startled them and diverted their attention. In an instant I had drawn my gun, and the arrest of the crowd followed. They were confined in jail overnight." Doc returned to the monte table, perhaps thinking this lawing stuff was not all that difficult to do if one timed his entrance and exit just right.

With the Indian threat gone, it was time to return to the usual chores of jailing bad guys. Soon, a tragic event would involve the cream of the local lawmen. Wyatt, Bat, Bassett, and Tilghman would ride together to capture the killer of Dora Hand.

In October, the seasonal rowdiness of the trail-driving cowboys was beginning to wind down. A new prairie season was taking hold, with cooler breezes being more prominent than long sun-baked days, and autumn rains began to refill streams and watering holes. The cattle drives that had begun in Texas were soon to finish up for the year. Only the most drunken or foolish required accommodations in the calaboose. Sheriff Masterson and Marshal Bassett and their deputies could lounge in tilted-back wooden chairs outside their respective offices and contemplate with more confidence getting through another night without any trouble.

So the shooting in the early-morning hours of the fourth was indeed a surprise. More surprising was that the victim was a woman and that the crime involved Mayor Dog Kelley.

Dora Hand was a popular performer in Dodge City, singing and dancing in musical comedies on Ham Bell's stage and at the Theatre Comique and Lady Gay Dance Hall. Most audience members knew her as Fannie Keenan, her stage name. The scant information known about her is that she had been born in Boston thirty-four years earlier, her family had the ability to send her to Europe to study music, and she had been an aspiring opera singer in New York City. She had ended up on the frontier because she was fleeing her husband, an East Coast musician named Ted Hand. Another story claimed that, like Doc Holliday, she had headed west looking for a climate that would slow the progression of tuberculosis.

As Fannie Keenan, Dora had arrived earlier in the year with a friend and fellow performer, Fannie Garretson, who was already experienced in the ways of cow towns. In the expanding entertainment scene that was Dodge City, the two Fannies easily found steady work, at forty dollars a week. An article written at the time described Dora as being "of medium height and build, with a face of classic beauty. There was a grace and charm in her walk. She dressed plainly, usually in black, and this color seemed to accentuate the ivory whiteness of her soft skin."

Quickly, her popularity began to rival that of Eddie Foy earlier in the summer. Dora also acquired the reputation of kindness, especially toward the less fortunate in Dodge City. Several accounts have her bringing food to families and distributing candy to children "white, black or Mexican." She even would give money to broke cowboys so they could get back the saddles they lost in poker games to begin to ride back to their outfits and earn more wages.

No doubt quite a few men developed romantic feelings for Dora, but the one who counted most was the mayor. He squired her to dinners and shows at other theaters, and more important, at the summer's end Kelley arranged for the Alhambra on the north side of Front Street to hire her to sing and dance five nights a week for seventy-five dollars, which most likely made Dora Hand the highest-paid performer in Dodge

City that autumn. Some of the most elite women in city society were critical when they heard about her visiting a small house owned by the married mayor off of Front Street, behind the Great Western Hotel that looked out on the Arkansas River.

Though at least ten years younger than she was, James Kenedy, whom most people called Spike, fell hard for Dora. He was a half-Mexican and half-white son of a wealthy Texan. His father was Mifflin Kenedy, a Pennsylvanian who had traded in captaining a ship for heading west to become a rancher. He had hit the jackpot by being partners in the King Ranch, one of the largest in Texas, and then in 1868 had bought his own 172,000-acre spread near Corpus Christi. Kenedy regularly sent herds up the trail to Dodge City and was well known there. Spike's mother was Petra Vela de Vidal, the daughter of a Mexican provincial governor who had borne twelve children, six to a colonel in the Mexican Army and six to Kenedy.

To Spike, being the son of Texas privilege meant getting away with everything up to murder. He felt more at home in cow-town saloons and with the women who worked there than at his father's Laureles Ranch in South Texas. When too much revelry got him into trouble, either his father bailed him out or the local law cut him loose rather than risk the wrath of Mifflin Kenedy. For example, in one of his earliest escapades, in 1872, Spike had shot and wounded a man in Ellsworth, and that night he was allowed to flee the jail. Occasionally, Spike was chastised enough that he paid some dues as a ranch hand and trail rider, but Dodge City emitted a siren call that literally got him off the wagon. His escalating love for Dora Hand had him spending more time in town. That it was unrequited led to more bad behavior.

Late in July, Wyatt had found Kenedy walking down the street north of the Dead Line carrying a six-shooter. When the younger man refused the request to turn over the gun, he discovered the definition of buffaloing. The fine Kenedy had to pay in court probably didn't help his headache. But three weeks later he was back in court, brought there this time by Charlie Bassett, for disorderly conduct.

Predictably, Spike's antics were most often on display at the Alhambra, where he drank up Dora's stage charms along with the whiskey. He was very jealous of Dog Kelley, yet it was the mayor whom Spike approached to complain about the discipline doled out by Wyatt and Bassett. Kelley told the young man sternly that he would become increasingly familiar with the inside of the jailhouse if he didn't straighten out. Instead of heeding this advice, Spike attacked. Kelley was an experienced-enough frontier man that he knew how to handle himself. When he was finished spanking Spike about the face, the mayor dragged the lovelorn young man outside and dumped him in the street.

Though made of stern stuff, an intestinal ailment was what saved Dog Kelley's life. For weeks, a humiliated Spike Kenedy fine-tuned his plot to kill the mayor. He wouldn't make the mistake again of confronting Kelley; this time he would sneak up on him, kill him, and get clean away. Even if it got messy, no court would actually convict Mifflin Kenedy's second-oldest son of a serious offense. He stalked the mayor and realized the best opportunity would be when Kelley, instead of going home late at night, decided to stay at his cottage behind Front Street, which he did many nights. Spike's strategy became more sophisticated when he purchased a racehorse and was confident no lawman could run him down.

So it was at 4:30 on the morning of October 4 that Spike rode through the quiet streets of Dodge City, past the closed doors and drawn shades, and trotted behind the Great Western and up to the cabin. He knew which room Kelley slept in, and he fired two shots into it from a .44-caliber pistol.

However, the mayor was not inside. He was at Fort Dodge. After a few days of persistent abdominal pain, Kelley had gone to visit the army surgeon and would return the next day. He had offered use of the cabin to the two Fannies.

The first bullet entered the room but lodged harmlessly in one wall. The second bullet hit one of the sleeping women in the side, killing her. Responding to the shots, assistant marshals Wyatt Earp and Jim Masterson found a hysterical Fannie Garretson and a dead Dora Hand.

The crowd that convened at the marshal's office that morning had no other suspect in mind but Spike Kenedy, especially after a bartender, who had just closed up a nearby saloon, reported seeing the young Texan galloping away from the Great Western. Certain that he had fled well beyond the confines of Dodge City, Bat Masterson, as Ford County sheriff, chose to lead the posse. Riding out of town with him that afternoon were Wyatt, Charlie Bassett, Bill Duffey, and Bill Tilghman. If they couldn't get their man, no one could — even if it meant taking on Texans who worked for Spike's father.

Spike may not have known much about Bat, especially that he was an aggressive and relentless pursuer. He probably relished the fact that he had a ten-hour start on the posse on a horse that could not be caught. Relentlessly, though, the posse thundered south toward the Texas border. A powerful rainstorm following a bout of stinging hail did not slow them down.

The nasty weather had affected Spike and his more sensitive horse, however, so much so that thirty-five miles southwest of Dodge the following day, the killer came over a rise to find the five lawmen blocking the trail: they had ridden past him during the night. Well, this wouldn't do at all; Spike's only plan was to get to the safety of the Laureles Ranch, which required that his horse outride the posse.

He did not get far. As soon as his horse turned in the other direction, both Bat and Wyatt fired. The bullet from Bat's .50-caliber rifle struck Spike in the shoulder as Wyatt's pistol shot hit the horse. It could not outrace a bullet, and it died. As it did so, it fell on its wounded rider.

After Bat dismounted and began yanking Spike free, he was asked, "Did I kill him?"

The sheriff told him he had killed Dora Hand instead. A distraught Spike complained to Bat, "You ought to have made a better shot than you did!" Bat tugged Spike harder and responded, "Well, you damn murdering son of a bitch, I did the best I could."

About thirty hours after the murder, the suspect was in the Dodge City jail. Bassett, Wyatt, and Jim Masterson were on guard duty — not to prevent Spike's escape, but to dissuade the angry mob of citizens outside from trying to break him out and lynch him. The trial would take place in two weeks, presided over by Judge R. G. Cook. Before then, Dora Hand was buried. For the second time that year there was a big public funeral in Dodge City. Shops and saloons closed that day, and over four hundred people attended, including poor families who had experienced the performer's generosity.

The trial was held behind closed doors, and when it was over Spike was a free man and Mifflin Kenedy was twenty-five thousand dollars poorer — and presumably, the judge was twenty-five thousand dollars richer. Father and son hightailed it to Texas before a reconstituted angry mob could turn on them.

The Kenedy family was to pay in other ways. Thomas Kenedy, Mifflin's oldest son, was shot to death in Brownsville, Texas, in April 1888. That would have made Spike the top heir to the family fortune and property, but four years earlier he had been jailed for killing a man at Laureles Ranch. Before his father could buy that judge off, Spike died of typhoid fever, only two months before his thirtieth birthday.

It seemed like Bat had barely returned from one pursuit of outlaws when he was back on a horse chasing others. The first week of December found seven men accused of various crimes enjoying the hospitality of the Dodge City jail, the most recently arrested being W. H. Brown, whom Bat had collared as a suspected horse thief. Suddenly, though, the incarcerated population dwindled to three when Brown and a trio of others — Frank Jennings, James Bailey, and Skunk Curley — escaped. A none-too-bright jailer had sawed through one of the bars in the process of creating an opening to insert a food tray, and when he left to find more materials, the prisoners broke out.

Once again, Bat put a posse together, this one consisting of Bassett, Duffey, and Jim Masterson. They fanned out as late-autumn darkness descended. Skunk Curley did not get far, only a mile from Dodge City, where Jim found him in a muddy buffalo wallow. But the pitch darkness of the prairie in December allowed the other three escapees to go undetected. Bat and the other two deputies returned empty-handed. It was of some consolation that two of the outlaws were arrested in Kinsley four days later. The fleet Mr. Brown was never seen in Ford County again. The *Dodge City Times* advised that in the future "double caution will be used on the part of the jailor."

Even more consolation came when the new year began and Bat was able to celebrate it getting the one who had gotten away. Dutch Henry Born had been a buffalo-hunting buddy of Bat's, but in the years since, he had devoted his energies to hunting trouble. As 1878 drew to a close, he had deservedly acquired the reputation of being one of the busiest stealers of horses on the frontier, including in Ford County. When Bat heard that Dutch Henry had finally been corralled in Colorado, he wired the sheriff of Las Animas County to keep the cuffs on the miscreant, that he was coming for him.

On New Year's Day, Bat took the train west. When he arrived in the town of Trinidad, Colorado, the sheriff there surprised him by saying that it would cost Bat five hundred dollars to take custody of Dutch Henry because the prisoner was also wanted in Nevada, which would offer at least that for him. Bat did not have five hundred dollars on him and certainly was not about to go back to Dodge City to get it. He insisted on a court hearing.

One was held on January 4 with a Judge Walker presiding. According to a newspaper account, there was a lot of verbal sparring, with Bat getting the better of both the attorneys and the judge — one argument being that if Bat looked hard enough, he might find that one of the attorneys was also wanted in Kansas, and he might have to travel east in handcuffs along with Dutch Henry. Rather than have his court descend into a free-for-all, Walker declared that the outlaw should continue to enjoy the county jail's menu until who was wanted where was sorted out.

Knowing that the odds rarely benefited a visitor, Bat did not wait around. In a way he never explained, when the eastbound train left Trinidad the next day, he and Dutch Henry were on it. About the outlaw's return, the *Dodge City Times* intoned that Bat "is one of the most noted men of the southwest, as cool, brave and daring as any man who ever drew a pistol."

It sure looked like 1879 was going to be a better year, and for Bat, it was likely to include being reelected as the sheriff of Ford County. If Dodge City could be further tamed, as they intended, he and Wyatt could possibly settle down there for the rest of their lives.

TWENTY-FOUR

How Bat got possession of the prisoner without the payment of a reward and without a gubernatorial requisition will probably be explained in the pages of a yellow-backed storybook, which will detail the mysteries and crimes of the early settlement of this border. — *Dodge City Times*

Bat Masterson was not back in Ford County from Colorado long when, in a way, he would have to take on Indians again. First, though, there were more thieving varmints to attend to as well as a visit from Frank and Jesse James.

After rounding up a group of horses that did not belong to him, one of those varmints made for Colorado. Conditions were such on the frontier in January 1879 that Bat did not expect the chase to be a long one: either the outlaw would not get far across the snow-choked and frozen landscape or the posse wouldn't. There might not even be a posse. Once again, Wyatt was away for the winter, and even Bat's brother Jim Masterson had left town. A tad desperate, when that hypocrite-hating Mysterious Dave Mather reappeared in Dodge City expecting to ride out the coldest months there, Bat deputized him.

It is not known if this time Bat got his man, but Mysterious Dave's experience being in his posse must have raised the possibility that he had a future in lawing, because he kept pursuing it. He pushed on from Dodge City to Las Vegas, New Mexico, where he somehow wangled an appointment as a deputy U.S. marshal in addition to being a member of the city's police force. In the latter capacity, Mysterious Dave would have his first shoot-out, in January 1880, and it was a doozy.

The marshal whom Mather served under was a man named Joe Carson. There may have been a robbery under way or a warrant was being served when Carson encountered four men outside the Close & Patterson Variety Hall on the main street of East Las Vegas, and almost immediately there was gunplay. When he heard the shots, Mather ran toward them, but he was too late to save the marshal. Seeing Carson lying dead in the street, Mather jerked out his six-shooters and began firing. When the smoke cleared, one outlaw was dead, another was gravely wounded, and the two others, with minor wounds, had gotten on their horses and ridden away. It quickly spread through the New Mexico Territory that Mysterious Dave was quite the man killer.

It was not long before he burnished that reputation. Joseph Castello was a business owner in town, and one day a dispute with employees went completely off the rails. When Deputy U.S. Marshal Mather arrived, Castello had a gun out and was threatening to start filling the room with bullets. It may have been a bit painful for the closemouthed Mysterious Dave to try to talk Castello out of it. In any event, the tactic did not work, and when Castello began to squeeze the trigger, Mather drew his gun and killed him with one shot. After an inquest, the coroner ruled that the shooting was justified because lives were saved.

Las Vegas and its environs were turning out to be hotter than Mysterious Dave had anticipated. The breaking point for him came when the two men who had escaped after the January shooting that had killed

Marshal Carson were captured and brought back for trial. The outlaws did not get to enjoy the accommodations of the San Miguel County Jail for very long: a mob broke in, grabbed them and the third outlaw still recovering from his injuries, and strung them up. Soon after, when two murders were reported in the area, Mysterious Dave determined he wanted his life expectancy to be longer than Carson's, and he resigned.

He wandered throughout Texas, having several brushes with the law, including being charged with stealing a silk dress from a madam. One day, Mysterious Dave reappeared in Dodge City. He served for a year as an assistant marshal; then, after he shot and killed a man — even though he was acquitted of it — the citizens had tired of this kind of lawing, and he was replaced as assistant marshal with the old buffalo hunter Tom Nixon. This didn't sit well, and the two men feuded. The dispute ended when Mysterious Dave shot and killed Nixon. An indication of how well liked Nixon was: the jury took just seven minutes to find Mather not guilty. A few months later, when he killed another man, it was time to leave Dodge City for good.

In subsequent years there were Mather sightings elsewhere in Kansas and Nebraska. His ultimate fate remains, yes, a mystery.

After the capture of Dull Knife and the remnants of his band of Northern Cheyenne the previous autumn, the old warrior had been held prisoner at Fort Robinson in Nebraska, where Crazy Horse had surrendered, then been murdered, a year earlier. Several months later, in January 1879, Dull Knife escaped one more time, taking his wife and son and a handful of followers with him. For eighteen days they walked west, braving the bone-chilling prairie winds of winter and cloudbursts of sudden snow with only tree bark for food. They arrived at the Pine Ridge Reservation just east of the Black Hills, in South Dakota, hoping to be given the protection of Red Cloud. Though only a decade removed from winning a war against the U.S. government, the Lakota Sioux warrior, now fifty-eight, had become a figurehead, and his wishes did not count for much with federal authorities.

It was decided that the leaders of the September 1878 uprising would be put on trial, and Bat Masterson would be the man to make sure Dull Knife and his captured associates Wild Hog, Old Crow, Nosey-Walker, Porcupine, Left Hand, Blacksmith, and Tangled Head would be there when the proceedings began.

Major General John Pope, who had not distinguished himself as the commander of the Army of the Potomac in the Civil War, was now head of the military district that included Kansas. He ordered that the prisoners be housed at Fort Leavenworth until the state of Kansas took jurisdiction. In February, the governor, John St. John, notified Ford County that Dull Knife and the others were ready to be transported west for trial. The deputies who accompanied Sheriff Masterson were his brother Jim, Charlie Bassett, A. J. French, and the exotically named Kokomo Sullivan.

They traveled by train, arriving on February 15. A large crowd had gathered at the station, with people curious to eye the Indians who had frightened so many on the frontier and killed a few while they were at it. The transfer of the prisoners was done right there on the platform, and adorned with shackles and handcuffs, the eight Indians were brought onto the next westbound train.

It may not have been anticipated that as the train made its way through Kansas, some people wanted to greet Dull Knife and his colleagues with something other than

430

curiosity. There was enough lingering anger that when the train made stops, there were attempts to board it and show the prisoners a more immediate form of frontier justice. Bat and his deputies had to block the steps and push people off the train as it chugged out of each station.

There was an especially violent ruckus in Lawrence. The *Ford County Globe* would report that "the mob was almost overpowering, and our officers were involved in a fight which resulted in a victory for Dodge City." The lawmen not only had to battle with vigilantes but even the "Mayor, City Marshal and a large portion of the able bodied braves of Lawrence undertook to capture Masterson and his outfit." They were unsuccessful, and the train finally arrived in Topeka. There Bat and his men had to push their prisoners through a crowd estimated at a thousand people to the hoped-for safety of the Shawnee County Jail, where everyone spent the night.

There was some rough going at train stations again the next day, February 17, but the prisoners were safely delivered to the jail in Dodge City. Then, after all that, nothing happened. Dull Knife and the seven other Indians languished behind bars for four months. In June, the governor ordered

Bat to bring the prisoners back to Lawrence for trial. After he deposited them there, another four months passed, and then the charges were dropped.

In 1883, at seventy-three, Dull Knife died. Little Wolf did not die until 1904, and both he and his former coleader were buried on the grounds of what is now Chief Dull Knife College in Lame Deer, Montana. A year after Dull Knife's death, what was left of the Northern Cheyenne were finally allowed to return to Montana, to live on the Tongue River Reservation.

Surprisingly, in March 1879 there were still buffalo hunters showing up in Dodge City with a few hides in their wagons. One of them was Levi Richardson. He was viewed as a slow and awkward man, but no one was foolish enough to say anything derogatory about him within hearing range, because Richardson was known to use his guns on people as well as buffalo.

"He was a high strung fellow who was not afraid of any man," Bat would later recollect of Richardson, who had been a companion during buffalo-hunting days. Wyatt Earp thought of Richardson as "one of the best shots with rifle or pistol" and "he had a touchy disposition that often got him into trouble." A gambler named Loving — the same man who had lent Doc Holliday his gun the previous fall — found out about this one night at the Long Branch Saloon.

Given that he was known along Front Street as Cockeyed Frank Loving because his eyes were somewhat askew, it made sense that he was not a very good shot. No one felt sorry for him, though, because he made a decent living as a gambler and he had an attractive wife named Mattie — attractive enough to catch Richardson's eye. He and Loving were actually friends and would good-naturedly gamble together after Richardson had sold a haul of hides, but once the hunter indicated he wanted to get to know Mattie better, there was more friction than friendship.

Matters first came to a head during the day. The two men encountered each other on Front Street, and an argument began immediately. Richardson socked Loving in the jaw. He didn't have a gun but Richardson did, so Loving simply staggered away. Richardson shouted after him, "I'll blow the guts out of you, you cockeyed son of a bitch!"

Perhaps the buffalo hunter thought he had overreacted, because on a chilly night in the first week of April he walked into the Long Branch seeking Loving, intending to work out their conflict and resume being friends. The gambler was not there, so Richardson bought a drink and sat in front of the potbellied stove to wait. Loving finally arrived at 9 P.M., and Richardson asked if the two of them could sit down at a table together. They spoke quietly, and others in the saloon assumed their feud was ending.

Suddenly, Richardson said loudly, "You wouldn't fight anything, you damned . . ."

Loving yelled, "You try me and see!"

Both men drew pistols and began firing. As the percussion and smoke of gunshots filled the saloon, men dove under tables and behind the bar. Charlie Bassett was in the saloon owned by Dog Kelley and P. L. Beatty, and the instant the marshal heard the racket he bolted out the door and hustled down the street, marveling at how many shots were being fired. Entering the Long Branch, expecting a massacre, Bassett instead found in the clearing smoke just Richardson and Loving facing each other, both still standing, their guns emptied. Could the buffalo hunter be as bad a shot as the gambler?

Yes. Loving's only injury was a scratch on one hand. Bassett took his gun and had him sit down. When he took Richardson's gun, the man stumbled away, then collapsed.

Loving had turned out to be the better marksman: his adversary was hit in the chest, side, and arm. Within a few minutes, Richardson was dead. Loving was arrested, but two days later he was released after the coroner ruled he had acted in self-defense.

Bat was tempted to intervene. While Loving was not unknown to him, Richardson had been a friend. But Bat was the elected sheriff, and he hoped to be reelected that November. "I have never stood for murder and never will," Bat wrote about the incident, "but I firmly believe that a man who kills another in defense of his own life should always be held blameless."

Instead, he consoled himself by seeing Richardson's odd death as providing a lesson in being cool under pressure: "No one . . . who knew both men could truthfully say that Loving possessed a greater degree of courage than Richardson, or that under ordinary conditions he was a better marksman with a gun. He simply had the best nerve, which is a quality quite different from courage."

After this, Loving had the reputation of a man dangerous with a gun. This must have gone to his head because, with gun belts on, he hit the trail, in the process leaving behind his two children as well as Mattie.

He spent some time in Las Vegas, New Mexico, gambling and telling and retelling the tale of how he had gunned down the fearsome buffalo hunter Levi Richardson, and then he moved on to Trinidad, Colorado. There, his argumentative ways got him into trouble again, this time with the former Dodge City deputy Jack Allen. Gunfire was exchanged — one report claims there were sixteen shots — but neither man was hit.

Out of bullets, the two men went their separate ways. But the next day, April 16, 1882, when Allen encountered Loving on the street, he yanked out his pistol and let loose a single shot, ending Loving's life.

Members of one of the cattle drives to arrive in Dodge City early in the 1879 season were the James brothers. Frank and Jesse were taking one of their periodic time-outs from robbing trains and banks, and one of the best ways to lie low was to ride hundreds of miles on a cattle drive up from Texas, the days spent in choking dust and the nights under a star-filled sky far from civilization and temptation.

But it was a different environment in Dodge City. With a few fellow trail riders, the brothers were wetting their whistles in the Long Branch Saloon that April. One of the drovers suddenly jumped up from a gaming table, insisting one of the gamblers at it had just cheated him. Gamblers and cowboys began to square off, with the brothers from Missouri having little choice but to go for their guns to back their Texas friend's play. Then the Ford County sheriff entered, his intense dark eyes quickly scanning the room.

The Wild West would have been even wilder if its story could have included a gunfight between Bat Masterson and Frank and Jesse James. But it did not happen. Bat was a peace officer first and a gunman second. His six-shooters were in their holsters, and he kept his hands free of them as he approached the James brothers. There was a quiet conversation, and Frank and Jesse relaxed. They offered to buy everyone a drink, and the tinny piano music resumed and the tension dissipated.

The notorious brothers soon left Dodge City and returned to their criminal ways. But Bat and Frank James maintained something of a friendship, and they exchanged letters until the latter's death. Wyatt could have a polarizing effect on people, but it was difficult to stay mad at Bat, or be mad at all.

TWENTY-FIVE

We were down there again last week, and were surprised in the change in the city. It has built up wonderfully, has a fine court house, church, good schools, large business blocks, a good hall, first-class hotels, and two live newspapers. Dodge is coming out and is destined to be a city of considerable size. — Topeka Times

That well-dressed dandy strolling along Front Street one fine spring day in 1879 sure resembled Luke Short, and it was indeed him, after a lengthy absence. Given that the city suited a gambling and drinking and lecherous man so well, it's a wonder that Luke had left Dodge City at all. But his intention had been to make money, an understandable motivation for most frontiersmen. But along the way he wound up in the army.

Luke had set off the previous August with

a wagon full of whiskey. As good as the saloon business was, he had gotten a tad restless waiting for customers to come to him, so he decided to go to them. He filled up a long wagon with sturdy wooden barrels of cheap whiskey and drove around the frontier. He made good money by supplying thirsty men at hunting camps and even bands of Indians who were unwise enough to trade robes and horses for a fiery liquid that could destroy their minds and bodies.

During the uprising that September led by Dull Knife and Little Wolf, the army had been anxious for scouts. Luke had run out of whiskey, and when the 4th Infantry recruited him, he signed on. He didn't see much action and was not part of the final roundup of Indians. When the winter of 1878–1879 came on, Luke stayed warm by gambling in Deadwood, South Dakota, and Ogallala, Nebraska. When he finally did get back to Dodge City in the spring, he spent most of his days drinking and wagering at the Long Branch Saloon.

Luke's schedule did not call for him getting there early in the day. He lived in the Dodge House and preferred to sleep until late in the morning, shades drawn against any sunlight that tried to intrude. After rising, he'd chase down a good breakfast with a shot of whiskey. He then strolled to the Long Branch, but not in a direct way, enjoying the warming spring breezes as he stopped to chat with friends and acquaintances, visited Wyatt and Bat at their respective offices or as they patrolled the mud-filled streets, and perhaps paid a call on his favorite brothel before or after the barber-shop. Luke Short was not a member of the elite level of society in the city but he was comfortable enough and had few ambitions beyond remaining comfortable and being available if a friend needed help or there was a damsel in distress, though most of the damsels he knew were soiled doves experienced in taking care of themselves. When he did get to the Long Branch, he drank and dealt faro until it was time to call it a night.

Luke also liked a good practical joke — as evidenced by his encounter with Bill Tilghman — so it was no surprise that he was involved in one of the more famous ones played in Dodge City during its golden decade, and he was probably in on it from the beginning. It was a surprise that the usually serious Wyatt joined his pal in the festivities.

A minister named O. W. Wright (no relation to the businessman Robert Wright) had recently arrived and soon proved popular enough that he attracted a sizable congregation, including Wyatt and Bat as "deacons." When Reverend Wright wanted to build a church that would be home to the congregation, the two lawmen went along Front Street, putting the touch on Doc Holliday and most of the other gamblers. To top off the collection basket, the Dodge City Ladies Aid Society suggested that there be a beautiful-baby contest. Beauty was in the eye of the beholder or in this case the donor, because the winner would not necessarily be the most beautiful baby but the one who had attracted the most donations.

Seeming to suddenly find religion — or the deacons leaned on him — Luke Short told the ladies that he would put up one hundred dollars to go to the parents of the winning baby rather than have the prize come out of the proceeds.

Parents and other supporters of the future church sold ballots vigorously. The plan was that the ballots bearing the names of babies would go into a bin, and that at a big congregation dinner the ballots would be counted and the baby with the most ballots, or donations, would be declared the winner, with the proud parents becoming a hundred dollars richer. Parishioners were pleased when the presumably impeccable lawmen Earp and Masterson offered to tabulate the results.

During the night of the congregational dinner, Reverend Wright read out the names of the babies who had received the third- and second-highest numbers of votes, disappointing every parent whose child was not named. When the winner was finally announced, there was stunned silence and much turning of heads, because no one knew who that baby was. Finally, Wyatt and Bat stepped forward and announced they knew the winning baby and would go fetch it.

When they left, they marched across the Dead Line to a dance hall that catered only to black customers. A woman was waiting there, holding a baby, and the lawmen escorted them back to the congregational dinner. There, the black woman displayed the baby and declared it was the winner. Where was the hundred dollars?

One of the losing mothers stood up and demanded, "Who is the father of that child?"

A perplexed but gallant Reverend Wright responded, "That is the lady's business," and he handed over Luke's money. Sometime later, when the good pastor learned about the hoodwinking, he may have wondered *With deacons like that, who needs enemies?* In any case, the fund-raiser had been successful and the congregation's church was one of several constructed during the next few years.

Maybe Dodge City was getting too much religion to suit Luke Short because he left again, this time for Leadville, Colorado, where he resumed gambling. The following year, Luke was living in Buena Vista, also in Colorado and about thirty miles from Leadville. It is not known why he was there, but that is where the 1880 U.S. Census found him. He did not stay long; his next move was to drift eastward, to Kansas City. There he found more trouble. A Texan who went by the name of John Jones claimed that Luke had swindled him out of $280. Local lawmen must have believed him, because Luke ended up in jail.

When he was released on October 11, Luke lingered in Kansas City because he didn't have a hankering to go anyplace in particular. Finally, out of habit, he drifted back to Dodge City.

When Luke's most recent wanderings had begun in the spring of 1879, he missed out on a confrontation that almost cost Wyatt his life. This time it was Bat, not Doc, who had his back.

In May, three men from Missouri were passing through on their way to Leadville to find work in the booming mineral mines there. They decided to take full advantage of the saloons in Dodge City and raise a ruckus before the sun rose and it would be time to leave. They were in the midst of their revelry when, before they could do any real damage, Wyatt arrived on the scene. He sized up the person who he thought was the trio's leader and grabbed him by the ear. The man's yelps could be heard far and wide as the assistant marshal hauled him down Front Street toward the city jail.

If his companions had been smart, the arrest would have signaled it was time to call it a night — but they weren't very smart. They went back inside the saloon and demanded their guns from behind the bar. Armed, they hurried out to Front Street and in the direction Wyatt had gone. They came up behind him with guns drawn. Hearing their approach, Wyatt turned and drew his pistol. The Missouri men ordered that their friend be released. Wyatt smiled grimly, one fist clutching his prisoner, the other his six-shooter. It was their play.

Bat had heard the commotion and from across the street was quietly observing the standoff. His friend's physical strength and a loaded gun were probably plenty for three Missourians. But suddenly the prisoner quit his moaning and grabbed Wyatt's arm, struggling for the gun. His companions saw this as their opportunity and moved in.

They weren't quick enough. Appearing to have materialized out of the darkness, Bat was beside Wyatt with his own gun drawn. He reminded the assistant marshal what buffaloing was by applying it to the prisoner, who in the morning would have a headache to go with a very sore ear. Bat then fixed his gun on one Missourian, and Wyatt raised his to cover the other. Right then and there, the visitors may have vowed never to drink in Dodge City again if it meant taking on two men who by then had gained the inflated reputation of being the most feared and bloodthirsty lawmen on the frontier. In its next edition, the *Dodge City Times* crowed that the Missouri men "were no match for Dodge City officers."

Instead of having learned a lesson, the trio then displayed that they were even dumber. The first standoff ended when the two would-be rescuers surrendered their weapons and joined their groggy comrade in jail overnight. The next day they paid fines, saddled up, and rode west. But they did not go far, and after the sun set, the men doubled back into Dodge City, with the idea of ambushing Bat for interfering and turning the tables on them.

They broke into the back of a shop. Its windows allowed them to crouch out of sight with a good view of the dark alley behind it. When a young black boy wandered through the alley, the Missourians instructed him to find Sheriff Masterson and tell him a man wanted to meet him in the alley. The not-so-brilliant bushwhackers drew their pistols and waited. . . .

And waited. Everyone in town knew Bat, including the young messenger and his family. When he located the sheriff, he told him about three men setting up in the back of the shop. Bat's IQ had to be considerably higher than that of the Missourians, because he posted his brother Jim on one end of the alley and possibly Wyatt, returning the favor, or Bill Tilghman at the other end, while he eased himself into a chair outside the shop's front door.

After an hour or so, the frustrated and weary trio were out of patience. They would soon be out more money, too, because after spotting men at either end of the alley, they tried to sneak out the front door, where Bat and his ivory-handled pistols waited for them. Another night in jail, another fine, and this time when they left town, the Missourians stayed gone.

A short time later, Wyatt and Jim Masterson had each other's back in another confrontation. The *Ford County Globe* reported that a black man had done a job, possibly blacksmithing, for a couple of cowboys. Instead of paying the man, they got on their horses and left town. The workman visited the marshal's office to complain, and Wyatt and Jim rode out. They soon found the two cowboys — in the company of five of their friends. Two against seven were not good odds, but Wyatt, at least, had faced worse. He and Jim had their hands near their six-shooters as Wyatt calmly explained that if the money owed the workman was not ponied up, the jail would be crowded that evening. The lawmen, as the newspaper reported, returned to Dodge City, and the workman was paid in full.

In June 1879, Bat, perhaps after joshing with his lawmen friends that they could take care of themselves for a while, left Dodge City again. But this time it was not to chase an outlaw or gold — it was to go to war. It took place in Colorado and became known as the Royal Gorge War.

Leadville had been formed by miners and others in the Arkansas River Valley of central

Colorado. Tons of silver and lead were being gouged out of the earth. It had to be transported out and more men and supplies brought in. The Atchison, Topeka & Santa Fe wanted to lay tracks into Leadville, but so did the Denver & Rio Grande outfit. Only one could do so, because there was just one right-of-way through the Royal Gorge canyon, a chasm 1,250 feet deep and only 40 feet wide at its narrowest point. Instead of flipping a coin or in some other way determining who could have the right-of-way, both railroads tried to take it.

The Santa Fe Railroad sent crews to grade for a rail line at the mouth of the gorge, and they turned back Rio Grande crews when they arrived. The Rio Grande was also stymied by court orders the Santa Fe obtained. So the thwarted crews went upriver and built stone forts from which they could hurl huge rocks and sharp tools onto the Santa Fe crews as they tried to lay down tracks. While the lawyers continued to fight it out in court in Denver and elsewhere, the skirmishes between the crews escalated to rifles and pistols. On June 10, armed crews from both railroads attacked each other. Men were wounded, trains were taken over, and depots and equipment shacks were torched.

An indication of the reputation applied to Bat, still only twenty-five, was that the Santa Fe Railroad — the same one he and his late brother Ed had graded track for back in Buffalo City days — reached out to him to pull together an outfit that would protect its crews. Bat, as the sheriff of a county in Kansas, of course had no legal jurisdiction in Colorado, but along the way to further legitimize his hunting of horse and cattle thieves, he had been appointed a deputy U.S. marshal, and that gave him some standing in the dispute. And it wasn't too hard to organize an outfit, because he invited fellows he knew and had ridden with before — Ben Thompson, Mysterious Dave Mather (during a Colorado sojourn), and, in a rare collaboration, Doc Holliday. With them aboard, it was even easier to collect a small "army" of sixty or so men. Fortunately for everyone's safety, Eddie Foy turned down an invitation from Doc to go along for the ride, explaining that if he fired a gun, he had no idea if he'd hit friend or foe.

Bat led the charge into the Royal Gorge. He and his men occupied a Santa Fe round-house in Pueblo, a strategic position to prevent Rio Grande rail crews from working in the area. If any opposing worker showed himself, Bat had marksmen positioned atop the roundhouse, or he might be of a mind to take a shot himself and remind others what a good rifleman he was. There were attempts to dislodge the defenders that must have involved close combat, because one of the participants reported that Bat put a railroad policeman in the hospital by applying a gun barrel to his head.

Executives at the Rio Grande had a bright idea: remove a cannon from the state armory, set it up on some level ground, and blast the roundhouse into dust. However, Bat had had the same idea and had it first, so when crews went to the armory the cannon was gone, and sure enough, a couple of days later cannonballs were flying from the roundhouse to rain on Rio Grande crews.

After all that, it was a simple piece of paper that ended the war. The Rio Grande assembled its own attack force and took over a telegraph office manned by a handful of Santa Fe employees, including Henry Jenkins, who was shot in the back and died. Then the contingent moved on to the roundhouse. Maybe for Bat it seemed like the siege of Adobe Walls all over again. This time, though, he had a cannon, and when the defenders saw the Rio Grande men approach, it was made ready to fire. But what could have been a bloodbath was averted when R. F. Weitbrec, the treasurer of the Rio Grande Pacific Corporation, asked to meet with Bat. He showed the sheriff a decision just handed down by a federal court that the Denver & Rio Grande did have the right-of-way. As a federal peace officer, Bat could not reject it. A truce was declared, and the combatants all went their separate ways, which for Bat meant returning to his Ford County responsibilities.

Despite its contentious origins, the railroad line through the Royal Gorge in Colorado turned out to be one of the most unique and enduring in the United States. The Denver & Rio Grande paid the Atchison, Topeka & Santa Fe company almost two million dollars for its troubles and what it had constructed so far, and took over the track work. The goal of trains arriving in Leadville was achieved on July 20, 1880. The line included a hanging bridge suspended over the river on the north side of the gorge at its narrowest point. An engineer from Kansas designed a 175-foot plate girder suspended on one side by A-frame girders spanning the river, and it was anchored to the sheer rock walls. The hanging bridge carried trains for over a century. In 1989, the Denver & Rio Grande company was purchased by the Southern Pacific

Railroad, and seven years later, when the combined corporation merged with the Union Pacific Railroad, the route through the Royal Gorge was closed.

For Doc Holliday, the Royal Gorge War had been a detour during a fresh series of wanderings he had undertaken before and after the conflict. One motivation was that a reform movement under way in Dodge City made it feel less like home for a devout drinking and gambling man. Another was the deterioration of his health as the year went on.

The biographer Gary L. Roberts suggests that because the Kansas climate was not a congenial one for those suffering from a chronic lung disease, Doc was entering the " 'second phase' of consumption. His voice began to develop a deep hoarseness as the result of throat ulcers that would periodically make it difficult for him to speak above a whisper or to eat. His cough became more severe, constant, and debilitating, producing a thick dark mucus of greenish hue with yellow streaks and laced with pus. The cough was attended by hectic fever that rose and fell with an accelerating pulse rate. The fever contributed to a ruddy complexion that seemed deceptively healthy yet alternated with a death-like paleness."

Doc returned to Colorado, this time accompanied by Big Nose Kate, stopping in Trinidad. He required ten days to recover from the journey, then apparently felt well enough to shoot someone. He would later tell Wyatt and Bat that it was only over a "trivial matter" that he shot a man called Kid Colton. Nothing else is known of the incident other than that it persuaded Doc and Kate to get back on a train and head south. When the tracks ended in New Mexico, they were hauled by freight wagon to Las Vegas.

Just outside of that town was a facility for those with lung diseases. The Montezuma Hot Springs had been established during the Civil War, and patients from across the country made use of the bubbling, sulfur-scented waters. After a few weeks of treatments, Doc was well enough that he and Kate moved into Las Vegas and he opened a dental practice. He had to make some money from it because the entire New Mexico Territory must have been feeling the reform spirit, too: its lawmakers had outlawed gambling. After being fined for ignoring the ban, Doc left Las Vegas. He left Kate, too — presumably after one of their big fights.

He moved on to Otero County, which the

inexorable Atchison, Topeka & Santa Fe had by then reached. He once again opened a dental practice (it is doubtful that he was dragging the same chair from Texas around with him), and he befriended two men, Hurricane Bill Martin and T. O. Washington. One was the town marshal, the other was a physician. With the protection of the former and the care of the latter, Doc planned to resume his gambling ways.

But unlike with old friends Wyatt and Bat, he had not chosen his new friends well. The Otero administrators claimed that Hurricane Bill was too often drunk and always incompetent, and they fired him. The not-very-good doctor got into an altercation with a man and carved him up with a knife. Washington fled the murder charge to a nearby railroad town, Raton. His attempt to establish a medical practice was very short-lived because he tried to fondle a female patient, her fiancé alerted the local law, Washington was tossed in jail, and even before he could be formally charged, the physician was hauled out of his cell and hung from a water tower.

No longer finding Otero to his liking, Doc again headed south, back to Las Vegas. He opened a saloon with Jordan Webb, a younger brother of John Joshua Webb. A thirsty customer was Mike Gordon, a former army scout whose appearance was distinctive because in a fight his adversary had bitten his nose off.

Gordon had been on a bender for several days when on the night of July 19, 1879, he was in Doc's saloon and threatened to kill a prostitute who would not accompany him to another saloon. He then stepped out into the street, took out his gun, and fired. A Mexican standing near the entrance to the saloon was wounded slightly. Gordon fired off a few more shots. Aggravated, Doc appeared and fired back. The disfigured former scout staggered away. Later that night, he was found inside a tent, a bullet in his chest. Gordon was brought to the prostitute's room at Doc's saloon, where early the next morning he died. The coroner, Hoodoo Brown, who would later be a prominent personality in Dodge City, did not accuse Doc, and no witnesses testified about the incident.

Doc's next adventure was much less violent but, in hindsight, of greater interest. He had to have been one of the few gamblers to play cards with Jesse James and Billy the Kid. Both arrived, separately, the last week of July and visited Doc's saloon. Possibly in the company of the dentist, they visited the Montezuma Hot Springs and ate dinner together at the Las Vegas Hotel, which had just opened there. The Kid had visited Las Vegas before, and the owner of the hot springs, Winfield Scott Moore, had known Frank James and his brother since their childhood days in Missouri. Because no one wrote about the intersection of Billy the Kid, the James Brothers, and Doc Holliday, one has to imagine their conversations and that they apparently got on well enough that their pistols stayed in their holsters.

Sometime during his travels Doc and Kate Elder were reunited. It may have been simply the established scenario that when Doc was healthy and going good, he did not need her around, and when there was trouble, Kate showed up. They considered returning to Dodge City, where Wyatt was. Doc found out, however, that was not true when one afternoon in September 1879, while Doc was crossing the downtown plaza in Las Vegas, he found Wyatt standing there.

Twenty-Six

What made Dodge City so famous was that it was the last of the towns of the last big frontier of the United States. When this was settled, the frontier was gone, it was the passing of the frontier with the passing of the buffalo, and the Indian question was settled forever. — ROBERT WRIGHT

During the summer of 1879 in Dodge City the surrounding prairie was exceptionally dry. It put people on edge, especially the cowboys up from Texas. They, of course, were accustomed to hot, dry, dusty conditions, but Dodge City, even with the heat of a typical prairie summer, was the end of the trail and was not supposed to be as brutal. There was still an abundance of liquor to soothe dry throats, but what had become a drought reduced the number of cattle drives to the city — there were more lush grazing areas elsewhere, including to the north in

Nebraska — cutting into the drovers' pay and good times. This in turn cut into the peace officers' pay, because they made extra money per arrest, and fewer cowboys hurrahing the town meant fewer occupants of the calaboose.

For Wyatt, it was the slowest summer since he had come to Dodge City in 1876. He almost made up for it all in one day when, finally, in early September, there was a melee big enough to rival previous brawls. A number of proper citizens had organized a festival to put the best face on a desultory summer, and the festivities irritated some already surly cowboys. Words were exchanged, friction escalated, and suddenly fists were flying.

By now, Wyatt probably welcomed the action. When the assistant marshal arrived on the scene he got right into the thick of things, buffaloing the more extreme combatants and displaying his talent for fisticuffs. In its report on the wild scramble in the streets, the *Ford County Globe* commented that the "finest work and neatest polishes were executed by Mr. Wyatt Earp."

As Wyatt's actions demonstrate, it was more than the weather keeping a lid on lawlessness. Effective policing was having a big impact, aided by the reputations of the area's leading lawmen. Those reputations were not anything like what they would be after decades of dime-store novels, but they at least made troublemakers hesitate to go too far and risk being the victims of buffaloing or a bullet.

People had already begun to pass the word that Wyatt Earp was a tough, sober, and serious lawman, and then the story about the Clay Allison confrontation made the rounds. When newspapers associated him with sidewalks that streamed with blood, that made an impression, even though the only man Wyatt had killed to date — and that was iffy — was George Hoy.

Bat held the higher position of being a county sheriff, and he, too, was finding his reputation, some of it true, bandied about. In September 1879, he was still two months shy of his twenty-sixth birthday, yet he was one of the most feared lawmen on the western prairie. One writer would report that in "rough" Dodge City there was "a string of slaughters headed by 'Bat' Masterson, whose hands were red with the blood of no less than a score of his fellow-men." However, "a good majority of these men deserved killing." Another writer claimed that when "the main street echoed with the roaring of firearms . . . Bat Masterson subdued the rebels" and when "killing was done he did his full share."

Most of what was written and said about Bat outside of Dodge City was hogwash, but having a reputation as a tough gunslinger could be a good card to play. Nat Love found that out during one of his Dodge City adventures.

Born in 1854 in Tennessee, Love learned to read and write even though his family had been slaves. But he didn't take much advantage of his literacy until decades later when he wrote an autobiography. As a teenager after the Civil War, he wanted to go west and become a cowboy, so he did, working his way to the Dodge City area, where he was given a job at a nearby ranch. Depending on the season and the cattle drives, Love — given the nickname "Red River Dick" by other cowhands — split his time between Dodge City and the Texas Panhandle. A detour to South Dakota, where he won several rodeo contests, earned him the new nickname of "Deadwood Dick."

The color of his skin did not seem to have an impact on Nat Love's ability to make a living and ride with the other cowboys. He enjoyed his times in Dodge City with the rest of them, and he was befriended by Bat

Masterson, who admired Deadwood Dick's riding and roping abilities, friendly disposition, and aversion to getting into trouble. But the trail rider admitted to imbibing "more of the bad whiskey of Dodge than anyone," and one day Deadwood Dick did find trouble.

He had recently been slightly wounded in a run-in with a rogue Indian band on his way up from the Panhandle, and his idea of revenge almost doomed him. Dick and several cowhands were riding past Fort Dodge — after a stop in the city to wet their whistles — when Love determined that when he returned to Texas he wanted to teach those Indians a lesson. What better way than to blast the lot of them with a cannon? Dick rode up to one side of the fort and displayed his roping skills by lassoing one. The dilemma Dick faced was that the cannon was much heavier than he'd anticipated. While he was pondering this, an officer alerted to the odd activity just outside the walls led troopers out to the drunken cowboys, and a few minutes later Deadwood Dick was in the guardhouse.

The prisoner was informed that he faced federal charges of attempted theft of government property, and he was to be transported to the nearest U.S. district court for arraignment. Dick was sobering up fast and begged the officer to contact his friend Bat Masterson. In case the prisoner was telling the truth, and not wanting to irritate the Ford County sheriff, a messenger was sent. The response was, "Send the prisoner to me, I'll take care of it." Soon, Dick was back on his horse and being escorted to Dodge City.

As Nat Love would recall, "Bat asked me what I wanted with a cannon and what I intended to do with it. I told him I wanted to take it back to Texas with me to fight the Indians with; then they all laughed. Then Bat told them I was all right, the only trouble being that I had too much bad whiskey under my shirt."

Bat told the soldiers that Deadwood Dick was under his protection now and to go on back to the fort. They did. The former prisoner did have to pay a "fine," though, of buying drinks for all at the nearest saloon.

Love worked as a cowhand for many years, until his bones became a bit too brittle and the jobs too few. He spent the rest of his life as a porter on the Denver & Rio Grande Railroad and died in 1921 at the age of sixty-seven in Los Angeles.

Dodge City was growing. It was reported in 1879 that there were seven hundred residents, fourteen saloons, two dance halls, and four dozen prostitutes. Yet a reporter for *The Atchison Champion* who visited the city focused on other aspects in his article: "Another evidence of the permanence of Dodge City is the fact that many elegant residences and large, commodious business houses are in the course of construction at the present time. Looking through many of the business homes, and counting three and six in each, all busy, if indicative of good times, certainly Dodge cannot complain. 'Dull times' is scarce heard in Dodge; they are happy, good-natured and prosperous."

There was certainly no written code among the marshals and sheriffs of various jurisdictions on the frontier on how to co-operate as law enforcers. Some peace officers were corrupt or gunslingers protected by badges, but many were advocates or at least custodians of the justice systems taking hold throughout the West. This probably explains why Bat went on another rescue mission.

This time it was to help out the marshal of Hay City. A gathering of troopers from the 7th Cavalry — George Armstrong Custer's old outfit — at a saloon was getting out of hand, and the bartender sent a messenger to go fetch the marshal. His appearance was resented by the Bluebellies, and the situation escalated to the point at which guns came out and shots were fired. The marshal was outnumbered, but he was apparently not outgunned, because when the smoke cleared the troopers were clearing out, leaving two dead comrades behind.

That the marshal had just been doing his job and forced into a violent confrontation did not dim the anger of General Philip Sheridan, the commander of the army in that district. He had two dead soldiers, and the man who killed them was to be punished, preferably by being hung at the nearest fort. Sheridan ordered that the marshal be found immediately.

The marshal sent a telegram to Bat, telling him where he was and to please come find him before the army did. When Bat arrived in Hays City, he rented a wagon and casually steered it out of town to where the marshal was hiding out. Bat had brought a large blanket, and he wrapped the marshal in it. Most likely, the marshal never envisioned leaving Hays City this way, alive.

They got as far as Junction City before the wagon was stopped by roaming members of the 7th Cavalry, who asked what the cargo was. Bat told them his brother had just died, and he was about to bury him. When asked what his brother died of, Bat replied, "Smallpox." The troopers set records riding away. For several weeks, the marshal enjoyed the hospitality of Dodge City until Bat brokered a truce between him and General Sheridan.

The Atchison Champion reporter had written, " 'Dull times' is scarce heard" in the ever-more-civilized city, but he apparently had not spoken to Wyatt. The restless Earp blood still ran in him, and even though his stays in Dodge City had not been continuous, he had never called anyplace else home for as long in his adult life. The frontier had moved farther west, and Wyatt was beginning to itch to move with it. Later in life he recalled to an interviewer that by 1879 Dodge City "was beginning to lose much of the snap which had given it charm to men of restless blood."

Combine this with what Virgil had been writing him about, and there was a whole lot to consider. By that September of 1879, Wyatt had made up his mind. As he put it, "I was tired of the trials of a peace officer's life and wanted no more of it." That month, he resigned his position in Dodge City.

He bid farewell to Bat, hoping they would meet up again soon, and to Jim Masterson, Bill Tilghman, Charlie Bassett, and the other local lawmen. His eventual destination was to reunite with Virgil in Arizona. Mattie would accompany him every step of the way, but for her they were increasingly stumbling steps.

Perhaps believing it was a healthy switch, or simply no longer caring, Mattie had replaced some of her intake of whiskey with more drops of laudanum. How she obtained the opiate-based painkiller is unknown, but she would often complain of headaches and no doctor was going to refuse the increasing demands of Wyatt Earp's wife. She continued to function well enough in public, but Wyatt, who disliked intoxication in himself and others (with the notable exception of Doc Holliday), spent as little time with her as possible. When not on patrol or manning the marshal's office, he could be found in a saloon, drinking coffee or allowing himself an occasional small beer.

He had grown tired of this routine. It was time to pull up stakes and go. According to Casey Tefertiller, "The Wyatt Earp who left Kansas had matured markedly from the boy who found himself in trouble in Indian Territory. He had become a most self-assured man who stoutly believed in right and wrong — and in his ability to determine which was which. He loved to be amused,

yet almost never laughed; his dour counte-
nance covered an air of supreme confidence
in his ability to deal with just about any
problem."

Wyatt had probably heard reports that
Doc Holliday had spent the summer in Las
Vegas, and he had never been there himself,
so that was how it happened that on that
hot late-summer afternoon in New Mexico
Wyatt, allowing himself a rare smile, was
standing before his friend. He brought Doc
to the outskirts of town where the Earp
party was camped. There was a lot of catching up to do. Wyatt and Mattie were not
traveling alone. James and Bessie Earp had
also thought it was high time for another
family reunion.

Wyatt may have believed that at least for
the near future he was done with lawing.
The West offered opportunity, as it had
when he was younger, for someone with an
entrepreneurial spirit. He was not interested
in simply making a living; he wanted to
become wealthy. Surely a man with his
experience and fortitude would make progress toward that goal.

Apparently not seeing it as the troubled
town that Doc did, the Earps remained in
Las Vegas for almost a month. Wyatt may
have lingered there because he was on the

job. A newspaper account hinted that he was working for Wells Fargo and might be investigating the recent robberies of the stagecoaches. When in October there was another robbery, this time of a train, outside Las Vegas, a moonlighting Charlie Bassett showed up leading a posse hired by the Adams Express Company. Whatever investigating Wyatt was doing he turned over to Bassett, and he and Mattie and the others in his party pulled up stakes and headed for Arizona.

When they stopped in Tucson, Wyatt picked up some extra money by riding shotgun on stagecoaches. This lasted until he was approached by Charlie Shibell, the sheriff of Pima County, who asked Wyatt to be his deputy. He agreed, further delaying the reunion with Virgil.

Before he had left Dodge City, Wyatt had had a last get-together with Bat. Maybe by now Sheriff Masterson had grown equally weary of being a peace officer. Neither one of them was getting any younger, and opportunities to make good money might be passing them by. Well, in Bat's case, he would soon turn only twenty-six to Wyatt's thirty-one, but the point was that with more people and activity in the West, an enterprising man could be confined by wearing a badge and surviving on a lawman's modest salary and maybe catching a bullet while he was at it. Bat was welcome to come along to Arizona with the Earps.

However, he was not ready for that yet. Kansas was still home. He felt like his job was unfinished. When Wyatt rode off into the sunset, Bat had waved farewell.

If Bat's plan was to remain in Dodge City for as long as he wore a badge, the next step was to keep the badge by getting reelected in November 1879. As autumn began, it looked likely that his opponent would be George Hinkle. The bartender in George Hoover's saloon was a popular presence in Dodge City. Though eight years older than Bat, he did not have nearly the same amount of law-enforcement experience, but he had worked a variety of jobs that had toughened him up, including as an army scout, prize-fighter, railroad worker, and teamster.

In mid-October, the Independent Party in Ford County officially — and unanimously — nominated Bat to run for reelection. This action was greeted enthusiastically by the *Dodge City Times,* which contended that he was "acknowledged to be the best Sheriff in Kansas. He is the most successful officer in the State. He is immensely popular and generally well-liked. Horse thieves have a terror for the name of Masterson."

Hinkle was nominated by the People's Ticket, and the campaign swung into high gear. Bat reasonably relied on his solid reputation and experience and that he knew many of the voters. When opponents spread rumors that he was careless with county taxpayers' money and had even gambled with it in the local saloons, Bat ignored them, confident no one would believe such ridiculous lies. This was not a sound strategy. Citizens began to wonder about Bat's silence on the matter. There was also renewed criticism about his association with less-savory citizens, such as Ben and Billy Thompson and Doc Holliday. The sheriff assumed that if there was any defending to do, his associates and the Dodge City press would do it. They didn't.

To Bat's mind, his affability as well as his effectiveness would be enough for voters. "Bat did not take himself too seriously; there was little of the gimlet-eyed killer about him," analyzed Richard O'Connor in his chronicle of Bat's life. "He proposed to relax in between jobs of shooting it out with desperate characters or leading man hunts across the prairies, and tending to his gambling business. Bat was a familiar figure in all the bars, the Lady Gay, the Lone Star,

Peacock's, Hoover's, the Long Branch, Wright and Beverley's, and there is no reason to believe that he shunned feminine company."

By the time Bat realized that he needed to respond aggressively to the allegations, it was too late. On November 4, the vote was 404 for Hinkle and only 268 for Bat. A changing Ford County had allowed him only one term as sheriff.

His opponents were not done with him. A man named Charles Roden, who lived in Spearville in Ford County, claimed that Bat had launched an unprovoked attack on him and stolen his wallet during the tussle. However, an attorney who had witnessed the confrontation offered to set things straight. But at his office, when the two men encountered each other, things went south fast. Bat was upset that during the campaign Roden had been one of those spreading the false rumors in support of Hinkle.

Roden reached for his gun. Bat grabbed that hand and beat Roden with his other hand. "Pull it if you can," he said, getting a few last punches in. When Bat released him, a reeling Roden fled the lawyer's office.

Life only got worse for Roden. Later that month, items and cash that had gone missing after several recent robberies were found in his house, and he was arrested. He made bail, but rather than risk a trial, he disappeared.

Bat would remain sheriff until Hinkle was inaugurated in January 1880. He continued his routine duties and contemplated life as an exlawman. He had business interests in Dodge City, his brother Jim was still on the marshal's staff, and for the most part this had been home since he and Ed had been buffalo hunters. Bat had many fond memories of the area, which was not all that far from the Masterson family farm near Wichita.

But he was bitterly disappointed with how the people of the county had been so quick to reject him and his good name. He deserved better, as Robert Wright pointed out in his memoir of Dodge City: "Bat was a most loyal man to his friends. If anyone did him a favor, he never forgot it. I believe that if one of his friends was confined to jail and there was the least doubt of his innocence, he would take a crow-bar and 'jimmy' and fight his way out, at the dead hour of midnight; and, if there were determined men guarding him, he would take these desperate chances."

Wyatt had been right: it was time for Bat to put his skills and personality toward other pursuits, ones that would earn better money. Gambling could pay his way as he figured out what those pursuits would be, and there was not much of that in Dodge City in the winter. In February, a few weeks after Hinkle had become the new sheriff of Ford County, Bat hit the trail. Like Wyatt Earp and the hundreds if not thousands he had followed, Bat Masterson rode west.

ACT IV

The Dodge City Peace Commission, left to right: Charlie Bassett, W. H. Harris, Wyatt Earp, Luke Short, Frank McLain, Bat Masterson, Neil Brown, and W. F. Petillon. **Courtesy of Kansas State Historical Society**

Twenty-Seven

> They looked alike as three peas in a pod
> — the same height, size and mustaches.
> In Tombstone later men were always mis-
> takin' one for the other. — ALLIE EARP

Wyatt Earp and Bat Masterson would meet again in Dodge City, but they took very different paths to get there. Wyatt, as was his way when his mind was made up, was done with Dodge. He turned his eyes west, and his long journey would include Arizona, Colorado, California, and even Alaska. Bat traveled a lot, too, but he couldn't quit Kansas. As was his way when there were long friendships to preserve, he returned to Dodge City again and again to experience the charms of the saloons and gambling halls. Both men, as a new decade dawned, began to explore an American West that was striving to keep pace with the progress of an increasingly sophisticated civilization.

The year 1880 would see the first electric streetlight installed, in Wabash, Indiana, which by the end of March would be the first electrically lighted city in the world. With financial backing from Thomas Edison, the journal *Science* would first be published. James Garfield would defeat Winfield Hancock to become the twentieth president of the United States, the last Civil War general to attain that office. (He would hold it less than a year, becoming the second president to be assassinated.) The first cash register, in Dayton, Ohio, would be patented. The prolific Edison would perform the first test of an electric railway. And born that year would be Tom Mix, who would become Hollywood's most popular cowboy star and a good friend to both Wyatt Earp and Bat Masterson.

Virgil's letters from Arizona had set the Earp migration in motion. He had informed Wyatt that he was doing pretty well for himself as a lumberman. On land he owned west of Prescott he cut down pine trees, and he fashioned them into lumber in the sawmill he owned, which he sold to construction crews building new residences and shops, to a nearby army post, and to the many mining enterprises whose activity continued unabated. He also continued to work as a stage driver. Life was pretty satisfying for Virgil and Allie.

So it was a bit surprising that he kept his eye out for lawman positions. Back in September 1878, he had been appointed a night watchman. Two months later, he ran for constable in Prescott and came out on top in a three-man race and resigned the watchman job. As constable, Virgil earned seventy-five dollars a month, meaning he had to keep selling lumber and driving stages.

He found time to concoct the plan that would reunite most of the Earp clan and make them money. From what he was hearing from visitors to Prescott and during his stage-driving journeys, Tombstone was the next hot spot. The place was booming because of all the silver being scooped out of the brown windswept hills and was thus a fertile town for ambitious men, especially those willing to work together. Virgil was ready to give Tombstone a try, and maybe his brothers would do so, too.

The only real objection was from Allie, who was not inclined to be uprooted from Prescott. According to her reminiscences many years later, she said that they "had a good home right here" and she had no interest in "traipsin' round the country."

But as she and their other women knew, when the Earp brothers decided to do something, there was no use resisting. Allie, especially, recognized their "silence, secrecy, and clannish solidarity."

Tombstone had been founded by sheer luck. It was regarded as a godforsaken area thirty miles north of the Mexican border. Water was scarce. The only things there were plenty of were dirt and dust and scorpions and wandering bands of Apache, who were not intimidated by the presence of Fort Huachuca and its listless Bluebellies, who would rather not be out on patrol baking in the Southwest sun. There was little appeal to the area except to those seeking solitude or snakes.

But in 1877, a man named Ed Schieffelin, prospecting by himself, made a discovery. He had ignored the warning given to him at the fort that all he would find out in the scorched hills was his tombstone, and what he did find was a silver deposit. Subsequently, bigger and bigger ones were uncovered. There was still not much water, but the area was flooded by miners, and as money was made, all manner of entrepreneurs followed them. Two years later, the tongue-in-cheek name of Tombstone had stuck and it was becoming another in a long line of American frontier boomtowns.

Because their travels had taken a lot longer than they'd expected, Wyatt and Mattie and James and Bessie did not arrive in Tombstone until the spring of 1880. They had ridden past brush-filled hills blooming with mines that were offering up silver and gold to hardworking and hopeful men. Of course, most of the profits went into the deep pockets of the mining companies, with the larger ones paying their investors up to six hundred thousand dollars a year.

For such a young town, Tombstone had advanced swiftly as a community. The population had already exceeded five thousand, and it had churches and genteel hotels and saloons. The three wide main streets were named Allen, Fremont, and Toughnut. They also offered gambling dens and dance halls. Farther from downtown were dozens upon dozens of tents that housed small shops and residences. When the tents ended, the dusty desert with its endless supply of sagebrush and cacti began. To the newcomers the air was fresher than Dodge City's, thanks to the lack of cattle. It was a more ethnically diverse community, too, because of the presence of a large number of Mexicans and of Chinese, who were referred to by the local press as "celestials." (There were by now one hundred thousand Chinese men and three thousand Chinese women living in the western United States.) Some visitors went so far as to compare Tombstone to San Francisco.

Virgil and Allie had arrived from Prescott the previous autumn. Toward the end of November 1879, Crawley Dake — who in addition to being Virgil's politically connected friend was the U.S. marshal for the Arizona Territory — had appointed Virgil as deputy U.S. marshal for the Tombstone mining district. This meant that he represented federal law enforcement in all of southeast Arizona.

Here it was a few months later, and Virgil, Wyatt, and James were finally back together again and Morgan was said to be on his way to Tombstone. James became the bartender and manager of Vogan's Bowling Alley on Allen Street, but he would soon open his own watering hole called the Sampling Room. Wyatt and Mattie and James and Bessie rented nearby houses and began to seek their fortunes. Unlike James, Wyatt would not have much support from his wife. The traveling and uncertainty about the future — especially her future with Wyatt — had given Mattie chronic headaches, and she was relying even more on laudanum.

Perhaps Tombstone would provide a fresh start.

When Morgan, by then twenty-nine years old, finally did join his brothers, he was a married man. It may have been in Kansas but it was more likely in Montana that he had met Louisa Alice Houston. After serving as a sometime lawman in Dodge City and before traveling to Tombstone, Morgan had lived in Big Sky Country as a rancher and hunter, and he had considered staying there permanently. He had resumed lawing for a while, too, beginning in December 1879, when he had served as a policeman in the mining town of Butte, but he held on to the job for only three months.

Born in Wisconsin in January 1855, Louisa was the second child of H. Samuel Houston — there were unfounded rumors that he was related to the Texas rebellion hero — and Elizabeth Waughtal, and she would be followed by ten siblings. Louisa was often unwell and would be diagnosed with rheumatoid arthritis and edema. Still, by only age fifteen she had left her family behind, and in 1872 she was living in Iowa. She and Morgan may have met before he relocated to Montana in September 1877, but they were living together there. The Pipestone Hot Springs in Butte was known as a treatment for arthritis sufferers, and they may have traveled there, or Louisa did and she and Morgan crossed paths.

In April 1878, Morgan and Louisa were living on a ranch on the Tongue River just outside Miles City. That September, when he had taken the job as a peace officer in Butte, Louisa moved there with him. But early in 1880 they left Montana, working their way west to eventually wind up in Temescal, California, where Nicholas and Virginia Earp lived for a time, with Warren being the only one of their children still living with them or nearby. After a visit, Morgan heeded the call from Virgil and Wyatt and James to head southeast to Tombstone. There he would, like Wyatt, ride shotgun on stagecoaches, from time to time be deputized by Virgil, and rent a house and join the expanding Earp compound.

Louisa's health was too fragile that winter for her to travel, but she intended to join Morgan later. However, month after month went by and she continued to feel poorly. It would not be until December 1880 that she would be reunited with her husband and find herself surrounded by Earp brothers and their women. That would soon include Warren, too. The twenty-five-year-old had drifted down from California and would spend some time in Tombstone. When he did, that meant there were five Earp brothers in town making a living and looking for their piece of the mining boom.

All five were not alike, however. In her memoir, their sister Adelia gave her appraisal: "Wyatt and Virgil were not too much alike in nature. Wyatt and Jim were more alike, and Morg and Warren were too. Virgil was Virgil and there wasn't nobody much like him. He was the biggest and had a big booming voice and laugh and a real big heart too. You would really have to push him some to make him angry but then he really did explode. I guess Wyatt and Jim were the same way, like mother, and me, I reckon."

For Wyatt, someone in addition to Morgan had arrived in the area recently who would also have an impact on his personal life. Despite the fragile health of his third wife, Wyatt wasn't necessarily looking for a fourth one, and he especially could not have anticipated the most romantic relationship he would have since the tragic death of Aurilla.

According to the detailed research done by Sherry Monahan for her book *Mrs. Earp,* Josephine Sarah Marcuse was born in June 1861 to Hyman Henry Marcuse, a member of a Jewish family in Poland, and the former

Sophie Lewis-Levy, eight years his senior, who was from either Germany or Prussia. The two had met in New York after emigrating to the United States. The couple had three children and lived on Hester Street in New York City alongside many other European Jewish immigrants.

At some point before 1870, the Marcuse family uprooted itself and traveled completely across to the other side of the country and settled in San Francisco, where Hyman Marcuse worked as a baker. Because of the ebb and flow of making a living, the family moved from time to time, including living on Clara Street and Powell Street. Josephine went to public schools and took dancing classes. The latter proved to be more appealing because the teenager became involved in stage productions. It seems that around the time she was eighteen, Josephine had a choice to make: stay with her family in San Francisco and hope to find a suitable husband, or join a traveling show and hope to find adventure. She chose the latter.

Well, that is the version she told decades later. There is also evidence to suggest that when Josephine was only fourteen, she was recruited by a woman who ran a brothel in her family's neighborhood. Coming from a family that had always struggled to pay the rent may have made the girl desperate or just very practical. The madam took her stable of girls on the road to Arizona mining country, also fertile ground for entrepreneurial females. (Josephine's official story was that she had run off to join a traveling troupe of players performing the Gilbert and Sullivan musical *H.M.S. Pinafore.*) They had hardly shaken the dust of distance off their dresses when in or near Prescott, Josephine met John Harris Behan (everyone called him Johnny), probably as he was making the rounds campaigning for sheriff of Yavapai County. He was married with two children, but that did not stop Josephine from becoming infatuated with him.

However, the combination of the harsh life of being a hooker in the mining region, homesickness, and unrequited puppy love proved too much for the teenager. With the help of family members and friends of theirs in Prescott, Josephine left her life there, and in March 1876 she was back in San Francisco.

One of Behan's flaws was he could not stay away from houses of ill repute, and his wife demanded a divorce, which was granted. It had to be a pleasant surprise for Josephine when, three months before her eighteenth birthday, she encountered Behan in San Francisco. He must have been impressed with how she had bloomed into a fetching young woman, because he proposed to her. She must have refused, because in May 1879, Behan was in Phoenix with his son — his daughter had died two years earlier from meningitis — not a fiancée. Well, again, that's one version. The other one is that hiding under the name of Sadie Mansfield, which she may have used previously in the profession, Josephine followed Behan to Arizona. By November 1880, when Behan was in Tombstone as a deputy sheriff, Josephine Marcus, as her last name was spelled by then, was living with Behan and his son.

Alas, it was not marital bliss at last. Behan being Behan, he was soon back to his adulterous ways. One of his more scandalous affairs involved a married woman. A betrayed and embarrassed Josephine bore such bad behavior as long as she could, then began making plans to return to her family in San Francisco. But she met Wyatt Earp instead, and everything changed.

Wyatt's initial idea for a business in Tombstone was an old occupation. He said that from the time he left Dodge City, "I intended to start a stage line." But he found out right away in Tombstone that there were already two stage lines operating and thus no room for a third. Instead, he and his brothers put down money for mining claims and water rights, hoping to be swept up in the boom. They weren't. While waiting for any kind of profits, Virgil at least had a steady and decent-paying job as a federal peace officer and James had the saloon.

The Earps maintained some confidence that Tombstone would pay off for them. According to Casey Tefertiller, "All around was the banging of hammers and whizzing of saws, cutting and crafting to build a boom-town. The village with the odd-sounding name had a constant bustle about it: noise, excitement, anticipation. Optimism always flowed as freely as whiskey, for only the optimistic would chance their lives on an unproved hope of new riches."

Wyatt may have had too taciturn a personality to be optimistic, but he certainly had hopes of finally striking it rich. First, though, he had to support himself and his wife, especially with Mattie no longer able to work. When he took a job there was a "Dodge" connection, but not to the city: Frederick James Dodge was an agent for Wells Fargo, and he hired Wyatt to ride shotgun on the stagecoaches that carried the company's strongboxes. Wyatt could not have been too happy about this, because he had come to Tombstone to finally make his fortune and he was back to the same old risk-filled occupation. Maybe a lawing position should be looked at again.

The July 28, 1880, issue of the *Tombstone Daily Nugget* reported, "Sheriff Shibell has appointed Wyatt Earp Deputy Sheriff for this precinct." Probably what a lawman new to Tombstone did not need was a companion who was an alcoholic, sickly, gunslinging former dentist, but that is what Wyatt got.

Many years later, Wyatt claimed that "Doc Holliday thought he would move with me. Big Nose Kate had left him long before — they were always a quarrelsome couple — and settled in Las Vegas, New Mexico. He looked her up en route, and the old tenderness reasserted itself; she resolved to throw in her lot with us in Arizona."

However, when the Earps had left Las Vegas, Doc had remained. He soon came to regret the decision. On a slow afternoon in the fall of 1879, Charles White had been standing behind the bar when Doc entered the saloon. There must have been some unfinished business between the two men, because Doc had a six-shooter in his hand,

and as soon as White saw him, he produced one of his own. Doc fired. No serious damage was done. Doc did not initially know this, though. One of his bullets creased his adversary's scalp, and down he went. Doc had seen a flash of blood and hurried out of the saloon, believing he had sent the bartender to the great beyond. He set out for Arizona, hoping it was not too late to catch up to Wyatt.

It was, however, because by the time he arrived in Prescott, the Earps had moved on. Doc decided to stay for a bit, most likely because he needed rest and money, and maybe luck would be with him at the gaming tables there. He was right. He gambled for days on end, wisely doing more card playing than drinking and keeping his temper under wraps. Thus, without killing anyone or getting killed, Doc was up forty thousand dollars. That day, Big Nose Kate walked into the saloon.

It is possible this was a coincidence, with many people passing through Prescott for one reason or another. Or she'd gotten wind of Doc being there and missed the cantankerous bastard. In any event, by Doc's standards, he gave her an effusive welcome. Kate may have been as happy to see his winnings as she was to see him.

She had never been very fond of Wyatt, dating back to Wichita, yet she agreed to accompany Doc when he soon decided to pocket his winnings and push on to Tombstone. They arrived there in the summer of 1880. Doc may have felt safer in the company of the Earp brothers, but it seemed his life had shifted into a phase of trouble following him wherever he went.

On a Sunday night in October, Doc and a man the *Tombstone Daily Nugget* would tentatively identify as John Tyley got into an argument at the Oriental Saloon. Most likely, Doc was drunk, and Tyley may have been, too. Fearing an escalation, several other men in the saloon relieved the two men of their weapons, and Tyley left. One of the saloon's owners, a man named Joyce, gave Doc some guff for creating a disturbance. His pistol having been taken away, Doc left, then returned to the Oriental with another. When Joyce came out from behind the bar and was no more than ten feet away, Doc began firing. Once again, Doc's accuracy was open to question. He stopped shooting and Joyce advanced on him, wrested the gun away, and hit Doc in the head with it. Doc fell to the floor, and Joyce sat on him until peace officers arrived. The only damage Doc had inflicted was hitting

Joyce in one hand and another man in the big toe. The next day a sober and sore Doc was fined twenty dollars for assault.

Tombstone was not a fresh start for Doc and Kate. "Happily ever after" was never in the cards for them. She was not in Tombstone long before recognizing that with all these Earp brothers and their women around, there was little room for her. Doc was deeply loyal to Wyatt and by extension his brothers, and that did not allow for much regard left over for her. So Kate left. She wound up running a boardinghouse, which probably doubled as a cathouse, in Globe, Arizona, 180 miles north of Tombstone.

She was not done with Doc, though, which would turn out to be too bad for both of them. With travel becoming more difficult for Doc as his respiratory illness worsened, Kate made the trip as often as she could to visit, staying with Doc in his rooms in Tombstone. The reunions must not have been particularly warm ones, because Kate would get very drunk and then she would be much more inclined to dish it out than to take it. Even on his best days, Doc was not a patient man, so no wonder his limit was reached. Early in 1881, Doc ordered her to get out and stay out, and Kate did.

She did not go far. If she had the intention of retreating to the boardinghouse in Globe, whiskey persuaded her otherwise. Kate went on a bender. Doc had to know she had remained in Tombstone, and he made sure to avoid her. Still, on March 15, Big Nose Kate was around to get Doc into an even bigger heap of trouble.

On that day, four mask-wearing men held up a stagecoach near Contention, and in the process the driver and a passenger were shot dead. It somehow got into the heads of the local lawmen that Doc Holliday was involved. The sheriff heading the investigation of the holdup went to see Kate in Tombstone. In her drunken stupor and still angry with Doc for kicking her out, it was easy to convince her that she should sign a statement that Doc had been one of the thieves and had gunned down the stagecoach driver. He was not immediately arrested, however, because Wyatt and his brothers were gathering eyewitness accounts of Doc's whereabouts at the time of the robbery. And then Kate sobered up.

She found the sheriff who had taken the statement and told him to tear it up. The case against Doc, such as it was, fell apart. But there was not to be a tender reunion of the two onetime lovers. Doc gave Kate some money and stuck her on a stagecoach out of Tombstone, vowing to have nothing more to do with her.

While Tombstone was far from the hoof-beaten cattle trails of the Texas Panhandle and Kansas, cowboys could be found in Arizona, too. It could be said that during its boom years Dodge City had hosted a higher caliber of cowboy. There were plenty of yahoos and a few who were worse, but many of those trail hands wanted to make a living and had bosses to answer to, who in turn had the cattle owners to answer to. The cowboys who frequented Tombstone were mostly about getting what they could for themselves, and the law wasn't about to stop their harsh activities.

Many of them worked at the ranches surrounding the town, while others were drifters looking for a score near the Mexican border. The "score" was often rustling. Cowboys slipped into Mexico, cut out part of a herd, drove it north into Arizona, and sold the cattle to the ranchers who did not care where they came from. Whatever other crimes were committed in the process were none of the ranchers' business, either.

Local residents had an uneasy relationship with the cowboys. They disapproved of their criminal acts, especially when it escalated to robbing stages and wounding or killing guards and passengers. On the other hand, as in Dodge City, they helped to fuel the economy of Tombstone. And roaming cowboys were a line of defense against marauding Apache.

In an interview with the *San Francisco Examiner* in 1882, Virgil referred to the cowboys as "saddlers" because they spent most of their time in the saddle "largely engaged in raiding into Sonora and adjacent country and stealing cattle. When cattle are not handy the cowboys rob stages and engage in similar enterprises to raise money. As soon as they are in funds they ride into town, drink, gamble, and fight."

This caused a problem for the honest, hardworking cowboys, because they were lumped in with the bunch who were thieves and hurrahed the town late at night. There was also increasing rancor between those cowboys and peace officers like Virgil, and that conflict began to include the ranchers who did business with and offered protection to cattle rustlers. Two of the most well known ranching families in the area benefiting from the illegal raids of the cowboys were headed by Frank and Tom McLaury and Newman "Old Man" Clanton.

The first time the Earps came up against

the Clanton family was late in the summer of 1880. Camp Rucker was an army outpost seventy-five miles east of Tombstone, and one night six mules disappeared from it. Suspecting that they were stolen, the army requested that Deputy U.S. Marshal Virgil Earp accompany a contingent of troopers sent in search of the missing animals. He in turn recruited Wyatt and Morgan to go with him. Along the way the searchers were told that the mules had indeed been stolen, by the McLaury brothers and Billy Clanton, the Old Man's youngest son. When the Earps and the troopers arrived at the McLaury ranch, they spied the missing mules.

The matter was resolved without criminal charges, but a week later Frank McLaury came into Tombstone to tell Virgil never to come near his ranch again. Virgil replied, "If any warrant for your arrest were put into my hands, I would endeavor to catch you, and no compromise would be made."

While Charlie Shibell was the county sheriff, his deputies, Wyatt and Newton Babcock, did most of the patrolling and corralling of lawbreakers. There were shootings and stabbings and drunks to be hauled off to the calaboose. Wyatt was found to be a particularly effective lawman, thanks to his buffaloing skills and his experience in the ways of crooks. While a man named Roger King was being held for the shooting death of another man until Wyatt could transport him to Tucson, a telegram arrived from Shibell instructing Wyatt to turn custody over to a Tombstone resident. Wyatt knew this trick. He sent his own telegram to Shibell, who responded that he had not sent the first one. Wyatt made sure King was delivered for trial in Tucson.

The most serious trouble yet with the cowboys took place the last week of October 1880. By that time Tombstone had a marshal, Fred White. One night he made a mistake that got him killed.

A crowd of cowboys who considered Curly Bill Brocius their leader had congregated in a saloon because they could, and whiskey flowed. A tall man with a full head of black hair, Brocius was the head wrangler at the McLaury ranch. The job description included plenty of cattle rustling and intimidating anyone who objected to illegal cowboy activities. While he did not have the far-flung reputation of a Clay Allison, Curly Bill was known to have a quick temper and a deep reservoir of viciousness to draw from, so most people, including lawmen, kept their distance.

When he and the boys went out into a

night that was beginning to feel a winter chill, they fired a few rounds in the air, laughing and howling at the moon. Marshal White's mistake was not simply letting Curly Bill's crew get off that last bit of steam before hopping on their horses and riding back to the ranch. A second mistake was taking them on alone. White angrily told the cowboys to disperse, and when Curly Bill sassed him, the marshal lit after him, chasing him down an alley. Shots were fired.

Within seconds, Wyatt was on the scene, and he was joined moments later by Morgan. They saw cowboys running. Assuming they had fired the shots, the unarmed Wyatt borrowed a pistol, and he and his brother ran after them. Near the alley they heard Fred White demand a gun. Entering, Wyatt saw Curly Bill draw his gun and threw his arms around him. Snarling, "You goddamn son of a bitch, give me that gun," White grabbed the barrel of Brocius's gun and yanked it toward him. The gun fired. As had happened with Ed Masterson, White's clothes caught fire. The bullet hit him in the groin. Wyatt took his pistol and hit Curly Bill on the head, knocking him down.

As the stricken marshal was carried to the nearest doctor, Wyatt and Morgan hauled

Curly Bill off to jail. Suspecting that an angry mob could seek vengeance at the end of a rope, Wyatt deputized Doc Holliday and Turkey Creek Jack Johnson, and when Virgil joined them the five shotgun-toting officers stood guard outside the jail. After the hasty arraignment, Wyatt snuck Curly Bill out of Tombstone and brought him to the jail in Tucson. Two days later, at only age thirty-two, Fred White died.

A consequence of the shooting was that Virgil's lawing chores expanded to include being the acting marshal of Tombstone, and as a consequence of the confrontation between White and Curly Bill, Virgil ordered that carrying weapons in town was prohibited. That November, a special election was held and Ben Sippy was elected as the new marshal, returning Virgil to his previous responsibilities.

Two months later, in January 1881, Curly Bill would be acquitted of murder because the court believed the shooting was accidental. On the second Saturday of the new year, reunited with his crew, he wanted to celebrate. The cowboys rode into nearby Charleston, found a dance hall mostly frequented by Mexicans, and entered and drew their guns. They ordered the music to stop, the dancers to take off all their clothes, and the dancing to recommence.

In another election that November, this one for Pima County sheriff, the outcome between Charlie Shibell, running for reelection, and Bob Paul was in such dispute, with everyone from Ike Clanton — son of Old Man Clanton and older brother of Billy — to John Behan putting in their two cents, that it would not be decided until the following April, when a judge ruled in favor of Paul. Long before then, though, wanting to wash his hands of the mess and go back to focusing on making money with his brothers, Wyatt resigned. He was replaced as deputy sheriff by Behan.

Also aligning himself with the Clantons was Johnny Ringo. He was reputed to not have a typical outlaw pedigree. Stories claimed that he had attended William Jewell College in Missouri and enjoyed quoting from the plays of Shakespeare. In truth, he had never made it past elementary school, and with his sordid personality he was fated to drift over the line to the wrong side of the law. After being arrested for an unknown crime he committed with John Wesley Hardin and two others, he went west, winding up in the Tombstone area. He made his presence known there in December 1879. A man drinking next to him at a bar made a remark about a woman who had just passed by. Ringo took offense and beat the man with the butt of his pistol. When the victim began to shout for help, Ringo shot him in the throat. By 1880, he had found work rustling cattle and thus fell in with the Clantons and the McLaurys. He and Curly Bill Brocius made for a dynamic duo of evil who were not fans of the Earps.

Resigning as a lawman did not completely stop Wyatt from trying to see that justice was done. One day in January 1881, Virgil was out exercising a fast horse that belonged to his brother. He was hailed by two men in a buckboard bouncing along the dirt road. One was a constable who explained that he had helped his handcuffed prisoner escape a lynch mob in nearby Charleston, and he was afraid they were now on their horses and catching up. Virgil hauled the prisoner up on the saddle behind him and raced for Tombstone.

Wyatt was at the Wells Fargo office when they arrived, and he recognized Virgil's cuffed companion as a precocious eighteen-year-old gambler nicknamed for a certain faro wager, "Johnny-Behind-the Deuce." He admitted to killing a man in Charleston but insisted it was in self-defense. The mob had not been interested in his side of the story.

Wyatt borrowed a shotgun from the office, and he and Virgil took Johnny to the saloon where James Earp worked. Only a few minutes later the angry citizens from Charleston were advancing down Allen Street. The Earp brothers were joined by Marshal Ben Sippy, Behan, Morgan, Doc Holliday, and a few others. (In the account published in *The Tombstone Epitaph,* only the three lawmen are listed.) Very soon, the air could be filled with gunsmoke and lead.

So be it. Johnny's guardians surrounded him, and with Sippy, Virgil, and Wyatt in the lead brandishing their shotguns, they began walking toward the livery stable. "Stand back there and make passage," Wyatt ordered in a calm voice. "I am going to take this man to jail in Tucson."

Instead the mob advanced until the two sides met in the middle of the rutted street. Wyatt leveled his shotgun at the man who appeared to be leading the vengeful visitors, and told him that he would be the first to die if a battle began. Gazing into Wyatt's cold, steady eyes — and the not as cold but just as intimidating eyes of Virgil — the man believed him. He backed off and a path opened up through the crowd. A few minutes later, the prisoner was on his way to Tucson, and no one in the Charleston crowd was motivated to follow him. Months later, before he could stand trial, Johnny-Behind-the-Deuce, whose real name was Mike O'Rourke, escaped from the prison. He was last seen in the Dragoon Mountains, telling another traveler, "The climate of Arizona don't agree with me."

Thanks to Curly Bill Brocius, the cowboys were increasingly getting out of hand. He and his crew visited another church in Charleston during a service and chased the minister out of it with blazing six-shooters. In Contention, they robbed a man in the street, and when angry citizens banded together, the thieves escaped with another hail of gunfire. There was criticism of local law enforcement for being unable or unwilling to put a stop to the rampage. Tarnishing the badge further, in a bizarre twist Curly Bill was appointed an assistant tax collector for Pima County. His particularly persuasive way of making sure that residents paid their taxes succeeded in raising more revenue for the county, which in turn put more money in the pocket of Deputy Sheriff John Behan, who often accompanied the tax collector on his rounds.

For much of this time, Curly Bill was not the Earps' concern. The wrangler tended to stay away from Tombstone, and Virgil saw the depredations as a county matter — in other words, Ben Sippy's problem — that did not have to involve the deputy U.S. marshal. Wyatt and his brothers were finally seeing some profits from their investment in silver mines, and Wyatt used some of that revenue to buy an interest in the Oriental Saloon. Clara Brown, a visiting *San Diego Union* columnist, would tell her readers that the saloon was "simply gorgeous and is pronounced the finest place of the kind this side of San Francisco. The bar is a marvel of beauty; the sideboards were made for the Baldwin Hotel; the gaming room connected is brilliantly lighted, and furnished with reading matter and writing materials for its patrons." The male-only patrons enjoyed piano and violin music every evening.

Wyatt went to work every day as supervisor of the gambling operations. He was something of a frontier gentleman, dressed in black trousers and a black coat and groomed well, especially his thick dark mustache, in a respectable place of business that had a touch of elegance to it.

But this new occupation did not go smoothly. Even with Curly Bill not accompanying them in Tombstone, the cowboys were an increasing source of trouble, wanting to treat the Oriental just like any old saloon. And rival gambling operations sent yahoos into the saloon to disrupt the games. Patrons leaving the Oriental were being robbed in the alleys. Even with Morgan's help as a bouncer, Wyatt was concerned about keeping a secure saloon.

He decided to send for some help, someone he could trust, someone like . . . Bat Masterson.

Twenty-Eight

The years rolled back on my shoulders,
and my friends departed. I was alone —
alone in the dark hotel room, looking out
to the drug store where Wyatt Earp had
once been an owner of the luxurious
Oriental gambling palace. — JOSEPHINE
MARCUS EARP

In the months after Bat Masterson had left,
Ford County in Kansas did not descend
into chaos. But there were troubles aplenty
to keep the local lawmakers and their peace
officers busy.

The death of Dora Hand had not dimmed
the political prospects of Dog Kelley. He
had continued as mayor of Dodge City and
was reelected in April 1880. George Hinkle
had settled in as the Ford County sheriff.
The city council voted Jim Masterson to be
the city marshal, the position once held by
his late older brother, Ed. Another indica-

tion that Bat could not harbor angry feelings for long was that in March he returned to the area to attend the Ford County Republican Convention and then the state version in Topeka. Colorado became his new home that spring. Bat traveled to Leadville to enjoy the robust gambling scene there, and when he felt like a kid in a candy shop, it was good-bye to lawman responsibilities.

He was soon making the rounds in search of a saloon to invest in. With all the money being poured into Leadville and Gunnison County to the south, he wanted to be more on the receiving than giving end. However, in May, he was on another short visit to Dodge City — not so short, though, that he escaped the census takers.

Ever since the death of Mollie Brennan in Sweetwater, Bat had not been linked with any particular woman. Not being as domestically inclined as Wyatt, and certainly more of a lover of the nightlife, Bat took his pleasures in temporary doses. That may have changed by the time the 1880 census was conducted, because listed as sharing Bat's home was Annie Ladue, a nineteen-year-old whose occupation was reported as "keeping house" for the twenty-six-year-old former sheriff. That was also the occupation of sixteen-year-old Minnie Roberts, who the census found lived with Jim Masterson.

Whatever opportunity there was for domestic bliss was quashed when Ben Thompson buttonholed him: His brother was in big trouble with the law in Ogallala, Nebraska, 250 miles away. Maybe only another lawman could get him out of it, even if he had removed the badge four months earlier.

Billy Thompson had really done it this time. Thanks to the Union Pacific, the Nebraska town on the South Platte River had, like a few of its Kansas cousins, become a profitable cattle-shipping site. As such, Ogallala was a good town for gambling and drinking and whoring. All this appealed to Billy. One night in a saloon with the wry name of Cowboy's Rest, he and the owner, Bill Tucker, got into a dispute over a local soiled dove. Billy stormed out, got drunk at a rival saloon, and returned to the Cowboy's Rest with a gun. He fired at the bar, aiming for Tucker. The bullet found him, more specifically, his left hand, where it removed three fingers and the thumb. Billy then left.

He was followed out into the street by Tucker, whose right hand held a sawed-off shotgun. Forgoing the courtesy of asking Billy to turn around, Tucker jerked the trigger, and a swarm of pellets penetrated

Billy's back. Billy staggered to his room at the Ogallala Hotel, and a few hours later he had a message sent to his brother in Dodge City. Ben was informed that the good news was that his brother's wounds were not mortal, but the bad news was they might as well be because Billy had been told by the deputy standing outside his door that he would soon be dangling at the end of a rope for blowing off half of Bill Tucker's left hand. Worse, Billy was further advised that if his brother showed his top hat in town, his neck would be stretched, too.

So Ben was begging an old friend, one whose life he had saved, and of course Bat could not refuse. He set off on what would be perhaps his wildest adventure.

When Bat got off the train in Ogallala and went to the hotel, he found that the back-shot Billy was indeed under arrest. Tucker's friends were fixing to tie a rope to a high branch as soon as Billy was well enough to walk to the designated tree. Obviously, the justice system practiced in Dodge City to the south had skipped over Ogallala. In his career as a lawman, gentle persuasion had worked before, so Bat went to practice it on Tucker, whose left hand was swathed in bandages. The saloon owner agreed to ask that Billy be released without further harm

— then named an exorbitant sum of money for being so forgiving. Bat later reported that "my conference with the thumbless one was at an end."

Plan B was to sneak Billy out of Ogallala to the safety of either Kansas or Texas. As Bat developed this plan, he decided to enlist the assistance of Buffalo Bill Cody.

Bat had never hunted with the living legend, but he had raised a glass or two with Colonel Cody when the hunter had passed through Dodge City. He thought the former army scout, who lived in Nebraska, would be keen on such an escapade. The two biggest challenges were slipping Billy, still too injured to ride a horse, out of town, and finding Buffalo Bill at his home in North Platte fifty miles to the east when chances were he was gone on some escapade of his own. The badgeless Bat may not have fully considered that if he was caught helping a prisoner escape, his body could sway in the prairie breeze next to Billy's.

The Bat Masterson luck held. The bartender at the Ogallala Hotel was a man named Jim Dunn, who had served Bat many a time when he worked in Dodge City. Bat learned that coming up on Sunday night a dance would be held at the local schoolhouse, and even the sheriff would be there

511

because he was the town's only fiddler.

When Sunday night arrived, the sole obstacle remaining was the deputy guarding Billy's room. Once the dance was under way and the fiddling and the stomping on the hardwood floor were in full swing, Bat remarked that there was probably a lot of drinking going on at the schoolhouse, and wasn't it a shame they — and especially the deputy — were missing out on all the fun.

Well, one drink wouldn't hurt, the dutiful deputy allowed. Bat offered to buy, and on cue Dunn arrived with a couple of drinks. The deputy was still smacking his lips when he slumped to the floor. As Bat had remembered, one of Dunn's talents back in Dodge City was doctoring drinks.

Offering the now-dreaming deputy a drink had to have been timed just right so that the eastbound train would be arriving a few minutes later. Bat carried Billy out of the hotel and across the street to the station. The reliable railroad was on schedule, and as soon as the train slowed to a stop, Bat and Billy climbed aboard. At 2 A.M., they were climbing back down — in North Platte. In another stroke of luck, when Bat and his fragile friend entered the only saloon open, one owned by a man named Dave Perry, sitting within a circle of rapt listeners was Buffalo Bill Cody, just finishing up another tall tale.

Bat reported, "We were given a royal welcome," and Cody "found a safe place for us to remain until he could outfit us for the trip across the country to Dodge City. We slept quite comfortably."

The fugitives wouldn't remain comfortable if they overstayed their welcome in North Platte. They had to assume that at dawn or even before, the befuddled deputy would report the escape to his fiddle-playing boss and a posse would be gathered. The sheriff would not necessarily figure out that Bat and Billy had left by train and had disembarked in North Platte, but he could get lucky. And Buffalo Bill teaming up with Bat Masterson would set tongues to wagging.

Soon after sunup Bat went to Cody's house. There he was given, without Louisa Cody's knowledge, a horse attached to a carriage that the former hunter had just purchased for his wife's riding pleasure. Cody also provided a plan. A group of about twenty Europeans, honored guests of William Tecumseh Sherman, were soon to arrive, and Buffalo Bill was to take them on a trail ride to a ranch that was on the route to Dodge City. Bat and his friend should travel with them. No sheriff would dare interfere or even think that such distinguished company would be harboring outlaws. This made sense to Bat, as long as the sheriff and his posse did not arrive in North Platte first.

They did not, and Cody led the contingent of carriages and wagons south. A small ocean of alcohol had been brought along to keep everyone loose and convivial: "The caravan would stop every little while and liquor up," Bat recalled of the journey. At one point Buffalo Bill, having imbibed his limit, got off his horse and into Bat's wagon, where he passed out. A few miles later the mess wagon wandered off the trail a bit and it "was tipped completely upside down," wrote Bat. "I was pitched out on my head in the prairie, while Cody was buried beneath the wagon and its contents." Bat jumped up and got hold of the horses, while "other members of the party came and rescued Cody, who hadn't received as much as a scratch."

All arrived tipsy but safely at the ranch, and the next morning, in Mrs. Cody's buggy, Bat and Billy left for Dodge City. As luck would have it this time, the buggy and its occupants were battered by storms during most of the two-hundred-mile trip. The

514

two travelers arrived in Dodge City soaked, exhausted, hungry, and bruised in a vehicle that was barely sticking together. Bat wanted to head immediately to a saloon for drinks and a meal followed by a sound sleep, but Billy persuaded him to stop by the telegraph office. There, he sent a message to the sheriff "notifying him of his safe arrival and inviting him to come and get him." There was no response from Ogallala.

Bat later reported being informed by Buffalo Bill that in the interests of domestic tranquillity, he presented Mrs. Cody with "a much more expensive outfit [buggy] than the one he had given us."

Supposedly, Billy was in San Antonio in 1884 when Ben Thompson and King Fisher were murdered. One would think this would have set Billy off on a rampage of revenge, but apparently the death of his beloved brother had the opposite effect. He was seen weeping as he wandered the streets of San Antonio, and then one day Billy Thompson was gone. There were rumors that he killed a man in Corpus Christi and later was spotted in El Paso. In 1888, word spread that Billy, age forty-three, had been gunned down in Laredo.

Bat used this time back in Kansas to visit the Masterson homestead; then he moved on east to Kansas City. He remained there into early 1881, visiting Dodge City a couple of times to bend the elbow with friends there. It was during one of those visits, in February, that Bat received a wire from Wyatt informing him that he would appreciate his old friend's help in Tombstone. Bat paid off any gambling debts and bar tabs he had accrued and boarded a train at the Dodge City station. He traveled west and south, occupying a stagecoach for the last leg of the journey. It was during this trip that the man riding shotgun filled Bat in on the troubles the Earp clan was confronting in Tombstone.

Finally, Bat was reunited with Wyatt himself, who explained that he needed a loyal man who was good with a grin and a gun. Wyatt had also requested help from another old Dodge City friend, so right after Bat arrived in Tombstone, Luke Short did, too.

The two men went to work at the Oriental as well-armed faro dealers. Bat soon learned that there was more to the friction in Tombstone than trying to put the saloon out of business. He was filled in on the faction of rustlers, smugglers, thieves, and cowboys who not only outnumbered the Earps and their law-and-order allies but seemingly had the protection of the sheriff's office and the *Tombstone Daily Nugget* newspaper. Such odds did not faze Bat. He was probably more bothered by having to rub shoulders again with Wyatt's other loyal friend, Doc Holliday, who anchored one of the gaming tables with a pistol under his vest.

It was Luke Short, however, who caused the most immediate trouble. One morning in late February, Bat walked into the Oriental in time to break up a confrontation between Luke and Charlie Storms. The latter was a well-known gambler originally from New Orleans who had been involved in previous bouts of gunplay. According to Bat, he and Storms "were very close friends — as much so as Short and I were — and for that reason I didn't care to see him get into what I knew would be a very serious difficulty."

Bat did not know what the dispute between his two friends was about, but it was clear that they "were about to pull their pistols when I jumped between them and grabbed Storms, at the same time requesting Luke not to shoot." Luke could be a hothead, but not enough of one to risk shooting Bat. He kept his six-shooter holstered as Bat hustled Storms out of the saloon. "I advised him to go to his room and take a sleep, for I then learned that he had been up all night, and had been quarreling with other persons."

He left Storms in his room at the San Jose House. When Bat was back at the Oriental, he found Luke standing outside it on Allen Street. Bat was in the middle of explaining that Storms was sleeping it off when Storms suddenly appeared with a Colt .45 in his hand. Saying, "Come go with me," he yanked Luke off the sidewalk into the street. "Are you as good a man as you were this morning?"

Luke jerked his gun, pressed the muzzle against his assailant's chest, and replied, "Every bit as good," as he fired. The bullet tore through Storms's heart. He was dead before he hit the dusty ground. But Luke shot him again for good measure.

The killer was arrested, and a couple of days later a hearing was held. The chief witness was Bat, who described the sequence of events, and as a result, the ruling was self-defense and Luke was freed. Bat had lost a friend, but at least he hadn't lost two. An upside to the incident was that word went around Tombstone not to trifle with the fellows from Dodge City.

Soon after, Wyatt and Bat were working as

lawmen again. The stage from Benson was nearing Tombstone on the night of March 15, 1881, when as many as half a dozen men emerged from the desert darkness and began firing. The men driving the stage, Eli "Bud" Philpott and Bob Paul, returned fire, with Paul yelling, "I hold for no one!" The robbers were chased off but left two dead behind — Philpott and a passenger in the coach named Peter Roerig.

Within minutes of the stage arriving in Tombstone, two posses were formed. Sheriff Johnny Behan deputized several cowboys and, with them and his regular deputy, Harry Woods, set off in one direction. Going in another was Deputy U.S. Marshal Virgil Earp accompanied by his brothers Wyatt and Morgan, and Bat was deputized, too. Before long, one of the bandits, Luther King, had been run down. An interrogation that probably involved the butt ends of pistols revealed that at least three of the would-be robbers were Harry Head, Bill Leonard, and Jim Crane, all known cowboys.

Virgil and his posse returned to Tombstone and handed King over to Behan to be jailed, then set off again. They spent days trying to track the outlaws but were at a distinct disadvantage in that as their supplies and water ran out and their horses wearied, the bandits were being aided by fellow cowboys and allied ranchers. When Virgil telegraphed Behan to rendezvous with a new posse and bring fresh horses and supplies, it should have been no surprise to Virgil that Behan did not come through.

That night, instead of the posse's preparing to renew their search, one horse died. Wyatt and Bat set off for Tombstone, but they had to stop at a ranch along the way and leave their exhausted mounts. The two friends had to hike the eighteen miles remaining to Tombstone, most likely with Bat talking away and Wyatt contributing the occasional brief response. Virgil and the others tried to continue the search, but there was no sign of the other outlaws.

Finally, they, too, were back in Tombstone, having gone without water for the previous thirty-six hours. Not only were none of the other outlaws caught, but upon their return they learned that King had simply walked out of Behan's jail and disappeared.

Bat's opportunity to recuperate in Tombstone from the tough trail riding was a brief one. Having been away from Dodge City for quite a while, he might not have been aware that by then, troubles had returned there and reached the point at which factions were at war with each other, with those wanting stiff law and order pitted against the side who wanted a return to the Wild West. A letter to the editor asserted that Mayor Kelley was "a flannel mouthed Irishman and keeps a saloon and a gambling house which he attends to in person. The city marshal and assistant are gamblers and each keep a 'woman' — as does the mayor also. There are many good people here, but the bad ones are so numerous we almost lose sight of the good . . . the yellow fever, measles, smallpox and seven year itch combined would all be preferable to a civilized county to residence in this town."

That April, voters tossed Kelley out and voted A. B. Webster in as mayor. One of his first acts was to fire Jim Masterson and replace him with Fred Singer, whose qualifications included being a bartender at Webster's saloon. Stung, Jim turned his focus full-time to making money at the Lady Gay, which he now owned with A. J. Peacock. This effort did not get off to a smooth start when one of his own bartenders, Al Updegraph, picked an argument with him over a woman. Jim fired him. Peacock rehired him: Updegraph was his brother-in-law.

It should be pointed out that if this had been Bat instead of Jim, tempers probably would not have flared. Jim's personality was not as easygoing as Bat's and especially not like his late brother Ed's or the youngest's, Tom's, who did not find lawing more appealing than working on the family farm north of Wichita. Jim's personality was more like Wyatt's, a dour disposition, and he was less likely to nip a dawning dispute in the bud by buying a couple of drinks. Jim brooded over losing his lawman job and wasn't about to take any guff from an employee.

It was, presumably, a friend of Jim's who sent an anonymous telegram to Bat in Tombstone: "Come at once. Updegraff [*sic*] and Peacock are going to kill Jim." He showed the telegram to Wyatt, who noted that it "didn't say what kind of trouble Jim Masterson was mixed up in." Bat, he said, "took the first stage out of Tombstone to go back to Dodge City," no doubt praying that he would not again be too late to save a brother's life.

The stagecoach took Bat to the nearest train station, and counting the hours, he rode the rails north and then east. When he stepped off the train in Dodge City — as it happened, high noon on April 16 — he feared that Jim could already be dead. He might not be back to save his brother but to avenge him. As it turned out, though, Bat's timing was perfect.

The train pulling out of the station revealed two men on the other side of the tracks: Peacock and Updegraph, both armed. Bat faced them, his hands poised beside his ivory-handled pistols. "Hold on," he called to the two men. "I want to talk to you." Instead, they fled, instigating what came to be called the Battle of the Plaza.

Peacock and Updegraph at first hid behind one corner of the jail. Undaunted, Bat advanced on them and was about to cross the tracks when they began firing. Pulling out his pistols, Bat crouched, hoping the railroad embankment would provide some cover. The three men fired furiously, their bullets breaking windows and gouging chunks of wood out of buildings. One ricocheting bullet struck an onlooker. The streets cleared, men and women pulling their boots out of the mud created by spring rains, trying to gain traction and run into the closest doorways. Friends of Peacock and Updegraph arrived and joined the fray, the assault on Bat intensifying.

Suddenly, from behind him there were gunshots — friendly ones, possibly Jim Masterson and others. War had broken out in the center of Dodge City, and Bat was caught in the crossfire. He fired a couple of more shots and learned his guns were empty. But one of his main assailants, Updegraph, straightened, staggered out into the open, and fell to the wet ground. Everyone stopped shooting.

Mayor Webster appeared, carrying a shotgun. He walked up to Bat and said he was under arrest. Even without bullets, Bat thought of fighting on, probably wresting the shotgun away from the mayor if he wanted to. But when Webster told Bat that Jim was unharmed, that he had indeed arrived in time to prevent and possibly interrupt an ambush, Bat agreed to be escorted to the jail, where Jim soon joined him. Everyone else either went home or repaired to their favorite saloons to begin telling stories about what may have been the biggest gun battle in Dodge City's history.

A hearing was held that very afternoon. By then, it was determined that Updegraphs's wound was a serious but not mortal one. (Six days later, he wrote a letter to the *Ford County Globe* boasting, "I feel that I will be around again, and will not die as the party wished me to.") Bat was fined eight dollars for firing a weapon in the city limits, and released. Jim sold his interest in the Lady Gay, and by the next day the Masterson brothers were on a train out of Dodge City.

Unaware that dime-store novelists back east were portraying him as one of the most dangerous gunslingers of the Wild West, Bat resumed his wanderings, gambling his way through Colorado the rest of the year and into 1882; then he escaped a week or so of winter by traveling to New Orleans. There he watched a newcomer named John L. Sullivan dethrone the U.S. heavyweight boxing champion, Paddy Ryan, in what was then a bare-knuckle bout. Also in the crowd were two brothers escaping the winter and the law as well, Frank and Jesse James, and Bat may have renewed his acquaintance with them. Then he headed to Colorado and the gambling charms of Trinidad, where his brother Jim was a deputy sheriff. In April, Jim's responsibilities included arresting John Allen, who years earlier had worn a badge in Dodge City, for the shooting death of Cockeyed Frank Loving. (It was also in Trinidad that Bat helped Wyatt Earp recuperate from an ordeal related in the next chapter.)

By then, Bat was wearing a badge again. Trinidad had become an incorporated city, and it needed a marshal, and the city council had selected Bat Masterson. The more powerful faction in Trinidad wanted the city to make the sort of progress toward being civilized that Dodge City had done, and how convenient it was that the former sheriff of Ford County was in town. Why did Bat accept the position? It could not have been the money, a mere seventy-five dollars a month. Most likely, it was the challenge. He was restless and not yet thirty years old. It was flattering that word was being bandied about that Bat and Wyatt had tamed the frontier, so why not do it again?

Life in Trinidad was not completely quiet — most serious was an incident involving a deputy killing a man — but as in Ford County, Bat was viewed as an effective peace officer. But as in Ford County, in the early spring 1883 voting, when it came time to elect Bat to a full term, voters weren't completely sold and he was defeated. This time, voters agreed with his opponents that Bat spent too much time gambling. It may have rankled him a bit when the new marshal, Lou Kreeger, persuaded Jim Masterson to join his staff. As a peace officer, Kreeger would serve Trinidad and the county until 1913.

For Bat, it was, unexpectedly, time to figure out what to do next. He decided to do his deciding in Denver. Furthest from his mind was that he would soon be back in Dodge City for one last campaign.

Twenty-Nine

> But for the cornerstone of this episodic narrative, I cannot make a better choice than the bloody feud in Tombstone, Arizona, which cost me a brave brother and cost more than one worthless life among the murderous dogs who pursued me and mine only less bitterly than I pursued them.
> — WYATT EARP

The summer of 1881 saw tensions rising in Tombstone. It also saw the death of Billy the Kid. While this would have no direct impact on Wyatt Earp or Bat Masterson, the Kid's death was another indication of the Wild West moving toward becoming less wild, as one by one its most colorful outlaws exited the stage.

Before he had joined forces with Dirty Dave Rudabaugh, Billy had gotten involved in what had become known as the Lincoln County War, and that was why Sheriff Pat

Garrett had gone after him.

Billy was working in New Mexico Territory for the rancher John Tunstall. The wealthy Englishman had arrived in Lincoln County in 1876 to go into the cattle business with John Chisum, but their efforts were thwarted by a rival faction that wanted to control the business as well as the federal government contracts that went with it. The friction escalated, and by the time the Lincoln County War was over, fourteen men had been killed. One of them was Tunstall, in February 1878. Billy was a big part of the revenge action that followed; then, as the war drew to a close, he went on the run.

After being arrested by Garrett because of his adventures with Dirty Dave, Billy was put on trial in Mesilla, New Mexico, convicted, and sentenced to be hung. Though often debunked, the reported exchange was between the judge declaring that Billy would hang "until you are dead, dead, dead," and the Kid responding, "And you can go to hell, hell, hell." He was restrained by handcuffs and leg irons and locked in a room on the top floor of the courthouse in Lincoln, where he awaited execution, scheduled for May 13, 1881.

But Billy escaped. Early on the evening of April 28, a deputy, James Bell, escorted him downstairs to a privy. As they were going back upstairs, Billy managed to slip one hand out of the metal cuffs and bashed Bell over the head with them, also yanking out the deputy's pistol. As Bell staggered down the stairs, Billy shot him; the deputy was dead when he hit the street. Another deputy, Bob Olinger, who hated the Kid, and the feeling was mutual, came running. By the time he arrived at the courthouse, Billy had a shotgun pointed out one window. "Hello, Bob," he taunted, then pulled both triggers, killing him, too. The Kid forced a man bringing them food to help him out of the restraints, then stole a horse and rode out of town. When Garrett returned to Lincoln, instead of supervising the construction of the gallows, he had to put together another posse.

Almost three months later, and many miles of following the outlaw's trail, Garrett was in a cantina in Fort Sumner when Billy, still two months shy of his twenty-first birthday, entered. Supposedly, he was there to see a girl he claimed he loved. It was dark inside and Billy couldn't see well, but he sensed danger. "Quién es? Quién es?" he queried. There is some dispute as to whether Billy drew a gun or a knife, but in any case, Garrett fired, hitting Billy in the chest. He fell to the floor, took a couple of last breaths, and died. The following day, July 15, Billy was buried at the Fort Sumner cemetery. And only nine months later, Pat Garrett's book on the outlaw's life and death was published. (In 1908, Garrett was shot and killed by a ranch worker contending he had been cheated out of his wages.)

In Tombstone, Ben Sippy could see which way the dry desert wind was blowing, and on June 6 he requested a two-week leave of absence as the chief of police. The city council granted it. Members were probably unaware that Sippy, having the good sense to know what could happen in Tombstone between the cowboys, ranchers, and the opposing factions of law enforcement, had his saddlebags packed. The former sheriff and now chief (since the city had been incorporated in February) was getting out while the going was good. The council installed Virgil as the temporary chief of the police department. Three weeks later, when there was no sign of Sippy, Virgil had the job he had been unable to be elected to the previous fall.

His first major action was an auspicious one. That month, a fire had begun in Tombstone that ate up sixty of the mostly wooden buildings on the east side. It was reported that Wyatt was in the Oriental (which was to suffer some damage) when the fire broke out and spread, but he did not leave the building for a safer location until he made sure all the money left on the gaming tables by the safety-first gamblers was swept up and secured in the saloon's safe.

No sooner had the ashes cooled when displaced residents and others looking for quick accommodations pitched tents and began living in the streets. As both the police chief and a deputy U.S. marshal, Virgil deputized Wyatt, Morgan, and twenty-one other men, and they cleared all the squatters away without violence. *The Tombstone Epitaph* lauded Virgil as "fearless and impartial" and declared that "his force kept perfect order and protected life and property in a manner that deserves the highest praise."

The hope among many residents was that someone so fearless and impartial as Virgil in charge of the lawing in Tombstone — though at a modest $150 a month — would prevent an outbreak of hostilities. (So impartial was Virgil that he even arrested the city's mayor and editor of *The Tombstone Epitaph,* John Clum, for riding his horse too fast.) But there were problems Virgil could not control, one being the rampant rustling throughout Cochise

County.

The other was that as Virgil had to pay more attention to policing in Tombstone, Behan was not picking up the slack. That February, Governor Frémont had appointed Behan sheriff of Cochise County, another reason why Wyatt wanted no part of being a deputy. But Behan had continued down the path of being more friend than foe to the lawbreakers, especially the McLaurys and the Clantons and others who could act with impunity. That summer, adding to the dangerous atmosphere was the combination of Curly Bill and Johnny Ringo.

Things got more out of hand in the summer of 1881 when one of the frequent border crossings to steal cattle resulted in fifteen Mexicans left for dead. This was too much. The Mexican Army could disrespect a border, too. On August 13, a contingent of troops did a raid of their own on American soil, looking for outlaws. Old Man Clanton and four others were found with a herd of stolen cattle and were executed on the spot.

On the night of September 8, several masked men held up a stage near Bisbee and took a Wells Fargo box of money and whatever valuables the passengers had. Normally, this would be Behan's sole jurisdiction, and thus the robbery might well have been ignored, but also stolen was a bag of mail, making the offense federal, too, requiring the intervention of the deputy U.S. marshal. Virgil deputized Wyatt and Morgan and they hit the trail again. This posse was more successful, finding and apprehending Frank Stilwell and Pete Spence. They were brought back to Tombstone, where Stilwell was released on bail. Virgil arrested him a second time. He would be acquitted in October, but he vowed to repay the Earps for what he claimed was harassment. Taking things a step further, Frank McLaury took Morgan Earp aside to warn him that the brothers would be killed if they attempted any more arrests.

Even with the occasional appearance of Mexican troops, by October the cowboys and crooked ranchers had Cochise County to themselves, except for that burr under their saddles — Virgil and his peace officers, who more often than not included his deputized brothers. As Wyatt was to tell the *San Francisco Examiner* in 1896 about Ike Clanton, now the head of the larcenous clan, "He knew that his only alternative was to kill us or be killed by his own people."

If the Earps could be swept away as efficiently as those squatters had been after the fire in Tombstone, the only real law would be Behan, and that was pretty much no law at all. To give him some credit, the sheriff knew that he was far outmanned and outgunned and had a widespread county under his jurisdiction. Taking on the cowboys would have been a huge task and most likely suicidal.

It could not have helped Behan's disposition and lack of desire to side with Virgil Earp that he was losing his woman to the federal officer's brother. Wyatt's romance with Josephine was not necessarily motivated by being fed up with Mattie. She was fine with the domesticity of the Earp commune and the company of her sisters-in-law, especially Allie, who shared her fondness for having a drink or two in the afternoon. Mattie was over thirty now, and Tombstone had potential as a place to build a home and maybe a family. Her headaches and her intake of laudanum were manageable.

Wyatt's habits did not change. Between his peace officer duties and gambling and other business interests, he was gone from home most of the day and well into the night. Even surrounded by Earps, Mattie increasingly felt neglected and alone. The headaches became more frequent and severe, and gum disease added to her woes. Higher amounts of whiskey helped, but when Mattie woke up, the pains returned, and drinking in the morning was not abided even by Earp women. Laudanum was appealing because of its potent mix of opium and alcohol, and it was more discreetly consumed. Frontier doctors were free to dispense gallons of the liquid painkiller for a wide variety of ailments, and overdoses were either overlooked, misdiagnosed, or considered a blessing.

As the distance between Wyatt and Mattie grew, he and Josie grew closer. An especially colorful assessment can be found in E. C. Meyers's biography of Mattie: "From the moment Josephine decided Wyatt was the man most likely to rescue her from Behan the sparks of passion flew, but it was Mattie who was burned. Wyatt took up with the sagebrush seductress, secretly at first, but later quite openly."

Virgil tried not to involve himself in Wyatt's dizzying domestic issues, instead devoting himself to his own as well as lawing. Allie was not pleased to be constantly surrounded by Earps, with that circle widening when Warren arrived and stayed at her house. He told her that he wanted to learn how to deal faro like Morgan and Wyatt did and be a marshal and wear a gun like Virgil did. (Apparently, James's job as a bartender did not entice him.) To put some cash in the young man's pocket, Virgil deputized Warren from time to time, as long as the job was not dangerous. Sometimes the cash did not stay long in his pocket, such as when Warren was arrested and fined twenty-five dollars for discharging firearms within the city limits. Again impartial, Virgil did not interfere with compliance with the law.

That autumn, as cooler breezes began to replace the hot desert zephyrs, Tombstone itself, under Virgil's watch, was quiet. Arrests were for only petty theft, drunkenness, and the like. Cochise County, however, under Behan's benevolent neglect, was descending into chaos. The cowboys were stealing everything in sight and continuing to raid across the border. This was not the place the Earps wanted to live in, but they were not about to pick up stakes and leave, either. Virgil was not one to shirk responsibilities, and his brothers were not going to leave him to fend for himself.

There have been many accounts of the Gunfight at the O.K. Corral, ranging from as close to authentic as the facts and differing reminiscences will allow to deliberate and often mystifying flights of fancy. Many authors and filmmakers have treated the more reliable accounts as obstacles to be overcome. For the sake of brevity, the following account is what Virgil and Wyatt contend happened. There are inaccuracies, but we may wind up unearthing the true origins of Stonehenge before knowing what exactly happened on Wednesday, October 26, 1881, in Tombstone.

Early that morning, brothers Virgil and Wyatt were told that an angry and probably drunk Ike Clanton was looking for them. He had already stopped at the boarding-house where Doc Holliday had rooms, but he had not lingered there long enough for Doc to get dressed and come out to fight. Virgil would later testify that he encountered Ike Clanton on Fourth Street between Fremont and Allen. He was toting a Winchester rifle and had a six-shooter tucked into his pants belt. After Virgil went up to him and grabbed the rifle, Clanton "let loose and started to draw his six-shooter. I hit him over the head with mine and knocked him to his knees and took his six-shooter from him." It was fortuitous that Virgil had acted quickly, because Clanton said, "If I'd seen you a second sooner I would've killed you."

Arrested for disturbing the peace, Ike paid

a twenty-five-dollar fine and was released. He then sent word for his brother Billy and the McLaurys, telling them to come armed because it was time to get rid of that cursed Virgil Earp and his brothers.

That afternoon, word reached Virgil that cowboys were gathering off Fremont Street and that they carried guns. The marshal believed it was his duty to disarm them. To help him, he deputized Wyatt, Morgan, and Doc. They walked to a narrow vacant lot between the Harwood House and Fly's Boarding House and Photography Gallery and the rear entrance of the O.K. Corral. There they found Frank and Tom McLaury, Ike and Billy Clanton, and Billy Claiborne.

Virgil said evenly, "Boys, throw up your hands. I want your guns."

They stared back defiantly. "I've got you now!" Frank McLaury shouted, and Doc responded, "Blaze away. You're a daisy if you do!"

Wyatt announced, "You sons of bitches have been looking for a fight, and now you can have it!" He later recalled:

For answer, their six-shooters began to spit. Frank McLaury fired at me and Billy Clanton at Morgan. Both missed. I had a gun in my overcoat pocket and I jerked it out at Frank McLaury, hitting him in the stomach. At the same time Morgan shot Billy Clanton in the breast. So far we had got the best of it, but just then Tom Mc-Laury, who got behind his horse, fired under the animal's neck and bored a hole right through Morgan sideways. The bullet entered one shoulder and came out at the other.

"I got hit, Wyatt!" said Morgan.

"Then get behind me and keep quiet," I said — but he didn't.

By this time bullets were flying so fast that I could not keep track of them. Frank McLaury had given a yell when I shot him, and made for the street, with his hand over his stomach. Ike Clanton and Billy Clanton were shooting fast, and so was Virgil, and the two latter made a break for the street. I fired a shot which hit Tom McLaury's horse and made it break away, and Doc Holliday took the opportunity to pump a charge of buckshot out of a Wells Fargo shotgun into Tom McLaury, who promptly fell dead. In the excitement of the moment, Doc Holliday didn't know what he had done and flung away the shotgun in disgust, pulling his six-shooter instead.

No doubt, every surviving member of that

gunfight would have a recollection that differs from another's. For example, supposedly Ike Clanton did not fire a weapon during the fight. Instead, he ran toward Wyatt, who said, "The fight has commenced. Go to fighting or get away."

The McLaurys and Billy Clanton died from their wounds. Virgil was shot in the left leg, Morgan in the shoulder, and a bullet grazed Doc's hip. Wyatt was not wounded. He and Doc were arrested, and three days after the gunfight Virgil was suspended as chief of police.

Following that a monthlong preliminary hearing before Justice of the Peace Wells Spicer was conducted. During it, testimony was given that supported the Earps and Doc Holliday, and other testimony placed the blame for the gunfight on them. On November 30, Spicer ordered the release of the defendants, declaring that based on what he had heard, no jury in the territory would find them guilty.

But the Earps were judged guilty by an outlaw jury. In a letter dated April 13, 1884, Will McLaury revealed to his father that he hired "assassins" to avenge his two younger brothers. The group included Pete Spence, Florentino Cruz, Hank Swilling, and Indian Charley, and their mission was to kill the

Earp brothers and any others, such as Doc, associated with them.

The first attempt came on December 28, 1881. Virgil was on patrol that night, and as he walked along Allen Street, the post-Christmas quiet was shattered by shotgun blasts. Virgil was hit, most of the damage done to his left arm. As he was being treated, Virgil managed to say to Allie, "Never mind, I've got one arm left to hug you with."

For weeks reports circulated that Virgil was near death, but he gradually improved. U.S. Marshal Dake appointed Wyatt to take his brother's place, and he assumed the role of federal peace officer. Peace was not necessarily uppermost in his mind, but he was not about to instigate a conflict, either. Doc took care of that, on January 17, 1882. In the middle of the street he faced off against Johnny Ringo. Both men were moments away from jerking their pistols when a peace officer, Joe Flynn, grabbed Ringo, and Wyatt wrapped his arms around Doc. Sheriff Behan was nowhere to be found.

There was a concern that it was now open season on the Earps and anyone could be a target. All the family members took up residence at the Cosmopolitan Hotel, which could be more easily defended than individual cottages. But they could not simply hide inside the building. And after almost three months without violence, on the evening of March 18, it did not seem too risky for Wyatt and Morgan to go shoot pool.

Across the street from the parlor was a saloon owned by Bob Hatch and John Campbell. From inside it, a man fired a rifle twice through a window in the back door. The second bullet just missed Wyatt, plunging into the wall behind where he was sitting. The first bullet had already torn into Morgan, severing his spine. As had happened with Bat Masterson four years earlier in Dodge City, in Tombstone Wyatt watched a brother die. Morgan, only thirty, breathed his last shortly after midnight, on Wyatt's thirty-fourth birthday.

There were several accounts of Morgan's last words. The biographer Casey Tefertiller sides with what Wyatt reportedly offered two months later: "I promised my brother to get even, and I've kept my word so far. When they shot him he said the only thing he regretted was that he wouldn't have a chance to get even. I told him I'd attend to that for him."

Later that day, Wyatt and James escorted a wagon bearing Morgan's casket to the train station in Benson. When the next westbound train came through, James and his dead brother were on it, bound for the Earp homestead in Colton, California. Next was to get Virgil along with Allie, Bessie, and Mattie to safety. Two nights later, they were put on a train in Contention, with Wyatt, his brother Warren, and Doc providing protection.

After the train pulled out, Wyatt spotted Ike Clanton and another man believed responsible for the shootings — Frank Stilwell — with shotguns. Firing erupted, and Stilwell was killed. Again, Clanton had run off. What became known as the Earp Vendetta Ride had begun. Wyatt would recall, "For a long time thereafter I occupied the anomalous position of being a fugitive from the county authorities, and performing the duties of Deputy United States Marshal, with the sanction and moral support of my chief." Wyatt had lost faith in the court system. He had always upheld the decisions of the system in Dodge City, even those he disagreed with, but in Arizona it was a different story.

The vendetta lasted several weeks, and during it the posse led by Wyatt was credited with killing three more men — Curly Bill Brocius, Indian Charlie, and Johnny Barnes. That July, Johnny Ringo was shot and killed,

544

and some accused Wyatt of doing it, but by then the vendetta was over and Wyatt was in Colorado. In an odd twist, during the rest of March and into April, the two Earp brothers and Doc and a few fellow riders were being pursued by a posse formed by Behan. When he drew close, though, courage failed him. He and his half hearted helpers gave up when Wyatt's posse left Arizona.

When all was said and done, the fight that began at the O.K. Corral culminated with at least eight men dead. Morgan was the only Earp to die, though Virgil would be disabled the rest of his life.

Wyatt and his posse were worn out and certain that whoever was left worth killing was long gone. Doc's declining health was another reason to call it quits. Arriving in Silver City, New Mexico, they sold their horses and took a stagecoach to where they could get a train to Trinidad, Colorado. For all his previous attempts at bravado, Warren had seen enough killing. Even Doc had. He split off from the others, to gamble his way to Denver. By the end of April, Wyatt had arrived by train in Gunnison, Colorado. He was sick at heart and exhausted, and he needed to reunite with an old friend.

It had to be a bittersweet get-together for Bat and Wyatt when the latter arrived in

Trinidad, where Bat was the city marshal. The last time Bat had seen his close friend, in Tombstone, Virgil and Morgan had been hale and hearty. At least now, Wyatt could recover under Bat's protection. He found a job dealing faro at a Trinidad saloon. He was done with lawing. For that reason, and Wyatt still being a wanted man himself, it was Bat who had to rescue Doc when he was arrested.

In Denver, Doc had been corralled by a lawman from Arizona named Perry Mallan, and the Denver authorities were content to be bystanders and watch the deadly dentist be extradited. Bat knew the marshal in Pueblo — Henry Jamieson — and wired him, asking a favor. Sure enough, Jamieson arrived in Denver with an arrest warrant, claiming that Doc had swindled a Pueblo man out of $150. But the Denver authorities refused to release Doc, insisting they would hold him until Arizona lawmen arrived to take custody.

So Doc sat in jail, with *The Denver Republican* reporting about him that "murders committed by him are counted by the scores and his other crimes are legion. For years he has roamed the West, gaining his living by gambling, robbery and murder. In the Southwest his name is a terror."

Bat's second ploy was to confront Mallan in the Denver sheriff's office, and he must have been pretty intimidated, because he confessed to not being a lawman at all but a swindler who was hoping to make money off his sudden fame as the man who had arrested the terror who was Doc Holliday. Bat then went to Colorado Governor Frederick Pitkin, who agreed to stall the extradition request from Arizona. He also agreed to have the custody of Doc transferred to Jamieson. No sooner was that done than the marshal, Doc, and Bat were on a train to Pueblo.

THIRTY

Now, gentlemen, there being nothing
further to do, suppose we adjourn to the
bar and take a little something just for old
time's sake. — LUKE SHORT

The Dodge City War had its roots in an action taken by nervous ranchers later backed by the law. Cattle coming up from South Texas were transmitting splenic fever to the longhorns in the Panhandle. When Governor Oran Roberts failed to quarantine cattle in the south, the rancher Charles Goodnight led a "Winchester Quarantine," a line of defense consisting of armed men with orders to shoot any cattle and cowboys who tried to enter West Texas or the Panhandle. When the Kansas legislature contemplated (and would later issue) a ban on the importation of all Texas cattle, wherever they were from, and prohibited shipping them across the state in railroad cars, Dodge City waned as a cow town. The summer of 1881 saw the last big cattle drive along what had become known as the Great Western Trail.

It was a step away from the wide-open frontier but another one toward civilization. Dodge City still had the railroad, at least, but by 1883, so did just about every place else of consequence. That November, to help organize and coordinate the shipping of passengers and freight every day over the thousands of miles of rail line that covered North America, at noon on the eighteenth the railroad companies in the United States and Canada would implement time zones. Timetables could then allow for there being an hour difference from Eastern to Central to Mountain to Pacific time zones.

No longer being in a cow town, Dodge City saloon owners and some other businessmen had to figure out a future with far fewer cowboys spending their money fast and furiously. About the same time as this uncertain future was being pondered, Luke Short returned to town. He spent enough time at the Long Branch Saloon and did well enough at gambling and other pursuits that he would buy a piece of the place. And one indication of the hopes that the city would have a stable environment and truly leave the "wicked" days behind was the opening of the Bank of Dodge City, the first such institution. In 1882, with the surrounding frontier deemed safe enough, Fort Dodge closed its gates for good.

It is one of those delicious ironies of history that such milestones pretty much coincided with the death of America's most famous bank robber. By 1882, many of the outlaws who had put Dodge City and other notorious frontier towns on the map were in prison or dead. That April, they would be joined by one more.

After the disastrous bank robbery attempt in Northfield, Minnesota in 1876, Jesse James and his brother Frank had spent several years under assumed names farming in the Nashville area. They probably could have lived out the rest of their lives there as history moved on, raising families. Frank had married seventeen-year-old Annie Ralston, and in 1878 the two had a son, Robert. But the brothers were not very good at farming, and in October 1879, the pockets of their overalls empty, a new James Gang was formed, and they robbed a train near Glendale, Missouri, hauling in a handsome thirty-five thousand dollars.

This obviously held them over for a time because the gang's next robbery was not until 1881, when they robbed a stage in

Muscle Shoals, Alabama. That July, during a robbery of a train back in Missouri, two men were shot dead, reportedly both by Jesse. There was a big public outcry, and Governor Thomas Crittenden offered a ten-thousand-dollar reward for the capture and conviction of the James brothers. However, this did not stop them from thievery. Jesse had even taken to reading dime-store novels about himself and no longer bothered to wear a mask. During another train robbery in Missouri, he entered a passenger car, announced, "I'm Jesse James," and as if hosting a stage show, he introduced the other members of his gang. They took fifteen hundred dollars and rode off.

The gang fell apart soon after, though, and the only two men left riding with the James brothers were Bob and Charlie Ford. On April 3, 1882, Jesse was at home in St. Joseph, Missouri, with his wife, Zee, and their two children. He invited the Ford brothers there to plan a robbery of the Platte County Bank. Jesse did not know that the Fords had secretly met with Crittenden about betraying Frank and his younger brother. After sharing a meal, the three men went into the parlor. Jesse stepped up on a stool to straighten a framed picture on the wall, and Bob Ford moved close behind him with a pistol and fired several times. Jesse was dead when he hit the floor. As the Fords ran from the house, Bob kept shouting, "I killed him! I killed Jesse James!" They went to the nearest telegraph office and wired the news to Crittenden.

They were charged with murder, but the governor had the charges dropped and the ten-thousand-dollar reward was paid. The Fords lived in fear that Frank James would avenge his murdered brother, but five months later, he walked into Crittenden's office, took off his gun belt, and surrendered. Still, Charlie Ford remained so frightened that he committed suicide. The "cowardly Bob Ford," as he was known, made his way farther and farther west, through Kansas and into Colorado, working in saloons. In Creede, in 1892, he was shot to death.

The tours that Frank led on the family farm in Kearney, Missouri, until his death at seventy-two in 1915 (with he and Bat Masterson still corresponding) included Jesse's grave site. Visitors could buy stones right from the site. Whenever there were only a handful of stones left, Frank replaced them with more from a nearby creek. Ultimately, enough stones were sold to have covered dozens of graves.

Luke Short was not the sole owner of the Long Branch, because in February 1883, when he bought out the interest of Chalk Beeson, Beeson's partner, William Harris, became Luke's partner. That was fine with both men, who had last done business together when Harris and Wyatt were partners in the Oriental Saloon back in Tombstone. Harris was a solid businessman and founder of the Bank of Dodge City. But when he ran for mayor, trouble followed.

In the election that April, Harris lost to a familiar figure in Dodge City, Lawrence Edward Deger, the count being 214–143. Just beating Harris at the ballot box was not enough for the rotund new mayor: he wanted to put him — and by extension Luke — out of business. The campaign began on April 26 when it was decreed that brothel keepers and their prostitutes would be fined and other forms of unsavory entertainment were no longer welcome in Dodge City. That apparently included singing, because two days later, three women performing in the Long Branch Saloon were hauled off to jail. Singing wasn't the primary way that girls in saloons brought in money, everyone knew, but it was a tad too vindictive to, as Bat put it, have them "locked up in the city calaboose."

When Luke Short learned that no other singers at the saloons in the city had been arrested, he strapped on his guns and headed for the jail to get them out. Once that task was attended to, Luke would take his grievances to the new mayor. He knew that Deger was the handpicked successor of the outgoing mayor, Ab Webster, who owned the Stock Exchange, a rival saloon one door east of the Long Branch. And word around town was that Harris had been defeated thanks to railroad workers casting illegal ballots. The Atchison, Topeka & Santa Fe Railroad wanted Dodge City even more tamed than it was when Wyatt Earp and Bat Masterson had removed their badges and left it several years earlier. Other sins to be outlawed were "loitering, loafing, or wandering," the idea being to get rid of vagrants and any others not contributing to the local economy.

Deger knew that Short was a friend of Bat Masterson's, and that alone put him on the wrong side of the law. He still bore a grudge over Bat defeating him for Ford County sheriff in November 1877 and then losing his deputy job soon afterward. Let Luke Short and his six-shooters come on. If Deger couldn't get Bat, he'd get one of his good friends.

It was moonless and dark that cool late-April night when Luke marched toward the jail. Lou Hartman had the bad luck of being on the wooden sidewalk outside of it. He had been hired as a city policeman by Deger within the last couple of days, and here was a known killer coming his way. Not taking any chances, Hartman drew his gun and fired. His bad luck continued, because he missed his diminutive target, the bullet kicking up dust behind him. Luke whipped out his pistols. Clearly, Hartman had not signed up for this, and he turned and ran. His one piece of good luck was that he tripped and fell off the sidewalk, so that when Luke fired, the bullets flew overhead.

Seeing the policeman topple out of sight caused Luke to think he'd killed Hartman, meaning he'd sure done more damage than he'd intended to do. He hightailed it back to the closed-up Long Branch and fortified it further by piling chairs and a table up against the door. He grabbed the shotgun from behind the bar, made sure it was loaded, and waited. Deger and his remaining crooked lackeys would have to come and get him.

Luke needn't have bothered erecting the barricade and, no doubt, losing a night's sleep. Hartman was not hurt, just embarrassed. In the morning, a messenger was sent by City Marshal Jack Bridges, whom *The Kansas City Evening Star* would soon describe as "a well-known character"; whatever that meant, it wasn't good. The deputy shouted the news about the resurrected Hartman through the saloon's door. And, the groggy Luke was told, if he surrendered peacefully, the only punishment would be a small fine for shooting off his guns.

The gambler in him saw this as a winning hand and not for the bluff it was. Down came the barricade, and Luke emerged, leaving his pistols on the bar along with the shotgun. But policemen took him into custody and he was tossed in jail. Luke was charged with assault — though the sidewalk had done more damage to Hartman than he had — and was released only when he put up two thousand dollars as bond.

That wasn't enough for Webster, Deger, and the other "reformers," some of whom had been deputized by Bridges. They were now riding roughshod over the town government and what had once been a pretty impartial law-enforcement system. Short and his gambler pals were viewed as a reminder of past evils as well as future rivals. Best to be rid of them altogether; so a couple of days after his assault arrest, Luke was again taken into custody. Five friends shared his cell. They were charged as being "undesirables," which sounded more like a social gaffe than a crime. Even so, they were not allowed to see lawyers. The six prisoners may have felt their necks itching as they wondered how far the reformers would go.

One morning, a group of deputies and others recruited for the task showed up at the jail and escorted the six men out of it and through town to the train station. Webster and Deger may have recognized how fitting it was that the railroad would remove the problem from Dodge City. The men were told it didn't matter which way they went, they should just get on a train. Three men chose to head west. Luke Short, accompanied by two others, took the eastbound train, to Kansas City.

From there he sent a telegram to Bat Masterson. Luke Short's wire found him in Denver. Ever loyal to friends, Bat hopped on a train and joined Luke in Kansas City, where he also found his old undersheriff, Charlie Bassett, who had been helping his brother at a saloon there. Bat's advice was that Luke should head to Topeka and plead his case to the governor of Kansas. George

Washington Glick was an opponent of prohibition, which appeared to be what the reformers in Dodge City were trying to impose. While Luke was on that mission, Bat's would be to round up supporters in case the governor failed to act.

Luke would learn that Governor Glick was already aware that things might get out of hand there. A Kansas City newspaper reported that "prominent Kansas City attorneys left to-day for Topeka to petition Gov. Glick in the interest of Dodge City property owners that the town be placed under martial law." It further informed readers, "The place is practically in the hands of the 'vigilantes' and the situation is more serious. The trains are watched and armed men guard the town while a list of others who would be ordered out has been prepared. Every source of reliable information indicates that Dodge is now in the hands of desperadoes [and] the lives and property of the citizens are by no means safe."

Luke did petition the governor, who in turn wired George Hinkle, still the sheriff of Ford County, requesting his view of the situation. Hinkle responded that it had been blown all out of proportion, and if need be he could take on any troublemakers. Glick was not convinced, but he was reluctant to send a contingent of Kansas militia to Dodge City and round all the reformers up. He suggested to Luke that he return to Dodge City under the protection of the governor and with a ten-day grace period, during which he would settle up his business affairs and leave.

This was not a smart suggestion. *The Kansas City Evening Star* emphasized that after the ouster of Short and other business rivals of the Webster/Deger faction, "vigilantes took possession of the town." A reporter in Dodge City sent by *The Chicago Times* had been warned not to send any telegrams notifying his newspaper of what was transpiring, and "a body of armed men watched the arrival of each train to see that there was no interference. That there will be trouble of a very serious character there, is anticipated."

Luke was no rube. He saw the grace period as a death sentence. He would return to Dodge City, all right, but not alone. Once more, he sent a telegram to Bat Masterson.

Within days, Bat was back in Kansas City, and rendezvousing with him, Luke, and Bassett there were Wyatt Earp, Doc Holliday, and others with a thirst for a new adventure in old surroundings. Getting wind of this, *The Kansas City Journal* predicted "a great tragedy" once these tough men answered the call, referring to Bat as "one of the most dangerous men the West has ever produced," adding, "For the good of the state of Kansas, it is hoped the governor will prevent violence."

Given that the two years since the Gunfight at the O.K. Corral had not been easy ones, Wyatt was not fixing for a new gunfight. But when Bat's telegram found him in Colorado, working full-time as a faro dealer, because his code called for not letting a friend down, he made ready for his return to Dodge City to make sure Luke Short received a fair shake.

Wyatt may have looked forward to him and Bat setting things right in Dodge City again, to experience once more having each other's back. Most of the time in the "old" days, the good guys had won. Here was another opportunity. But Luke Short's troubles meant the good guys weren't winning. The ending in Dodge City had yet to be written. The six-shooters on their belts might be the pens that would do it. More old acquaintances flocked to Kansas City or headed directly to Dodge City to follow Bat and Wyatt.

If Webster and Deger and their armed

supporters weren't yet aware of the force being arrayed against them, it had to be an unpleasant surprise when words drifted west that gathering in Kansas City were Wyatt, Bat, Doc, Luke, Bassett, Shotgun Collins, Rowdy Joe Lowe, and like-minded adventurers and that they were armed and ready for action. Newspapers in several major cities reported on the imminent "Dodge City War."

The Kansas City Evening Star had a ringside seat, and it told readers that "those who are acquainted with the party and their disposition are at no hesitancy in predicting that there is going to be trouble of a bloody nature if resistance is offered to Short's return." It further reported that when Hinkle "learned of this threat from Kansas City, he gathered a posse to meet all incoming trains." *The Daily Commonwealth* of Topeka chimed in, "The plan is to drive all of Short's enemies out of Dodge at the mouth of the revolvers."

Several accounts have Wyatt traveling to Dodge City before the others. *The Daily Commonwealth* even confided that "Doc Holliday and Wyatt Earp are now secretly in Dodge City, watching matters," and when showdown time came, a telegram would be sent to the others containing a coded message. This was as silly as it was untrue. Wyatt did go to Dodge City, accompanied by Dan Tipton, Johnny Green, Texas Jack Vermillion, and Johnny Millsap. It is not known why Doc did not make the trip. One possibility is that he may have been too ill to be of much good should there be a showdown. It was reported — more accurately — that Bat and Luke had stayed behind to welcome supporters who were still trickling in from all over the West.

According to Wyatt's recollection offered to Stuart Lake, waiting for him and his group when they stepped off the train from Kansas City was Prairie Dog Dave Morrow, who was a member of the police force. Wyatt was thirty-five then, still lean and handsome with his blond hair and dark mustache, wearing a black vest, coat, hat, trousers, and a crisp white shirt. If he had to return to Dodge City for some unofficial lawing, he wanted to make an immediate impression.

Prairie Dog, not at all happy that he was the only lawman who had shown up at the station, had a choice: try to disarm the men who were weighed down by rifles and six-shooters, or listen to what Wyatt had to say. Wyatt said he did not want trouble, he was there only to see that his friend Luke Short was treated like everyone else. If Morrow would deputize him and his companions, that would resolve the problem of carrying guns in public. He may not have had the legal authority to actually do that, but Prairie Dog saw the wisdom of Wyatt's way, and Dodge City had five new deputies.

Wyatt directed his men to take up lookout stations in case the Webster-Deger alliance was dismayed about the sudden expansion of the police force. They sure were. According to Bat, "It finally became whispered about that Wyatt Earp had a strong force of desperate men. When [Webster] learned that he had been trapped by Earp, he hunted up the sheriff and prosecuting attorney and sent a hurry-up telegram to the governor." They begged the governor for two companies of militia or "a great tragedy would be enacted on the streets of Dodge City."

When the next train arrived, it carried Bassett, Collins, Frank McLain, and others. There was no need to deputize them, because no local lawman could be found to greet them. Wyatt would have to go look for one. He sauntered to Deger's office and told the sweating marshal, "Bat will arrive at noon tomorrow, and upon [his] arrival we expect to open up hostilities."

"News" spread fast. One report being passed among Dodge City residents was that ruthless men, including Dirty Sock Jack, Cold Chuck Johnny, Black Jack Bill, and Dynamite Sam were also on their way to Dodge City to back Wyatt up. And about the former lawman himself, *The Kansas City Journal* was colorfully reporting that Wyatt "is equally famous in the cheerful business of depopulating the country. He has killed within our personal knowledge six men, and he is popularly credited with relegating to the dust no less than ten of his fellow men."

When Luke Short, the reason for all the fuss, arrived, *The Kansas City Evening Star* reporter informed that "he slung a 6-shooter on each hip, and with a double barreled shot gun in his hands, walked down the street to the Long Branch saloon, carefully watching the corners." He also announced to anyone within earshot that Bat Masterson was on his way.

The *Dodge City Times* would later report, "For a number of days the city was like a powder magazine, the slightest spark would have caused a concussion fearful in consequences and revolting in details."

All this was a lot more than Mayor Deger had bargained for, and even Sheriff Hinkle found his former confidence evaporating.

With some satisfaction, Glick rejected the feverish request for troops. He wired back that instead he would dispatch Thomas Moonlight, his adjutant general, to Dodge City to size up the situation. When Webster and Deger heard about this, they realized their goose was cooked. Within hours, their vigilante followers melted away.

As promised, Bat arrived, carrying a loaded shotgun, and Wyatt greeted him at the station. There were at least fifty men in town now ready to back their play. It was time to take back Dodge City.

For purely dramatic purposes, it would be wonderful to describe the wild shoot-out that followed, one that would make the Battle of the Plaza or the Gunfight at the O.K. Corral pale in comparison. And where better could it take place than Dodge City, whose law-and-order system emerged after the high body count of its first years.

But Webster and his supporters wanted to live, not die in a blaze of bullets. As Bat later described events, "The Mayor called a hasty meeting of his friends, and after they had all assembled in City Hall, he informed them of what he had heard about the Earp invasion. Anyone who was present at the meeting could easily see that anything BUT a fight was what the Mayor and his friends were looking for, now that a fight was not altogether improbable."

Harris and Webster pulled Wyatt and Bat aside and told them that Luke could stay in Dodge City and return to what he was doing. Gambling could resume in all the saloons as long as the gaming rooms were screened off from the barrooms and dance halls. Women would be welcome in the saloons. Without exactly doing so, the former mayor apologized for all the inconvenience he and Deger and their supporters had caused.

Wyatt consulted with Bat and the others, then responded that this return to normal was fine with them. Bat had arrived fully loaded and expecting a furious fight, but he later wrote that "if at any time they did 'don the war paint,' it was completely washed off before I reached here." To his observation, and with a touch of sarcasm, Bat contended that most of the people in Dodge City "hailed the return of Short and friends with exultant joy."

When Moonlight, the governor's emissary, arrived all was well. To be on the safe side he formed a group composed of friends of Webster's and friends of Luke's and dubbed them "Glick's Guards." Such a committee could settle disputes instead of needing a nail-biting confrontation. Eight members of what had been dubbed, with some tongue in cheek, the Dodge City Peace Commission — Wyatt, Bat, Bassett, Frank McLain, W. F. Petillon, Neil Brown, William Harris, and Luke — posed for a photograph on June 7. Luke invited everyone for a drink, and the following day most of the old acquaintances began to go their separate ways.

The *Ford County Globe* "regretted" the peaceful conclusion to the war, according to its June 12 editorial: "To make this abrupt settlement is very agreeable to our people, but rather rough on the press at large which has so gloriously feasted on our misfortune, to be so ingloriously cut off from publishing any further soul-stirring scenes from the late battlefield of Dodge City."

A rather deflated Deger continued as mayor, but perhaps soured by the experience or afraid of being someone else's rather large target, he did not remain a public servant the rest of his life. After marrying Etta Engleman in Dodge City, he relocated to Velasco, Texas, near the mouth of the Brazos River, and operated a lumber company. In 1898, when government pay became enticing again, he secured the position of postmaster, and he held on to it for sixteen years. He and Etta and their daughter, Bessie, moved on to Houston. Lawrence Deger died there in 1924 at the ripe age of eighty-nine.

Luke Short could have continued to enjoy the gambling and other charms of Dodge City indefinitely, but he chose not to. Later that year, in November, he sold his share of the Long Branch and relocated to Fort Worth. He opened a new saloon, the White Elephant, in that Texas town, and with the subsequent profits he invested in brothels and other gambling operations. When Fort Worth reformers outlawed gambling, Luke simply became more discreet and his revenue stream kept flowing.

Like Doc Holliday, Luke was a heavy drinker who had the deserved reputation as a hot-tempered gunslinger. Unlike Doc, Luke could shoot straight. One day in 1887, he was approached by Longhair Jim Courtright, a former Fort Worth marshal who was shaking down illegal saloon owners for protection money. Luke told him to get lost. Longhair Jim jerked his gun and was pulling the hammer back when Luke shot his thumb off. When the ex-lawman went for a second gun, Luke shot three more times, killing him. Three years later another man, Charles Wright, tried to take over Luke's business interests. He too died from gunshot wounds.

There is a postscript to the White Elephant killing of Courtright. When the ex-marshal entered the saloon, the by-then-well-traveled Bat Masterson was sitting with Luke. "It was not a parley that he came for, but a fight," Bat observed. A grand jury would not indict Luke after he spent a night in jail. But Bat feared that one night could be the last one for Luke because he overheard friends of Courtright planning to lynch the prisoner. As soon as the sun set, Bat showed up at the jail, and with the sheriff's permission he conspicuously sat out front, his ivory-handled six-shooters prominently displayed. Any men who approached the building that night just kept walking.

On a happier note, Luke had gotten married in March 1887, to Harriet Beatrice Buck, in Oswego, Kansas. There were only six years of wedded bliss, however. It was not a gunman but his own unhealthy habits that caught up with Luke Short. In September 1893, while seeking relief from various ailments at a mineral spa in Geuda Springs, Kansas, he died of dropsy, or Bright's disease. He was only thirty-nine years old, and was buried in Oakwood Cemetery in

Fort Worth, Texas.

By this time, Dodge City had found itself settling into early middle age, far from being the wickedest city in the West. In November 1883, the same month that Luke sold his interest in the Long Branch and left town, Patrick Sughrue was elected sheriff of Ford County, replacing Hinkle. The following April, George Hoover was elected mayor, and he chose Bill Tilghman to be the new marshal. He helped to insure that the rowdy hurrahing days were over.

As Odie B. Faulk put it, "By 1885, the boom period was ending — and with it the gunfighting, gambling, prostitution, and fist fighting that had characterized Dodge City. Several factors in combination forced the city to become what several editors had been demanding for years: civilized."

THIRTY-ONE

Notoriety has been the bane of my life. —
WYATT EARP

As Wyatt and Bat and other members of the Peace Commission went their separate ways, much of the frontier was giving way to the same civilizing forces affecting Dodge City. That same year, 1883, Buffalo Bill Cody staged his first Wild West show, in Omaha, Nebraska. Over the years it and similar extravaganzas and relentless dime-store novelists following in Ned Buntline's ink-stained steps would provide the public with their versions of what the frontier had once been.

That year also saw the last mass killing of buffalo in the United States. One of the participants was Theodore Roosevelt. This was the last blow that put the American bison close to extinction. By then, even Buffalo Bill was calling for protection of the animal, but it would still be years before adequate preservation efforts took hold. One of their champions would be President Roosevelt, who by then was friends with the former buffalo hunter Bat Masterson.

The cowboy way of life was nearing extinction, too. Fewer cattle drives meant fewer jobs for trail riders, and wages were low for pretty much anything cowboys did. In the Texas Panhandle in 1883, two hundred of them attempted to strike as the spring rodeo season was about to begin. A ranchers cooperative easily broke their resistance.

After escorting Morgan Earp's body to California in March 1882, Virgil and Allie had decided to remain in Colton. As he recuperated, he was able to get regular medical attention in San Francisco. In an interview with the *San Francisco Examiner* that May, Virgil explained what had led to the now-famous gunfight in Tombstone: "My brother Wyatt and myself were fairly well treated for a time, but when the desperate characters who were congregated there, and who had been unaccustomed to troublesome molestation by the authorities, learned that we meant business and were determined to stop their rascality if possible, they began to make it warm for us."

When Virgil was arrested in August for

operating a faro game, it was apparent he was seeking more than treatment in San Francisco. Perhaps best to stick to lawing, or something like it, even with a crippled left arm. He opened a detective agency in Colton, and in 1886 he was elected constable there, with his seventy-three-year-old father being justice of the peace. The following year, Virgil became the city's marshal. But in 1893, now fifty and no doubt to Allie's dismay, he became restless.

The couple moved to the mining town of Vanderbilt, California, and built Earp's Hall, a gambling emporium that also featured Saturday boxing matches and Sunday church services. When the Vanderbilt boom went bust, Virgil reunited with Wyatt in Cripple Creek, Colorado, but it already had all the liquor and gaming it could handle, so Virgil and Allie returned to the familiar environs of Prescott. He invested in what was called the Grizzly Mine, which promised to produce profits, until it collapsed — literally. Virgil was in the mine that day in November 1896 and was knocked down and out for a few hours after a tunnel gave way. Several broken bones and bad bruises required months of recuperation.

He had a much more enjoyable experience in 1898, when he was fifty-five. That autumn, a letter from a woman with the delightfully coincidental name of Jane Law, mailed from Portland, Oregon, found him. Virgil was informed that she was his daughter, the one born to Ellen Rysdam in 1862, who had given him a purpose other than patriotism to join the Union Army. A few months later, he and Allie traveled to Oregon and father and daughter and Ellen were reunited. Allie commented, "It was a meeting of great feelings and after these had been dispensed with, they went to her home." Virgil also met his three grandchildren for the first time. In the following years he and his daughter would exchange visits.

Allie was not jealous but overjoyed. She would write, "All these years and me and Virge never had a baby, and here was Virge finding out for the first time in his life he had a grown-up young lady daughter, Jane!"

Virgil and his third wife divided their time between Prescott and Colton. In Colton in 1901, he and Wyatt reunited to operate a gambling hall. However, after determining the city already had enough such establishments, town fathers rejected the brothers' application.

Presumably, while Wyatt was in Colton he visited his father and his stepmother. Virginia Ann Cooksey Earp had passed away in January 1893, and Nicholas had remarried nine months later. In 1901, at eighty-eight, he was placed in the Veterans Home in Sawtelle, which was on the western fringe of Los Angeles. He lived long enough to be part of an Earp reunion a couple of years later, which included Virgil, Wyatt, James, Adelia, and probably Newton and their spouses and children. In February 1907, shortly after being elected to the Los Angeles County Court and having outlived six of his ten children, Nicholas Earp died at ninety-four.

A couple of years earlier, reports of new gold strikes had brought Virgil and Wyatt to southwestern Nevada. It would be the last time those two brothers were together. They did not stay long, and when Wyatt and Josephine moved on, Virgil and Allie stayed put.

Early in 1905, Virgil became a peace officer again when he was appointed a deputy sheriff of Esmeralda County, in Nevada. And even with just one functioning arm, he also served as a bouncer in one of the saloons in Goldfield. Next door was the Northern, built by Tex Rickard, and it soon became very successful, boasting the longest bar in the West. Virgil did not keep both positions very long because his health became more fragile. He was just plain worn out, and a bout of pneumonia tipped the scales.

Lying in bed in a hospital in Goldfield, Virgil asked Allie for a cigar. Then he asked her to place a grandniece's letter to him under his pillow, and to "light my cigar, and stay here and hold my hand." On October 19, 1905, at age sixty-two, Virgil Earp died. He was buried in the Riverview Cemetery in Portland, where he could be near his daughter when her turn came.

Allie and Virgil had been together for thirty years, and she outlived him by forty-two more. For some of those years she lived in San Bernardino and was a close friend of Adelia Earp Edwards, and then she moved to Los Angeles. She died there in November 1947 at age ninety-eight, and she and Adelia share a grave site in the Mountain View Cemetery in San Bernardino.

The older and youngest of the Earp brothers had very different lives and endings, with the oldest living the longest. Newton continued to avoid lawing, content to be a carpenter and builder in northern California and Nevada. He and his wife, Jennie, raised five children, who in turn married and had families of their own, mostly on the West

Coast. Jennie and their daughter Effie May both died on March 29, 1898. A heartbroken Newton outlived them by two decades. He died at age ninety-one in December 1928 and was buried at the East Lawn Memorial Park Cemetery in Sacramento.

Perhaps never recovering from the brutality of the vendetta his brother Wyatt involved him in, Warren's life was much more troubled as time passed. He drifted from town to town across the frontier, not returning to Arizona until 1891, when he found work as a driver of stages that transported the U.S. mail, interspersed with stints as a range detective. He may have had contact with his brothers during his travels, and if so they might not have been pleasant reunions. Warren had acquired the reputation of being something of a bully and exaggerated the exploits of Wyatt and Virgil, probably for free drinks and other favors. Virgil contended that Warren "is too hasty, quick-tempered and too ready to pick a quarrel. Besides he will not let bygones be bygones, and on that account, I expect that he will meet a violent death."

In July 1900, Warren was doing some detecting work for Henry Hooker, a prominent rancher in Cochise County, Arizona. Because of an interest in the same woman, and because they simply rubbed each other the wrong way, Warren and Johnny Boyett, Hooker's range boss, were often in conflict. One day in Brown's Saloon in Willcox, Arizona, the two men argued. The argument reignited that night in the same saloon, and this time both men were drunk. Warren said he had a gun and that Boyett should get one of his own.

He went and got two, both .45-caliber Colts. When Warren appeared in the saloon doorway, Boyett fired twice and missed twice. Warren left and reentered. Boyett fired two more times and missed twice more. Warren advanced on him, opened his coat and vest, and said, "I have not got arms. You have a good deal the best of this." Boyett either did not believe that Warren was unarmed or was too unhinged by the advancing Earp, because he fired a fifth time. This time the bullet went true, striking Warren in the chest, and moments later he was dead.

He was buried in the Pioneer Cemetery in Willcox. One account has Virgil, under an assumed name, spending time in Willcox questioning witnesses and finding that his brother's death was murder. However, none of the other Earps followed up, and though Boyett was arrested he was never tried. He continued his job at Hooker's ranch, later moved to Redlands, California, and died in Texas. Unlike the assassins in Tombstone, he killed an Earp brother and got away with it.

After the events in Tombstone, James and Bessie stayed put in California. She died only five years later, in 1887. James lived quietly well into old age, dying in January 1926 at eighty-four. He was buried in the Mountain View Cemetery, near Adelia and Allie.

Mattie had been another casualty of events in Tombstone. Seemingly for her protection in the aftermath of Morgan's murder, Wyatt had her accompany James and Bessie and their daughter Hattie to the Earp family farm. Mattie believed that after the expected bloody business was finished, Wyatt would come to Colton to collect her.

She was mistaken. Leaving Tombstone meant the end of her life with Wyatt. She remained at the Earp farm until August, when she boarded a train to begin a return journey to Arizona. Wyatt and Josephine had moved on, and there was nothing left for her in Tombstone, so Mattie looked up Big Nose Kate, who took her in. The two women lived in the Globe boardinghouse. The first three years of her stay, Mattie lived a quiet life and her use of laudanum may have diminished or stopped. But in 1885 — soon after a photo of her was taken in a studio showing a reasonably healthy frontier woman in her midthirties — Mattie spied Wyatt and Josephine in Globe. That they looked happy and prosperous was a blow to her, and Mattie went into a tailspin.

She began to drink heavily and returned to using opium and laudanum in ever-increasing doses. Months later, in another blow, Kate Elder informed her that Doc Holliday was on his last legs in Colorado and she was going to him. Mattie remained in Globe until October 1887, when she boarded a stage for a smaller Arizona town, Pinal. The only aspect that may have appealed to her about the dusty and derelict postboom mining community, with ghost town in its future, was anonymity. No one would care what or how much she drank, there was one doctor who could prescribe laudanum, and she even could return to being a prostitute if need be.

By the late winter of 1888, Mattie was in severe pain, and this time it was more physical than emotional. Her teeth were decaying and Pinal did not have a dentist. Increasing abdominal anguish and decreasing appetite indicated she could have cancer, cervical or intestinal, or there was the possibility of a late-stage sexually transmitted disease. She required more and more laudanum to dull the pain, month after month. Finally, on the night of July 3, Mattie mixed an overdose of laudanum with whiskey, drank it down, passed out, and did not wake up.

After Bat Masterson, putting aside his personal feelings, had delivered Doc from custody in Denver and deposited him in Pueblo, Doc spent the rest of his days in Colorado. It was reported that he and Wyatt got together in Gunnison, perhaps to gamble or to resolve any conflicts lingering from the vendetta ride, and if so, that would be the last time the two close friends would see each other.

Doc was living in Leadville — his health declining and his dependence on alcohol and now laudanum increasing — when he had his last gunfight. A man named Billy Allen, looking to earn a reputation, challenged Doc in a saloon. Doc demurred, but when Allen drew his gun Doc drew faster, firing twice and hitting Allen in his shooting arm. Doc could have killed him, but the last thing he needed was more trouble from the law.

Entering 1887, Doc was gravely ill and he moved to Glenwood Springs, hoping the sulfurous waters would offer some relief. However, they failed to extend his life. According to Kate Elder, it was here the longtime lovers said their good-byes. She claims to have nursed him during Doc's last weeks that autumn, which were mostly spent in bed because he was too weak to do anything else, even drink alcohol. But on November 8, he asked a nurse for whiskey, and he drank it down in two gulps. He looked at his feet and said, "Damn, this is funny," probably thinking of the prediction given to him years earlier that he would never die in bed with his boots off. By dying that day, he proved the prediction false. Dr. John Holliday was thirty-six.

A hastily arranged funeral was held that very afternoon, presided over by a local minister, W. S. Rudolph. Because Doc had died flat broke, a collection was taken up by gamblers and bartenders to pay for the expenses of the funeral and interment. Doc was buried at the Linwood Cemetery. His tombstone reads he died in bed.

The following year, Kate married George Cummings, a blacksmith. They settled in Arizona, but a year later the restless Kate moved from Bisbee to Cochise, alone. She found work at the one-floor, ramshackle Cochise Hotel, and in 1900 she moved in with a man reputed to be a mining executive, John J. Howard. When he died thirty years later, she went to live in the Arizona Pioneers' Home, an old-age facility. There Kate Elder remained until November 1940, when she died five days before her ninetieth birthday. Her tombstone at the facility's cemetery in Prescott has MARY K. CUMMINGS carved into it.

After leaving Dodge City in 1883 for what would be the last time, Wyatt collected Josephine, and she became his fourth wife, though it is unclear when or if that became official. He called her "Sadie," after her middle name of Sarah, even though that was also the name of his second wife and the one Josephine had used as a pseudonym while being courted by Johnny Behan and possibly being a prostitute.

The couple began a wandering journey through the West, a combination of Wyatt's ongoing search for wealth and the inherent Earp restlessness. During the 1880s they spent time in Galveston, Texas, Salt Lake City, Los Angeles, San Francisco, and Idaho, where for a time Wyatt owned a saloon. In San Diego, Wyatt was a real estate speculator and he owned racehorses, none of which were fast enough to be consistent winners. Around this time Sadie developed her own addiction, this one to gambling. Wyatt was constantly buying jewelry back from pawnshops and regifting it to his wife.

In the 1890s, while living in Arizona, Wyatt heard about the gold strikes in the Klondike area of Alaska and decided that would be their next adventure. He did not find gold in the hills, but apparently a saloon he owned in Nome did a brisk business. In 1901, he cashed out and he and his wife relocated to Los Angeles, where one newspaper referred to him as "the well-known sporting authority," alluding to his connection to boxing. Like Bat, he enjoyed the sport and had found work as a referee. Then there was Nevada, his last get-together with Virgil, and back to California. Wyatt and Sadie finally settled down for good in Los Angeles.

Over the next two decades Wyatt was approached to cooperate on writing projects. This would mean talking, not his strong suit, and perhaps revealing more about his life than he cared to. He could use money, though, because ill-advised investments had taken most of what he'd previously earned. In fact, he was arrested for "bunco steering" in 1911, when he was sixty-three. Wyatt cooperated with writer and friend John Flood, but his much-exaggerated "biography" was never published. Next up was Stuart Lake, and he and Wyatt exchanged letters throughout 1928, until Wyatt was too unwell to continue.

When 1929 began, Wyatt was very ill. He had prostate cancer, and whatever treatment existed at the time would have been too late anyway given his late-stage condition. He would not see his eighty-first birthday two months later. One day, the ex-lawman, who had made buffaloing an art form, could not get out of bed, and that is where he remained, with his wife of forty-seven years (give or take a few) at his side.

Sadie continued her vigil day after day. At one point, Wyatt woke up. He appeared thoughtful and said, "Supposing . . . supposing. . . ." He was quiet for a few moments then added, "Oh, well," and fell back asleep. He died on January 13, 1929.

The services were held at the Pierce Brothers chapel in Los Angeles. Sadie was too overcome with grief to attend. Among those who did attend were John Clum from Tombstone and the cowboy stars William S. Hart and Tom Mix. Wyatt's body was cremated. Six months later, Sadie brought the ashes to the Marcus family plot at Hills of Eternity, a Jewish cemetery in Colma, California.

Wyatt's reputation as one of the greatest gunslinging marshals of the American West, even though a lot of it was not true, was safe with Sadie. As Stuart Lake and others published material about him, or tried to, she was quick to attempt to correct and refute anything negative and approve anything positive. This was the approach to her own, mostly fabricated, book titled *I Married Wyatt Earp.* However, she was not interested in discussing her own life before Wyatt, letting people think what they wanted to.

Josephine remained in Los Angeles and would never allow herself to be called Sadie again. She was close to being penniless when World War II began. On December 19, 1944, she died of a heart attack, at eighty-three. She was buried next to Wyatt and they share a headstone. (It was stolen in 1957 but recovered.) William S. Hart and Sid Grauman of Grauman's Chinese Theater paid for the funeral.

Thirty-Two

Every dog has his day, unless there are more dogs than days.

— BAT MASTERSON

Wyatt Earp may have outlived Bat Masterson in years but perhaps not in life experiences. For Bat, the Dodge City years were a first act, and his life was a three-act play.

His departure from Dodge City after the "war" there led to years of itinerant travel. He turned thirty in November 1883 but was not the least bit inclined to settle down somewhere. Though occasionally swinging through Dodge City — such as an 1884 visit to organize a baseball team and a short stint as Patrick Sughrue's deputy in 1886 — Bat traveled from boomtown to boomtown, wherever the gambling was reasonably honest and profitable. For the adventure as well as the money, he occasionally worked as a hired gun. One job had him and twenty men

— one of them his old friend Bill Tilghman — guarding polling places as a hotly contested campaign concluded in Kansas.

From time to time, Bat would spend time in Kansas, not just on a job but to visit with family near Wichita and look up old acquaintances in Dodge City. In 1884, he became a newspaper publisher. *Vox Populi* was the publication's name, but it didn't last the year. Still, Bat retained an abiding interest in newspapers, which he would be able to put to better use later. In 1885, he was listed as a Dodge City farmer, though it's very unlikely he spent any time trudging behind a plow. That summer, as part of the Fourth of July celebration, Bat was given a gold watch and a gold-topped cane upon being voted the "most popular man in Dodge City." Then he was on his way again.

From Kansas, Bat went west to Denver. For several months he served as a deputy sheriff of Arapahoe County, and then he traded that in for a much more lucrative job as a faro dealer at the high-tone Arcade gambling house. If he and Wyatt had been concerned about never crossing trails again, that evaporated when Bat learned that his friend was dealing faro at another of Denver's top sporting establishments, the Central. Wyatt and Sadie and Bat found rooms in the same boardinghouse, and during off-hours they reminisced about the Dodge City days. It was after Wyatt moved on, he and his wife always chasing that elusive fortune, that for the first time in many years, Bat Masterson fell in love.

Her name was Emma Walters. As with his first romance a good fifteen years earlier, she was a showgirl. Unlike the ill-fated Mollie Brennan, Emma did not also double as a prostitute. The blond singer and dancer must have been quite the knockout because Bat's occupation at the time was managing the burlesque troupe that performed at the Palace Variety Theater in Denver (booked regularly there was his old pal Eddie Foy), and thus he had access to plenty of pretty women.

Emma was different. She hailed from Philadelphia, and her father had the distinction of being the first Civil War veteran buried in that city; he died not in battle, though, but of typhoid fever. There were many difficult years for Mrs. Walters and her three daughters. Six months shy of her sixteenth birthday, Emma saw a way out, and his name was Ed "Gopher Boy" Moulton. He had served in the 1st Minnesota Heavy Artillery, and after the war had become a professional foot racer. He ran away with Emma after the two married.

The bride became an adept racer herself, competing in events with her husband, and she took up Indian-club swinging, too. When she turned twenty in 1877, Emma was getting booked into theaters to perform as the "Queen of Clubs," demonstrating her dexterity with what were purported to be actual clubs taken from Indians in battle. She and Ed traveled throughout the Midwest and to New Orleans, and her popularity grew. She was especially popular with Frank Clifton, a performer on stages and in the circus. While the Queen of Clubs was in Chicago, Ed accused her of adultery. The affair ended, however, when it was learned that Clifton was married, and Emma returned to Gopher Boy.

The marriage continued but it was a rocky one. Ed trained athletes, Emma branched out to singing and dancing, and she got into trouble with other performers, one time running off to Los Angeles with a blackface minstrel named Ed Sheehan. She was still married to Ed Moulton, though, in March 1889 when she played the Palace in Denver and met Bat Masterson.

By then, Emma was no longer a show business ingenue but, at thirty-two, a veteran stage performer, adulterer, and soon-to-be bigamist. On November 21, 1891, five days shy of his thirty-eighth birthday, Bat married Emma. However, Emma did not file for divorce until June 1893. Ed, who was by then coach of the University of Michigan football team, did not contest it, and the divorce was granted in November. Given Emma's track record, the marriage may not have appeared to be a match made in heaven, and Bat was not inclined to give up his night-crawling ways in theaters and saloons, but he and Emma would be together the rest of his life.

For the couple, Denver soon paled in comparison to Creede, Colorado, after a huge silver strike there. Unlike Wyatt, Bat was not necessarily looking to get rich but to be where the action was and make a nice-enough living. In Creede, he managed a saloon and gambling hall and was a notable presence, sporting a lavender-colored corduroy suit and black tie. His reputation as a gunslinger, however inaccurate it was, came in handy when a tense situation developed, because a shout of "Here comes Masterson!" was known to calm down the potential combatants. Creede was a boomtown that appealed to some uncivilized elements, but in Bat's place of business, most of the time all was serene.

When the nearby silver mines began to play out, Bat and Emma returned to Denver. There, his next venture was as a boxing promoter. If Bat had only promoted and not bet on fights, he might have made out okay. But he wagered on the fighter who lost in John L. Sullivan's next match, did the same against James J. Corbett, and then backed Corbett in his losing bout with the Australian Bob Fitzsimmons. To many people at the time, Bat Masterson was not a famous former peace officer but a boxing impresario who could also compose colorful prose out of pugilism. In 1893, *The National Police Gazette* saluted him as "king of Western Sporting Men" who "backs pugilists, can play any game on the green with a full deck and handles a bowie or a revolver with the determination of a Napoleon."

Despite the praise, various business ventures connected to boxing and gambling went south for Bat. When the twentieth century began, he found himself forty-six years old and broke. Then Teddy Roosevelt reached out to him.

They had first encountered each other in 1884. Roosevelt, who had failed in a bid to be elected mayor of New York City, experienced the double tragedy of his mother and his young wife dying in his home on the same night, his wife during childbirth. He fled New York, heading to the Dakota Territory to take up ranching. While trying to scratch out a living in rough country, Roosevelt met Bat Masterson.

"Although their backgrounds were worlds apart, their personalities were quite similar in many respects," wrote Robert DeArment. "Both were extreme individualists who held firm convictions and were ready at all times to fight in defense of their beliefs, both were full of a love of adventure and were utterly fearless, both deplored sham and pretense in any form, and both were staunchly Republican in their political outlook." Though Roosevelt would last only a couple of years as a rancher in the West, the friendship he formed with Bat "grew stronger with the passing years."

By this time, Bat and Jim Masterson had drifted apart. Jim would spend more years wearing a badge than Bat did, having begun as a teenager in Dodge City and continuing to 1895. He was often identified only as the brother of Bat Masterson, yet he was a very fine lawman in his own right.

A year after Jim had become deputy in Trinidad, Colorado, he was a participant in the Maxwell Land Grant War, as a captain of thirty-five state militiamen, as under-sheriff of Colfax County, and as a deputy U.S. marshal. The "war" was essentially a fight between two factions over who owned two million acres in northern New Mexico. Jim survived several close scrapes, and in 1885 he was glad to return to Trinidad.

Jim, Neal Brown, and Bill Tilghman were part of the Oklahoma Land Rush in 1887, and when the town of Guthrie was founded, Jim and Tilghman were appointed its first peace officers, charged with clearing out squatters so that proper streets could be laid out. Guthrie became Jim's home, and he served as deputy sheriff of Logan County. But sometime lawing or opportunities to make money took him elsewhere. In Cimarron in 1889, he was involved in a bullet-riddled battle over the courthouse as a deputy to Sheriff Tilghman, who was wounded. At one point, Jim and Neal Brown and several others were holed up and surrounded by their adversaries. The stand-off continued until a telegram from Denver arrived with a warning from Bat Masterson that if the captives were not allowed to leave unharmed, the big brother would jump on a train and "come in with enough men to blow Cimarron off the face of Kansas." The message proved persuasive.

In August 1893, again as a deputy U.S. marshal, Jim was second in command in a posse organized to capture the Doolin-Dalton Gang, a particularly violent outfit of outlaws terrorizing parts of Kansas, including Dodge City. The first confrontation was the Battle of Ingalls in September, in which Jim survived, but three of his colleagues were killed, and most of the Doolin-Dalton Gang escaped. Between then and August 1896, when Bill Doolin was killed by a shotgun, the outlaws were either arrested or met their demise.

By then, Jim Masterson had forged as fine a reputation as any frontier lawman, and it would outlast him. He was only thirty-nine in 1895 when he contracted galloping consumption while living in Guthrie, and he died there. An obituary seemed to describe a man who was a blend of his brother and Wyatt Earp: "He was considered here the bravest of the marshals. Every man has his virtues and his faults. Jim Masterson was a man who never went back on a friend, and never forgot an obligation. He never pretended to keep up the conventional social amenities; but yet there was a man whom money could absolutely never make break a trust."

His body was shipped to Wichita and was

buried on the Masterson farm.

In June 1902, acting upon a suggestion from President Roosevelt, Bat and his wife traveled to New York City. For many people coming from the frontier, even a reputed gunslinger, the tall buildings and rushing people and cacophonous clashing of sounds would have been too intimidating. Bat could simply have turned around and gotten back on the train, returning to the wide-open West, where he was a big fish in a large but comparatively shallow pond. But he liked what he saw. Always a man who sought action, Bat believed there was more action in New York than anywhere else. Maybe it was not too late to start over in the big city. There was little left for him but a penny-pinching retirement back in the West, and too many of his friends and acquaintances there, as well as two brothers, were by now six feet under.

Bat's ambitions received a jolt when barely clapping the dust of the prairie off his clothes, he was arrested. The charge was grand larceny, and there was an additional charge when the New York City detectives found a .45-caliber gun holstered at his hip. An elder of the Mormon Church had reported that Bat had cheated him at a card game on the train between Chicago and

New York. However, when the confused man recanted, the charges were dropped and Bat's welcome to New York became a warm one.

Bat and Emma rented an apartment at 300 West Forty-ninth Street. This offered easy access to the expanding theater district and its restaurants and saloons, which provided free sandwiches to those who purchased whiskey or beer at lunchtime. His traveling days were not completely over because from time to time he took the train down to Washington to accept Roosevelt's invitation to visit. The former frontier buddies recalled mutual acquaintances, favorite boxing matches they had attended, and inevitably some of Bat's adventures chasing down bad guys and tossing them in the calaboose.

Roosevelt would make two offers. The first was for Bat to become the U.S. marshal for the Oklahoma Territory. This he rejected, claiming his gunslinging days were over but "some drunken boy" would not believe that and would try to make a reputation for himself by shooting Bat. The second offer Bat accepted: U.S. marshal for the Southern District of New York, which included a steady paycheck and the freedom to carry a weapon.

During one later get-together, in April 1908, the election-challenged former sheriff urged Roosevelt to run for a third term. Upon his return to the city that would be his home longer than any other place in his life, Bat told *The New York Times* that the president "displayed the fact he was suffering from an attack of 'third termitis' in its most virulent form." Apparently, Roosevelt overcame it because he chose not to run for reelection that year.

By then, Bat had been a newspaperman, working for *The Morning Telegraph.* In 1903, he had renewed a friendship from days past with two brothers, William E. Lewis and Alfred Henry Lewis. The former was editor and general manager of the New York *Morning Telegraph;* the latter, a book and magazine writer, became a frequent carousing partner. Until Richard O'Connor's book was published in 1957, Alfred Lewis's book, *The Sunset Trail,* issued in 1905, would be the only biography of Bat, though it is more of a novel than nonfiction. When William Lewis offered Bat a job, he became the sports editor of *The Morning Telegraph.* At age fifty, the third act of his life began.

Bat fully embraced the position and the events and social life that went with it. He did very little actual editing; instead, his duties were to write a column several times a week about sports, with many of them about boxing. "By W. B. 'Bat' Masterson" was his byline. He came to know and swap stories with many of the major sports figures of the day passing through New York. The baseball great Ty Cobb wrote of Bat that with his physique, despite the smart clothes and bowler hat, he "more nearly approximated the conception of a steamfitter's helper on a holiday than the authentic person who'd helped to clean up Dodge City with a Colt forty-five for his broom." His eyes, however, were "smoothed ovals of gray schist with flecks of mica glittering in them if he were aroused. And some of the men who faced him through the smoke fogs of cow-town melees hadn't lived long enough to get a good look."

Before long, Bat's column was a must-read for sports aficionados and rival columnists. He became known as the Wise Man of Longacre Square, referring to *The Morning Telegraph*'s headquarters at Eighth Avenue and Fiftieth Street. He had a routine that suited him well: breakfast at home with Emma at noon, a meander to the office to write and file his column, off to Belmont Racetrack if the horses were running or to the Polo Grounds to watch a New York Giants game, then back to Manhattan to take in a boxing match or a play, concluding with a late supper, often at Shanley's Grill at Broadway and Forty-third Street. This was followed by drinks with friends in the sports and Broadway worlds after the theaters had shut for the night, with a favorite haunt being the Metropole on Forty-second Street and Broadway. There and at adjacent watering holes Bat stood leaning at the bar and rubbing shoulders with George M. Cohan, Stanford White, John McGraw, Jimmy Walker, Arnold Rothstein, boxer and future actor Victor McLaglen, and, when his Wild West show was in town, his old friend Buffalo Bill Cody. Bat may have had to duck and cover like the other patrons on the night of July 16, 1912, when the gangster Herman Rosenthal was shot to death in the Metropole's doorway; a police lieutenant friend of Bat's and four other men went to the electric chair for the murder.

Whatever useful material he gathered would go into the next column, which could sometimes be as much about the theater and its stars as sports. Bat was a respected and a bit feared elder presence who was quick to champion causes, especially the fleeting examples of honesty in boxing. According to Bat's newspaper protégé Damon

Runyon, "He gained a wide reputation for his fearless writing. Four square to all the winds that blew, he despised hypocrisy and dishonesty, and he had a forceful way of expressing his feelings." When Runyon wrote the short stories that would be adapted into the huge stage success *Guys and Dolls,* he saluted Bat by naming his main character Sky Masterson.

By the eve of World War I, Bat's reputation as a Wild West gunslinger had ballooned to legendary proportions, and it was believed that even at sixty he could slap leather as quick as any murderous outlaw. Bat did not encourage this outlook, but he didn't go out of his way to discourage it, either. It intrigued people, and more potential sources eased into his orbit. And there was a profitable part of it, too. It was generally reported that Bat's trusty Colt .45 had twenty notches in it, each representing a man who deserved killing. An article that appeared in *The New York Sun* years earlier had been headlined A MILD EYED MAN WHO KILLED TWENTY-SIX PERSONS. Every so often an awestruck visitor would beg Bat to sell his gun and it would be honored and protected as a collectible. After careful consideration and with some reluctance, Bat would give in, negotiate a price, and turn over the coveted pistol. The next day, he would stop at a pawnshop, buy a Colt .45, and cut twenty notches in it.

From time to time, his reputation helped Bat avoid fights. One day a former lawman whom he had known in Creede, Richard Plunkett — mostly known for arresting the man who had killed Bob Ford, who had killed Jesse James — arrived in New York. He and a man named Dinklesheets hit the saloons, boasting they would settle some old grievance against Bat Masterson. They finally found him in the crowded café at the Waldorf Astoria Hotel. Dinklesheets went at Bat first and was knocked to the floor for his trouble. Bat went to his pocket, then drew and pressed something against Plunkett's stomach. As the petrified ex–peace officer trembled, the crowd raced for the doors, shouting for the police and that Masterson was about to put another notch on his six-shooter. When the cops arrived, no one was more grateful than Plunkett, who had run out of prayers to say. Bat took his hand away and displayed a package of cigarettes.

Having left the showgirl life behind long ago, Emma busied herself with reading and housekeeping. A reporter who had interviewed her in 1905 wrote, "If anyone expects to see in her a typical Westerner, he will be much mistaken. Of medium height, Mrs. Masterson is a woman of retiring disposition."

There was very little interruption to Bat's daily life and his contented marriage to Emma during the World War I years and immediately after. He had kept up a lively correspondence with the cowboy matinee idol William S. Hart. In September 1921, creating quite the commotion and sending secretaries swooning, Hart visited Bat at *The Morning Telegraph.* "I play the hero that Bat Masterson inspired," he told Louella Parsons. "More than any other man I have ever met, I admire and respect him." Bat had recently entertained another visitor, Bill Tilghman, who had come to New York to see the heavyweight championship bout between Jack Dempsey and George Carpentier. The staff marveled at two legendary lawmen in the same New York building.

That October, Bat was approaching his sixty-eighth birthday and thirtieth wedding anniversary. He held a senior administrative position at *The Morning Telegraph,* which also employed aspiring actor John Barrymore and the reporters Heywood Broun and Stuart Lake, and Bat mentored such new young staffers as the future writer and activist Dorothy Day and Parsons, who would become one of Hollywood's most powerful gossip columnists. It was estimated that in the eighteen years since he had begun his column, titled "Masterson's Views on Timely Topics," he had written at least four million words. Life had been full during his New York years, and even with mobsters, such as Al Capone and the precocious Dutch Schultz, taking over some sections of the city, it was a safe existence compared to the Dodge City of a half century earlier.

Around noon on October 25, after the usual breakfast with Emma, Bat walked down to his office at the newspaper, greeting familiar faces along the way, tipping the white short-brimmed hat he had exchanged for his bowler to ladies and children. Seated at his wooden rolltop desk, he wrote a column on the previous night's bout, which, coincidentally, had seen Rocky Kansas defeat Lew Tendler. Perhaps thinking of his father, Thomas, Bat wrote about the disparity between boxers making thousands of dollars per fight while a hardworking farmer labors "from daylight to dark for forty of the best years of his life, and lucky if he finishes with as much as one of these birds gets in an hour. Yet there are those who argue that everything breaks even in this old dump of a world of ours."

He continued, "I suppose these ginks who argue that way hold that because the rich man gets ice in the summer and the poor man gets it in the winter things are breaking even for both. Maybe so, but I can't see it that way."

Moments after concluding his column, Bat Masterson slumped over and his broad forehead rested gently on the scarred desktop. He was dead from a heart attack.

His passing was front-page news. Runyon's tribute that Bat was "a 100 percent, 22-karat real man" was typical of the tributes. He was one of several friends and admirers who remained by Bat's casket as hundreds of mourners filed past it at the Campbell Funeral Home on Broadway. The funeral service was attended by five hundred people. Among the pallbearers were Runyon, William Lewis, saloon owner turned boxing promoter Tex Rickard, New York Giants owner Charles Stoneham, and William S. Hart, back again after having made the round-trip from Los Angeles only the month before. The former sheriff of Ford County was buried at Woodlawn Cemetery in the Bronx. His headstone reads WILLIAM BARCLAY MASTERSON and LOVED BY

EVERYONE.

A month after her husband's death, Emma wrote to a friend, "I hope I will die soon to be with him." But she would live quietly for another eleven years, first at the Martha Washington Hotel, then at the Hotel Stratford. She died alone there in July 1932, two days after her seventy-fifth birthday, and was buried next to Bat.

In 1910, there had been one last visit to Dodge City. Bat was returning from covering the boxing battle between Jack Johnson and Jim Jeffries in Reno, Nevada. On a July morning, the train steamed through southwest Kansas. Bat would later write in his newspaper column that during the last leg of the trip, down the Arkansas River Valley from Pueblo to Dodge City, seeing the vast, grass-filled prairie he had first witnessed four decades earlier, "I could not help wondering at the marvelous change that had come over the country in the last twenty years. As I looked from the car window, I saw in all directions groves of trees, orchards and fields bearing abundant crops of corn, wheat and alfalfa. The idea that the plains of Western Kansas could ever be made fertile was something I had never dreamed of."

ACKNOWLEDGMENTS

While working on this book, many kind and generous people stepped forward to provide assistance with the research, fact-checking, and double-checking, along with support and encouragement. The concept of telling the stories of Wyatt Earp and Bat Masterson when they were young and serving as lawmen in Dodge City, plus their impact on frontier justice in its formative years and the colorful characters whom they came in contact with, was greeted with enthusiasm, much to my benefit.

To me, reference librarians and curators at historical collections are the people who truly keep nonfiction writers in business. No wonder, then, that in previous books, I've placed them at or near the top of the list of people and others in similar positions who hold the keys to their collections of fascinating material and are available to help just for the asking. I will certainly not stray from that token of gratitude here. Arizona Historical Society, Boot Hill Museum, Denver Public Library, Dodge City Public Library, Kansas Heritage Center, and Kansas State Historical Society (especially Nancy Sherbert) are simply wonderful repositories of information. *Dodge City* would not exist without them and their staffs. On the local level, doing the heavy lifting for me after I cast a wide research net was the John Jermain Memorial Library, especially Sue Mullin.

Invaluable contemporary information was provided by several of the daily and weekly newspapers of the time. At the top of that list were the *Dodge City Times* and the *Ford County Globe,* but also providing eyewitness and sometimes amusing descriptions of events and people were the *Atchison Patriot, Atwood Pioneer, Barbour County Mail, Daily Kansas City Journal, The Eureka Herald, The Girard Press, The Hutchinson News, Inland Tribune, Junction City Statesman, The Kansas City Evening Star, The Kansas Daily Commonwealth, Leavenworth Daily Commercial, The New York Times, St. Louis Western Journal of Commerce, Stillwater News Press, The Tombstone Epitaph, The Topeka Daily Capital,* and *The Evening Star* (Washington, D.C.). I am grateful for their editors and reporters for their efforts in the evolution of journalism in the United States — and for having some fun while they were at it.

I want to express my appreciation to the members of the Western Writers of America for being champions of the truth about the American West. Some of them write for such enjoyable and reliable publications as *True West, Wild West,* and various state and regional publications, and the effort to combine smart and thorough scholarship with telling darn good tales is truly inspiring.

A big thank-you goes to Nancy Jo Trauer of Dodge City. When I "asked around" for someone who would be able to read an early draft of the manuscript and give me incisive feedback, Nancy Jo was the one recommended. I am very glad I followed that advice. Also, the supportive Sally McKee of Brighton, Michigan, was an early reader and was generous in her comments.

My editor, Marc Resnick, was a joy to work with, always supportive and encouraging and available for any necessary handholding. Sally Richardson, Tracy Guest, Rebecca Lang, Jaime Coyne, and the rest of the team at St. Martin's Press have been generous with their time and I am grateful for their efforts on behalf of this book.

Hand-holding has also been a specialty for quite a few years now of Scott Gould of RLR Associates. Most of all, the embrace of family and friends — you know who you are — makes all the difference in any writer's life, especially mine.

ABOUT THE AUTHOR

Tom Clavin is a *New York Times* bestselling author and has worked as a newspaper, and website editor, magazine writer, TV and radio commentator, and a reporter for *The New York Times.* He has received awards from the Society of Professional Journalists, Marine Corps Heritage Foundation, and National Newspaper Association. His books include *Halsey's Typhoon, Reckless,* and *The DiMaggios.* He lives in Sag Harbor, New York.

The employees of Thorndike Press hope you have enjoyed this Large Print book. All our Thorndike, Wheeler, and Kennebec Large Print titles are designed for easy reading, and all our books are made to last. Other Thorndike Press Large Print books are available at your library, through selected bookstores, or directly from us.

For information about titles, please call:
(800) 223-1244

or visit our website at:
gale.com/thorndike

To share your comments, please write:
Publisher
Thorndike Press
10 Water St., Suite 310
Waterville, ME 04901